All inquiries should be addressed to:
Barron's Educational Series, Inc.
250 Wireless Boulevard
Hauppauge, New York 11788

Library of Congress Catalog Card No. 90-423

International Standard Book No. 0-8120-4382-0

Library of Congress Cataloging in Publication Data

Brownstein, Samuel C., 1909-
    A pocket guide to vocabulary / Samuel C. Brownstein, Mitchel
Weiner, Sharon Weiner Green. — 2nd ed.
        p.   cm.
    ISBN 0-8120-4382-0
    1. Vocabulary.   I. Weiner, Mitchel.   II. Green, Sharon.
III. Title.
PE1449.B765   1990   90-423
428.1—dc20   CIP

PRINTED IN THE UNITED STATES OF AMERICA
012   5500   987654321

A Pocket Guide to
Vocabulary

Second Edition

Samuel C. Brownstein
Former Chairman, Science Department
George W. Wingate High School, Brooklyn, New York

Mitchel Weiner
Former Member, Department of English
James Madison High School, Brooklyn, New York

Sharon Weiner Green
Former Instructor in English
Merritt College, Oakland, California

BARRON'S EDUCATIONAL SERIES, INC.
New York • London • Toronto • Sydney

Contents

Acknowledgments

Special acknowledgment is made to the following organization for allowing us to reprint copyrighted or previously published material.

Pronunciation symbols and pronunciation respellings used by permission from *Webster's Ninth New Collegiate Dictionary*. © 1990 by Merriam-Webster Inc., publishers of the Merriam-Webster® Dictionaries.

Preface

This book is designed to serve as a handy reference to the spelling, syllabication, pronunciation, part of speech, and meaning of over 3,000 words that appear most frequently on standardized exams like the SAT, PSAT, GMAT, and GRE. It is intended for use by students, executives, secretaries, proofreaders, writers, or anyone else in need of a quick, easy-to-use word reference book.

The plan of *A Pocket Guide to Vocabulary* is straightforward. Designed in dictionary format, each entry contains the word broken into syllables, its preferred pronunciation based on *Webster's Ninth New Collegiate Dictionary,* its part of speech, its meaning, and a sentence illustrating its use. Some entries contain other forms of the word as well.

A detailed explanation of the pronunciation symbols precedes the full list of words; a concise pronunciation key appears at the bottom of each page of the list.

A Pocket Guide to Vocabulary is a power tool. Based on computer analysis of actual published standardized tests, *A Pocket Guide* enables its users to reach their goal: a strong working vocabulary of college-level words.

Pronunciation Symbols

ə .... banana, collide, abut

ˈə, ˌə .... humdrum, abut

ᵊ .... immediately preceding \l\, \n\, \m\, \ŋ\, as in battle, mitten, eaten, and sometimes open \ˈōp-ᵊn\, lock and key \-ᵊŋ-\; immediately following \l\, \m\, \r\, as often in French table, prisme, titre

ər .... further, merger, bird

ˈər-
ˈə-r .... as in two different pronunciations of hurry \ˈhər-ē, ˈhə-rē\

a .... mat, map, mad, gag, snap, patch

ā .... day, fade, date, aorta, drape, cape

ä .... bother, cot, and, with most American speakers, father, cart

ȧ .... father as pronounced by speakers who do not rhyme it with *bother*; French patte

au̇ .... now, loud, out

b .... baby, rib

ch .... chin, nature \ˈnā-chər\ (actually, this sound is \t\ + \sh\)

d .... did, adder

e .... bet, bed, peck

ˈē, ˌē .... beat, nosebleed, evenly, easy

ē .... easy, mealy

f .... fifty, cuff

g .... go, big, gift

h .... hat, ahead

hw .... whale as pronounced by those who do not have the same pronunciation for both *whale* and *wail*

i .... tip, banish, active

ī .... site, side, buy, tripe (actually, this sound is \ä\ + \i\, or \ȧ\ + \i\)

j .... job, gem, edge, join, judge (actually, this sound is \d\ + \zh\)

k .... kin, cook, ache

k̲ .... German ich, Buch; one pronunciation of loch

l .... lily, pool

m .... murmur, dim, nymph

n .... no, own

ⁿ .... indicates that a preceding vowel or diphthong is pronounced with the nasal passages open, as in French un bon vin blanc \œⁿ-bōⁿ-vaⁿ-bläⁿ\

ŋ .... sing \'siŋ\, singer \'siŋ-ər\, finger \'fiŋ-gər\, ink \'iŋk\

ō .... bone, know, beau

ȯ .... saw, all, gnaw, caught

œ .... French boeuf, German Hölle

œ̄ .... French feu, German Höhle

ȯi .... coin, destroy

p .... pepper, lip

r .... red, car, rarity

s .... source, less

sh .... as in shy, mission, machine, special (actually, this is a single sound, not two); with a hyphen between, two sounds as in grasshopper \'gras-ˌhäp-ər\

t .... tie, attack, late, later, latter

th .... as in thin, ether (actually, this is a single sound, not two); with a hyphen between, two sounds as in knighthood \'nīt-ˌhu̇d\

t̲h̲ .... then, either, this (actually, this is a single sound, not two)

ü .... rule, youth, union \'yün-yən\, few \'fyü\

u̇ .... pull, wood, book, curable \'kyu̇r-ə-bəl\, fury \'fyu̇(ə)r-ē\

ue .... German füllen, hübsch

ūe .... French rue, German fühlen

v .... vivid, give

w .... we, away; in some words having final \(,)ō\, \(,)yü\, or \(,)ü\ a variant \ə-w\ occurs before vowels, as in \'fäl-ə-wiŋ\, covered by the variant \ə(-w)\ or \yə(-w)\ at the entry word

y .... yard, young, cue \'kyü\, mute \'myüt\, union \'yün-yən\

ʸ .... indicates that during the articulation of the sound represented by the preceding character the front of the tongue has substantially the position it has for the articulation of the first sound of *yard*, as in French *digne* \dēnʸ\

z .... zone, raise

zh .... as in vision, azure \'azhər\ (actually, this is a single sound, not two); with a hyphen between, two sounds as in *hogshead* \'hȯgz-,hed, 'hägz-\

**** .... slant line used in pairs to mark the beginning and end of a transcription: \'pen\

ˈ .... mark preceding a syllable with primary (strongest) stress: \'pen-mən-,ship\

ˌ .... mark preceding a syllable with secondary (medium) stress: \'pen-mən-,ship\

- .... mark of syllable division

( ) .... indicate that what is symbolized between is present in some utterances but not in others: *factory* \'fak-t(ə-)rē\

÷ .... indicates that many regard as unacceptable the pronunciation variant immediately following: *cupola* \'kyü-pə-lə, ÷-,lō\

—a—

a-base\ə-ˈbās \v. lower; humiliate. His refusal to *abase* himself in the eyes of his followers irritated the king, who wanted to humiliate the proud leader.

a-bash\ə-ˈbash \v. embarrass. He was not at all *abashed* by her open admiration.

abate\ə-ˈbāt \v. subside; decrease, lessen. Rather than leaving immediately, they waited for the storm to *abate*. **abate-ment**\ə-ˈbāt-mənt\N.

ab-bre-vi-ate\ə-ˈbrē-vē-ˌāt\v. shorten. Because we were running out of time, the lecturer had to *abbreviate* her speech.

ab-di-cate\ˈab -di₁kāt \ v. renounce; give up. When Edward VIII *abdicated* the British throne, he surprised the entire world.

ab-er-ra-tion\ab -ə-ˈrā -shən\N. wandering or straying away; in optics, failure of rays to focus. In designing a good lens for a camera, the problem of correcting chromatic and rectilinear *aberration* was a serious one. **ab-er-rant**\a-ˈber -ənt\ADJ. and N.

a-bet-tor\ə-ˈbet -ər\N. encourager. He was accused of being an aider and *abettor* of the criminal. **a-bet** (ə-ˈbet) v.

a-bey-ance \ə-ˈbā -ən(t)s\ N. suspended action. The deal was held in *abeyance* until his arrival.

ab-hor\əb-ˈhȯ(ə)r \v. detest; hate. He *abhorred* all forms of bigotry. **ab-hor-rence**\əb-ˈhȯr -ən(t)s\N.

ab-jure\ab-ˈju̇(ə)r \v. renounce upon oath. He *abjured* his allegiance to the king. **ab-ju-ra-tion**\ab -jə-ˈrā -shən\N.

ab-lu-tion\ə-ˈblü -shən\N. washing. His daily *ablutions* were accompanied by loud noises which he humorously labeled "Opera in the Bath."

ab-ne-ga-tion\ab -ni-ˈgā -shən\N. repudiation; self-sacrifice. No act of *abnegation* was more pronounced than his refusal of any rewards for his discovery.

abol-ish\ə-ˈbäl-ish \v. cancel; put an end to. The president of the college refused to *abolish* the physical education requirement. **ab-o-li-tion**\ˌab-ə-ˈlish-ən \N.

\ə\ abut	\ᵊ\ kitten, F table	\ər\ further	\a\ ash	\ā\ ace	\ä\ cot, cart
\au̇\ out	\ch\ chin	\e\ bet	\ē\ easy	\g\ go	\i\ hit	\ī\ ice	\j\ job
\ŋ\ sing	\ō\ go	\ȯ\ law	\ȯi\ boy	\th\ thin	\t͟h\ the	\ü\ loot	\u̇\ foot
\y\ yet	\zh\ vision	\à, k̲, ⁿ, œ, œ̄, ue, ū̄e, ʸ\ *see* Pronunciation Symbols

a-bom-i-nate\ə-'bäm -ə-ˌnāt \v. loathe; hate. Moses scolded the idol worshippers in the tribe because he *abominated* the custom.

ab-o-rig-i-nal\ˌab -ə-'rij -nəl\ADJ., N. being the first of its kind in a region; primitive; native. His studies of the primitive art forms of the *aboriginal* Indians were widely reported in the scientific journals. **ab-orig-i-ne**\ˌab -ə-'rij -ə-(ˌ)nē\N.

a-bor-tive\ə-'bȯrt -iv\ADJ. unsuccessful; fruitless. We had to abandon our *abortive* attempts.

a-brade\ə-'brād \v. wear away by friction; erode. The skin of his leg was *abraded* by the sharp rocks. **a-bra-sion**\ə-'brā -zhən\N.

abridge\ə-'brij\v. condense or shorten. Because the publishers felt the public wanted a shorter version of *War and Peace*, they proceeded to *abridge* the novel.

ab-ro-gate\ˈab -rə-ˌgāt \v. abolish. He intended to *abrogate* the decree issued by his predecessor.

ab-scond\ab-'skänd \v. depart secretly and hide. The teller *absconded* with the bonds and was not found.

ab-solve\əb-'zälv \v. pardon (an offense). The father confessor *absolved* him of his sins. **ab-so-lu-tion**\ˌab -sə-'lü -shən\N.

ab-ste-mi-ous\ab-'stē -mē -əs\ADJ. temperate; sparing in drink, etc. The drunkards mocked him because of his *abstemious* habits.

ab-sti-nence\'ab -stə-nən(t)s\N. restraint from eating or drinking. The doctor recommended total *abstinence* from salted foods. **ab-stain**\əb-'stān \v.

ab-stract\ab-'strakt\ADJ. theoretical; not concrete; non-representational. To him, hunger was an *abstract* concept; he had never missed a meal.

ab-struse\əb-'strüs \ADJ. obscure; profound; difficult to understand. He read *abstruse* works in philosophy.

abu-sive\ə-'byü-siv\ADJ. coarsely insulting; physically harmful. An *abusive* parent damages a child both mentally and physically.

a-but\ə-'bət \v. border upon; adjoin. Where our estates *abut*, we must build a fence.

\ə\ abut	\ᵊ\ kitten, F table	\ər\ further	\a\ ash	\ā\ ace	\ä\ cot, cart
\aů\ out	\ch\ chin	\e\ bet	\ē\ easy	\g\ go	\i\ hit	\ī\ ice	\j\ job

a-bys-mal \ə-'biz -məl\ ADJ. bottomless. His arrogance is exceeded only by his *abysmal* ignorance.

ac-cede\ak-sēd \v. agree. If I *accede* to this demand for blackmail, I am afraid that I will be the victim of future demands.

ac-cel-er-ate\ik-'sel -ə-rāt \v. move faster. In our science class, we learn how falling bodies *accelerate*.

ac-ces-si-ble\ik-'ses-a-bal\ ADJ. easy to approach; obtainable. We asked our guide whether the ruins were *accessible* on foot.

ac-ces-so-ry\ik-'ses -(ə-)rē\ N. additional object; useful but not essential thing. The *accessories* she bought cost more than the dress. also ADJ.

ac-claim\ə-'klām\ v. applaud; announce with great approval. The NBC sportscasters *acclaimed* every American victory in the Olympics and decried every American defeat. also N.

ac-cli-mate\'ak -lə-mmāt \v. adjust to climate. One of the difficulties of our present air age is the need of travelers to *acclimate* themselves to their new and often strange environments.

ac-cliv-i-ty\ə-'kliv -ət-ē\ N. sharp upslope of a hill. The car could not go up the *acclivity* in high gear.

ac-co-lade\'ak -ə-ʃlād \ N. award of merit. In Hollywood, an "Oscar" is the highest *accolade*.

ac-com-plice\ə-'käm -pləs\ N. partner in crime. Because he had provided the criminal with the lethal weapon, he was arrested as an *accomplice* in the murder.

ac-cord\ə-'kȯ(ə)rd \ N. agreement. He was in complete *accord* with the verdict.

ac-cost\ə-'kȯst \ v. approach and speak first to a person. When the two young men *accosted* me, I was frightened because I thought they were going to attack me.

ac-cou-tre \ə-'küt -ər\ v. equip. The fisherman was *accoutred* with the best that the sporting goods store could supply. **ac-cou-tre-ment**\ə-'kü -trə-mənt\ N.

ac-cre-tion\ə-'krē -shən\ N. growth; increase. The *accretion* of wealth marked the family's rise in power.

\ŋ\ sing \ō\ go \ȯ\ law \ȯi\ boy \th\ thin \<u>th</u>\ the \ü\ loot \u̇\ foot
\y\ yet \zh\ vision \à, <u>k</u>, ⁿ, œ, œ̄, ue, ūe\, ʌ\ *see* Pronunciation Symbols

ac-crue\ə-ˈkrü \v. come about by addition. You must pay the interest which has *accrued* on your debt as well as the principal sum. **ac-cru-al**\ə-ˈkrü -əl\N.

a-cer-bi-ty\ə-ˈsər -bət-ē\N. bitterness of speech and temper. The meeting of the United Nations Assembly was marked with such *acerbity* that little hope of reaching any useful settlement of the problem could be held.

a-ce-tic\ə-ˈsēt -ik\ADJ. vinegary. The salad had an exceedingly *acetic* flavor.

a-cid-u-lous\ə-ˈsij -ə-ləs\ADJ. slightly sour; sharp, caustic. James was unpopular because of his sarcastic and *acidulous* remarks.

ac-knowl-edge \ik-ˈnäl -ij\ v. recognize; admit. When pressed for an answer, he *acknowledged* the existence of another motive for the crime.

ac-me\ˈak -mē\N. top; pinnacle. His success in this role marked his *acme* as an actor.

a-cous-tic\ə-ˈkü -stik\N. science of sound; quality that makes a room easy or hard to hear in. Carnegie Hall is liked by music lovers because of its fine *acoustics*.

ac-qui-esce\ˌak -wē-ˈes\v. assent; agree passively. Although she appeared to *acquiesce* to her employer's suggestions, I could tell she had reservations about the changes he wanted made. **ac-qui-es-cence**\ak-wē-ˈes-ᵊn(t)s\N; **ac-qui-es-cent**\ak-wē'es-ᵊnt\ADJ.

ac-quit-tal\ə-ˈkwit -ᵊl\ N. deliverance from a charge. His *acquittal* by the jury surprised those who had thought him guilty. **ac-quit**\ə-ˈkwit \V.

ac-rid\ˈak -rəd\ADJ. sharp; bitterly pungent. The *acrid* odor of burnt gunpowder filled the room after the pistol had been fired.

ac-ri-mo-ni-ous\ˌak -rə-ˈmō -nē-əs\ADJ. stinging; caustic. His tendency to utter *acrimonious* remarks alienated his audience. **ac-ri-mo-ny**\ˈak -rə-ˌmō -nē\N.

ac-tu-ar-i-al \ˌak -chə-ˈwer -ē-əl\ ADJ. calculating; pertaining to insurance statistics. According to recent *actuarial* tables, life expectancy is greater today than it was a century ago.

---

ac-tu-ate \ak -chə-wāt \ v. motivate. I fail to understand what *actuated* you to reply to this letter so nastily.

acu-ity \ə-'kyü-ət-ē\ N. sharpness. In time his youthful *acuity* of vision failed him, and he needed glasses.

a-cu-men \ə-'kyü-mən\ N. mental keenness. His business *acumen* helped him to succeed where others had failed.

ad-age \ad -ij\ N. wise saying; proverb. There is much truth in the old *adage* about fools and their money.

ad-a-mant \ad -ə-mənt\ ADJ. hard; inflexible. He was *adamant* in his determination to punish the wrongdoer. **ad-a-man-tine** \ad -ə-man -tēn \ ADJ.

a-dapt \ə-dapt \ v. alter; modify. Some species of animals have become extinct because they could not *adapt* to a changing environment.

ad-dic-tion \ə-dik -shən\ N. compulsive, habitual need. His *addiction* to drugs caused his friends much grief.

ad-dle \ad -ᵊl\ ADJ. rotten; muddled; crazy. This *addle*-headed plan is so preposterous that it does not deserve any consideration. also v.

ad-duce \ə-d(y)üs \ v. present as evidence. When you *adduce* evidence of this nature, you must be sure of your sources.

a-dept \ə-dept \ ADJ. expert at. He was *adept* at the fine art of irritating people. **ad-ept** \ad -ept \ N.

ad-here \ad-'hi(ə)r \ v. stick fast to. I will *adhere* to this opinion until proof that I am wrong is presented. **ad-he-sion** \ad-hē -zhən\ N.

ad-i-pose \ad -ə-pōs \ ADJ. fatty. Excess *adipose* tissue should be avoided by middle-aged people.

ad-junct \aj -əŋ(k)t \ N. something attached to but holding an inferior position. I will entertain this concept as an *adjunct* to the main proposal.

ad-ju-ra-tion \aj -ə-rā -shən \ N. solemn urging. His *adjuration* to tell the truth did not change the witnesses' testimony.

ad-jure \ə-'jü(ə)r \ v. request solemnly. I must *adjure* you to consider this matter carefully as it is of utmost importance to all of us.

\ŋ\ sing   \ō\ go   \o\ law   \oi\ boy   \th\ thin   \th\ the   \ü\ loot   \u\ foot
\y\ yet   \zh\ vision   \à, k, ⁿ, œ, œ̄, ue, ūe, ʸ\ *see* Pronunciation Symbols

ad·mon·ish\ad-'män -ish\v. warn; reprove. He *admonished* his listeners to change their wicked ways.

ad·mo·ni·tion \ad -mə-'nish -ən\ N. warning. After repeated rejections of its *admonitions,* the country was forced to issue an ultimatum.

adorn\ə-'dȯ(ə)rn\v. decorate. Wall paintings and carved statues *adorned* the temple. **adorn·ment,**\ə-'dȯ(ə)rn-mant\N.

a·droit \ə-'drȯit \ADJ. skillful. His *adroit* handling of the delicate situation pleased his employers.

ad·u·la·tion \aj -ə-'lā -shən\ N. flattery; admiration. He thrived on the *adulation* of his henchmen.

a·dul·ter·ate\ə-'dəl -tə-ṛāt \v. make impure by mixing with baser substances. It is a crime to *adulterate* foods without informing the buyer. also ADJ.

ad·um·bra·tion \ad -(ı)əm-'brä -shən\ N. foreshadowing; outlining. The *adumbration* of the future in science fiction is often extremely fantastic.

ad·vent\'ad -ṿent \ N. arrival. Most Americans were unaware of the *advent* of the Nuclear Age until the news of Hiroshima reached them.

ad·ven·ti·tious \ad -vən-'tish -əs\ ADJ. accidental; casual. He found this *adventitious* meeting with his friend extremely fortunate.

ad·verse \ad-'vərs \ ADJ. unfavorable; hostile. *Adverse* circumstances compelled him to close his business.

ad·ver·si·ty\ad-'vər -sət-ē\N. poverty; misfortune. We must learn to meet *adversity* gracefully.

ad·vert\ad-'vərt \v. refer to. Since you *advert* to this matter so frequently, you must regard it as important.

ad·vo·cate\'ad -və-ṛkāt \v. urge; plead for. The abolitionists *advocated* freedom for the slaves. also N.

ae·gis\'ē -jəs\N. shield; defense. Under the *aegis* of the Bill of Rights, we enjoy our most treasured freedoms.

ae·on\'ē -ən\N. long period of time; an age. It has taken *aeons* for our civilization to develop.

aes·thet·ic\es-'thet -ik\ADJ. artistic; dealing with or capable of appreciation of the beautiful. Because of his *aesthetic* nature, he was emotionally disturbed by ugly things. **aes·thete**\'es -ṛthēt \N.

\ə\ abut	\ə\ kitten, F table	\ər\ further	\a\ ash	\ā\ ace	\ä\ cot, cart
\au̇\ out	\ch\ chin	\e\ bet	\ē\ easy	\g\ go	\i\ hit	\ī\ ice	\j\ job

af-fa-ble \ˈaf -ə-bəl\ ADJ. courteous. Although he held a position of responsibility, he was an *affable* individual and could be reached by anyone with a complaint.

af-fect-ed \ə-ˈfek -təd\ ADJ. artificial; pretended. His *affected* mannerisms irritated many of us who had known him before his promotion. **af-fec-ta-tion** \af -ek -ˈtā -shən\ N.

af-fi-da-vit \af -ə-ˈdā -vət\ N. written statement made under oath. The court refused to accept his statement unless he presented it in the form of an *affidavit*.

af-fil-i-a-tion \ə-ˈfil-ē-ā -shən\ N. joining; associating with. His *affiliation* with the political party was of short duration for he soon disagreed with his colleagues. **af-fil-i-ate** \ə-ˈfil -ē-āt \v.

af-fin-i-ty \ə-ˈfin -ət-ē\ N. kinship. He felt an *affinity* with all who suffered; their pains were his pains.

af-fir-ma-tion \af -ər-ˈmā -shən\ N. solemn pledge by one who refuses to take an oath. The Constitution of this country provides for oath or *affirmation* by officeholders.

af-flu-ence \ˈaf -ˌlü -ən(t)s\ N. abundance; wealth. Foreigners are amazed by the *affluence* and luxury of the American way of life.

af-fray \ə-ˈfrā \N. public brawl. He was badly mauled by the fighters in the *affray*.

a-gape \ə-ˈgāp \ADJ. openmouthed. He stared, *agape*, at the many strange animals in the zoo.

a-gen-da \ə-ˈjen -də\ N. items of business at a meeting. We had so much difficulty agreeing upon an *agenda* that there was very little time for the meeting.

ag-glom-er-a-tion \ə-ˌgläm -ə-ˈrā -shən\ N. collection; heap. It took weeks to assort the *agglomeration* of miscellaneous items he had collected on his trip.

ag-gran-dize \ə-ˈgran -ˌdīz \v. increase or intensify. The history of the past quarter century illustrates how a President may *aggrandize* his power to act aggressively in international affairs without considering the wishes of Congress.

ag-gre-gate \ˈag -ri-gət\ADJ. sum; total. The *aggregate* wealth of this country is staggering to the imagination. also v.

\ŋ\ sing   \ō\ go   \o\ law   \oi\ boy   \th\ thin   \th\ the   \ü\ loot   \u̇\ foot
\y\ yet   \zh\ vision   \à, ḵ, ⁿ, œ, œ̄, ue, ūe, ʸ\ *see* Pronunciation Symbols

a·ghast\ə-ˈgast \ADJ. horrified. He was *aghast* at the nerve of the speaker who had insulted his host.

a·gil·i·ty \ə-ˈjil -ət-ē\N. nimbleness. The *agility* of the acrobat amazed and thrilled the audience.

ag·i·tate\ˈaj -ə-ˌtāt \V. stir up; disturb. His fiery remarks *agitated* the already angry mob.

ag·i·ta·tion\aj -ə-ˈtā -shən\N. strong feeling; excitement. We felt that he was responsible for the *agitation* of the mob because of the inflammatory report he had issued.

ag·nos·tic\ag-ˈnäs -tik\N. one who is skeptical of the existence or knowability of a god or any ultimate reality. The *agnostic* demanded proof before he would accept the minister. also ADJ.

a·grar·i·an\ə-ˈgrer -ē-ən\ADJ. pertaining to land or its cultivation. The country is gradually losing its *agrarian* occupation and turning more and more to an industrial point of view. also N.

a·gron·o·mist\ə-ˈgrän -ə-məst\N. scientist engaged in the management of land. Because the country failed to heed the warnings of its *agronomists,* it was faced with serious famine.

a·lac·ri·ty\ə-ˈlak -rət-ē\N. cheerful promptness. He demonstrated his eagerness to serve by his *alacrity* in executing the orders of his master.

al·che·my\ˈal -kə-mē\N. medieval chemistry. The changing of baser metals into gold was the goal of the students of *alchemy.* **al·che·mist**\ˈal -kə-məst\N.

a·li·as \ˈā -lē-əs\N. an assumed name. John Smith's *alias* was Bob Jones. also ADV.

al·ien·ate\ˈal -yə-ˌnāt \V. make hostile; separate. His attempts to *alienate* the two friends failed because they had complete faith.

al·i·men·ta·ry \al -ə-ˈment -ə-rē\ADJ. supplying nourishment. The *alimentary* canal in our bodies is so named because digestion of foods occurs there.

al·i·mo·ny\ˈal -ə-ˌmō -nē\N. payment by a husband to his divorced wife. Mrs. Jones was awarded $200 monthly *alimony* by the court when she was divorced from her husband.

---

al-lay\ə-'lā\v. calm; pacify. The crew tried to *allay* the fears of the passengers by announcing that the fire had been controlled.

al-lege\ə-'lej\v. state without proof. It is *alleged* that he had worked for the enemy. **al-le-ga-tion**\al-i-'gā-shən\ N.

al-le-go-ry\'al-ə-gōr-ē\N. story in which characters are used as symbols; fable. *Pilgrim's Progress* is an *allegory* of the temptations and victories of man's soul. **al-le-gor-i-cal**\al-ə-'gȯr-i-kəl\ADJ.

al-le-vi-ate\ə-'lē-vē-āt\v. relieve. This should *alleviate* the pain; if it does not, we shall have to use stronger drugs.

al-lit-er-a-tion\ə-lit-ə-'rā-shən\ N. repetition of beginning sound in poetry. "The furrow followed free" is an example of *alliteration*.

al-lo-cate\'al-ə-kāt\v. assign. Even though the Red Cross had *allocated* a large sum for the relief of the sufferers of the disaster, many people perished.

al-loy\'al-ȯi\N. a mixture as of metals. *Alloys* of gold are used more frequently than the pure metal. **al-loy**\ə-'lȯi\ v.

al-lude\ə-'lüd\v. refer indirectly. Try not to *allude* to this matter in his presence because it annoys him to hear of it.

al-lu-sion\ə-'lü-zhən\N. indirect reference. The *allusions* to mythological characters in Milton's poems bewilder the reader who has not studied Latin.

al-lu-vi-al\ə-'lü-vē-əl\ADJ. pertaining to soil deposits left by rivers, etc. The farmers found the *alluvial* deposits at the mouth of the river very fertile.

aloft\ə-'lȯft\ADV. upward. The sailor climbed *aloft* into the rigging.

a-loof\ə-'lüf\ADJ. apart; reserved. He remained *aloof* while all the rest conversed.

al-ter-ca-tion\ȯl-tər-'kā-shən\N. wordy quarrel. Throughout the entire *altercation*, not one sensible word was uttered.

\ŋ\ sing   \ō\ go   \ȯ\ law   \ȯi\ boy   \th\ thin   \th\ the   \ü\ loot   \u̇\ foot
\y\ yet   \zh\ vision   \à, k̲, ⁿ, œ, œ̄, ue, ūe, ʸ\ *see* Pronunciation Symbols

al-tru-ism\ˈal -trü-ˌiz -əm\N. unselfish aid to others; generosity. The philanthropist was noted for his *altruism.* **al-tru-is-tic**\ˌal -trü-ˈis -tik\ADJ.

a-mal-gam-ate\ə-ˈmal -gə-ˌmāt \v. combine; unite in one body. The unions will attempt to *amalgamate* their groups into one national body.

a-mass\ə-ˈmas \v. collect. The miser's aim is to *amass* and hoard as much gold as possible.

am-a-zon\ˈam -ə-ˌzän \N. female warrior. Ever since the days of Greek mythology we refer to strong and aggressive women as *amazons.*

am-bi-dex-trous\ˌam-bi-ˈdek-strəs\ADJ. capable of using either hand with equal ease. A switch-hitter in baseball should be naturally *ambidextrous.*

am-bi-ence\ˈam-bē-ən(t)s\N. environment; atmosphere. She went to the restaurant not for the food but for the *ambience.*

am-big-u-ous\am-big -yə-wəs\ADJ. doubtful in meaning. His *ambiguous* direction misled us; we did not know which road to take. **am-bi-gu-i-ty**\ˌam -bə-ˈgyü -ət-ē\N.

am-biv-a-lence\am-ˈbiv-ə-lən(t)s\N. the state of having contradictory or conflicting emotional attitudes. Torn between loving her parents one minute and hating them the next, she was confused by the *ambivalence* of her feelings. **am-biv-a-lent**\am-ˈbiv-ə-lənt\ADJ.

am-ble\ˈam -bəl\N. moving at an easy pace. When she first mounted the horse, she was afraid to urge the animal to go faster than a gentle *amble.* also v.

am-bro-sia\am-ˈbrō -zh(ē-)ə\N. food of the gods. *Ambrosia* was supposed to give immortality to any human who ate it.

am-bu-la-to-ry\ˈam -byə-lə-ˌtōr -ē\ADJ. able to walk. He was described as an *ambulatory* patient because he was not confined to his bed.

a-me-lio-rate \ə-ˈmēl -yə-ˌrāt \ v. improve. Many social workers have attempted to *ameliorate* the conditions of people living in the slums.

a-me-na-ble\ə-ˈmē -nə-bəl\ADJ. readily managed; willing to be led. He was *amenable* to any suggestions which came from those he looked up to; he resented advice from his inferiors.

\ə\ abut　\ᵊ\ kitten, F table　\ər\ further　\a\ ash　\ā\ ace　\ä\ cot, cart
\aů\ out　\ch\ chin　\e\ bet　\ē\ easy　\g\ go　\i\ hit　\ī\ ice　\j\ job

amend\ə-'mend\v. correct; change, generally for the better. Hoping to *amend* his condition, he left Vietnam for the United States.

ame-ni-ties\ə-'men-ət-ēz\N. agreeable manners; courtesies. She observed the social *amenities*.

a-mi-a-ble\ā-mē-ə-bəl\ADJ. agreeable; lovable. His *amiable* disposition pleased all who had dealings with him.

am-i-ca-ble\am-i-kə-bəl\ADJ. friendly. The dispute was settled in an *amicable* manner with no harsh words.

amiss\ə-'mis\ADJ. wrong; faulty. Seeing her frown, he wondered if anything were *amiss*. also ADV.

am-i-ty\'am-ət-ē\N. friendship. Student exchange programs such as the Experiment in International Living were established to promote international *amity*.

am-ne-sia\am-hē-zhə\N. loss of memory. Because she was suffering from *amnesia*, the police could not get the young girl to identify herself.

am-nes-ty\am-nə-stē\N. pardon. When his first child was born, the king granted *amnesty* to all in prison.

a-mor-al\'(')ā-mȯr-əl\ADJ. nonmoral. The *amoral* individual lacks a code of ethics; he should not be classified as immoral.

a-mor-phous\ə-'mȯr-fəs\ADJ. shapeless. He was frightened by the *amorphous* mass which had floated in from the sea.

am-phib-i-an\am-'fib-ē-ən\ADJ. able to live both on land and in water. Frogs are classified as *amphibian*. also N.

am-phi-the-ater\am(p)-fə-thē-ət-ər\N. oval building with tiers of seats. The spectators in the *amphitheater* cheered the gladiators.

am-ple\am-pəl\ADJ. abundant. He had *ample* opportunity to dispose of his loot before the police caught up with him.

am-pli-fy\am-plə-fī\V. enlarge. His attempts to *amplify* his remarks were drowned out by the jeers of the audience.

am-pu-tate\am-pyə-tāt\V. cut off part of body; prune. When the doctors decided to *amputate* his leg to prevent the spread of gangrene, he cried that he preferred death to incapacity.

\ŋ\ **sing** \ō\ **go** \ȯ\ **law** \ȯi\ **boy** \th\ **thin** \th̲\ **the** \ü\ **loot** \u̇\ **foot**
\y\ **yet** \zh\ **vision** \à, k̲, ⁿ, œ, œ̄, ue, ūe, ʸ\ *see* Pronunciation Symbols

a-muck \ə-mək \ ADV. in a state of rage. The police had to be called in to restrain him after he ran *amuck* in the department store.

am-u-let \ăm -yə-lət\ N. charm; talisman. Around his neck he wore the *amulet* which the witch doctor had given him.

a-nach-ro-nism \ə-năk -rə-niz -əm\ N. an error involving time in a story. The reference to clocks in *Julius Caesar* is an *anachronism.*

an-al-ge-sic \ăn -ə̄l-jē -zik\ ADJ. causing insensitivity to pain. The *analgesic* qualities of this lotion will provide temporary relief. **an-al-ge-sia** \ăn -ə̄l-jē -zhə\ N.

a-nal-o-gous \ə-năl -ə-gəs\ ADJ. comparable. He called our attention to the things that had been done in an *analogous* situation and recommended that we do the same.

a-nal-o-gy \ə-năl -ə-jē\ N. similarity; parallelism. Your *analogy* is not a good one because the two situations are not similar.

an-ar-chist \ 'an-ər-kəst\ N. person who rebels against the established order. Only the total overthrow of all governmental regulations would satisfy the *anarchist.*

an-ar-chy \ăn -ər-kē\ N. absence of governing body; state of disorder. The assassination of the leaders led to a period of *anarchy.*

a-nath-e-ma \ə-năth -ə-mə\ N. solemn curse. He heaped *anathema* upon his foe.

an-chor \ 'aŋ-kər\ V. secure or fasten firmly; be fixed in place. We set the post in concrete to *anchor* it in place. **an-chor-age** \ 'aŋ-k(ə-)rij\ N.

an-cil-lar-y \ăn(t) -sə-ler -ē\ ADJ. serving as an aid or accessory; auxiliary. In an *ancillary* capacity he was helpful; however, he could not be entrusted with leadership. also N.

a-ne-mi-a \ə-nē -mē-ə\ N. condition in which blood lacks red corpuscles. The doctor ascribes his tiredness to *anemia.* **a-ne-mic** \ə-nē -mik\ ADJ.

an-es-thet-ic \ăn -əs-thet -ik\ N. substance that removes sensation with or without loss of consciousness. His monotonous voice acted like an *anesthetic;* his audience was soon asleep. **an-es-the-sia** \ăn -əs-thē -zhə\ N.

an-gu-lar\\'an-gyə-lər\\ADJ. sharp-cornered; stiff in manner. His features, though *angular*, were curiously attractive.

an-i-mad-ver-sion \\an -ə-mad -ˈvər -zhən\\ N. critical remark. He resented the *animadversions* of his critics, particularly because he realized they were true.

an-i-mat-ed \\ˈan -ə-ˌmāt -əd\\ ADJ. lively. Her *animated* expression indicated a keenness of intellect.

an-i-mos-i-ty \\an -ə-ˈmäs -ət-ē\\ N. active enmity. He incurred the *animosity* of the ruling class because he advocated limitations of their power.

an-i-mus\\an -ə-məs\\N. hostile feeling or intent. The *animus* of the speaker became obvious to all when he began to indulge in sarcastic and insulting remarks.

an-nals\\an -ᵊlz\\N. records; history. In the *annals* of this period, we find no mention of democratic movements.

an-neal \\ə-hē(ə)l \\ V. reduce brittleness and improve toughness by heating and cooling. After the glass is *annealed,* it will be less subject to chipping and cracking.

an-ni-hi-late\\ə-hī -ə-ˌlāt \\V. destroy. The enemy in its revenge tried to *annihilate* the entire population.

an-no-tate\\an -ə-ˌtāt \\V. comment; make explanatory notes. In the appendix to the novel, the critic sought to *annotate* many of the more esoteric references.

an-nu-i-ty\\ə-ˈn(y)ü -ət-ē\\N. yearly allowance. The *annuity* he set up with the insurance company supplements his social security benefits so that he can live very comfortably without working.

an-nul \\ə-ˈnəl \\V. make void. The parents of the eloped couple tried to *annul* the marriage.

anoint\\ə-ˈnöint\\V. consecrate. The prophet Samuel *anointed* David with oil, crowning him king of Israel.

a-nom-a-lous\\ə-ˈnäm -ə-ləs\\ADJ. abnormal; irregular. He was placed in the *anomalous* position of seeming to approve procedures which he despised.

a-nom-a-ly\\ə-ˈnäm -ə-lē\\N. irregularity. A bird that cannot fly is an *anomaly*.

a-non-y-mous\\ə-ˈnän -ə-məs\\ ADJ. having no name. He tried to ascertain the identity of the writer of the *anonymous* letter.

\\ŋ\\ sing	\\ō\\ go	\\ò\\ law	\\òi\\ boy	\\th\\ thin	\\th̲\\ the	\\ü\\ loot	\\u̇\\ foot
\\y\\ yet	\\zh\\ vision	\\à, k̲, ⁿ, œ, œ̄, ue, ūe, ʸ\\ *see* Pronunciation Symbols

an-tag-o-nism\an-tag -ə-ˌniz -əm\N. active resistance. We shall have to overcome the *antagonism* of the natives before our plans for settling this area can succeed.

an-te-cede\ˌant-ə-ˈsēd\v. precede. The invention of the radiotelegraph *anteceded* the development of television by a quarter of a century.

an-te-di-lu-vi-an\ant -i-də-ˈlü -vē-ən\ADJ. antiquated; ancient. The *antediluvian* customs had apparently not changed for thousands of years. also N.

an-thro-poid\ˈan(t) -thrə-ˌpòid \ADJ. manlike. The gorilla is the strongest of the *anthropoid* animals. also N.

an-thro-pol-o-gist\an(t) -thrə-ˈpäl -ə-jəst\N. a student of the history and science of mankind. *Anthropologists* have discovered several relics of prehistoric man in this area.

an-thro-po-mor-phic \an(t) -thrə-pə-ˈmor -fik\ADJ. having human form or characteristics. Primitive religions often have dieties with *anthropomorphic* characteristics.

an-ti-cli-max\ant -i-ˈklī -ˌmaks \N. letdown in thought or emotion. After the fine performance in the first act, the rest of the play was an *anticlimax*. **an-ti-cli-mac-tic**\ant -i-klī-ˈmak -tik\ADJ.

an-tip-a-thy \an-tip -ə-thē \N. aversion; dislike. His extreme *antipathy* to dispute caused him to avoid argumentative discussions with his friends.

an-ti-sep-tic\ant -ə-ˈsep -tik\N. substance that prevents infection. It is advisable to apply an *antiseptic* to any wound, no matter how slight or insignificant. also ADJ.

an-tith-e-sis\an-tith -ə-səs\N. contrast; direct opposite of or to. This tyranny was the *antithesis* of all that he had hoped for, and he fought it with all his strength.

ap-a-thy\ˈap-ə-thē \N. lack of caring; indifference. A firm believer in democratic government, she could not understand the *apathy* of people who never bothered to vote. **ap-a-thet-ic**\ˌàp-ə-ˈthet-ik \ADJ.

ape\āp\v. imitate or mimic. He was suspended for a week because he had *aped* the principal in front of the whole school.

ap-er-ture\ˈap -ə(r)-ˌchù(ə)r \N. opening; hole. He discovered a small *aperture* in the wall, through which the insects had entered the room.

\ə\ abut	\ᵊ\ kitten, F table	\ər\ further	\a\ ash	\ā\ ace	\ä\ cot, cart
\au̇\ out	\ch\ chin	\e\ bet	\ē\ easy	\g\ go	\i\ hit	\ī\ ice	\j\ job

a-pex \ˈā -peks \ N. tip; summit; climax. He was at the *apex* of his career.

a-pha-sia \ə-ˈfā -zh(ē-)ə\ N. loss of speech due to injury. After the automobile accident, the victim had periods of *aphasia* when he could not speak at all or could only mumble incoherently.

aph-o-rism \ˈaf -ə-ˌriz -əm\ N. pithy maxim. An *aphorism* differs from an adage in that it is more philosophical or scientific. **aph-o-ris-tic**\ˌaf -ə-ˈris -tik\ADJ.

a-pi-ar-y\ˈā -pē-ˌer -ē\N. a place where bees are kept. Although he spent many hours daily in the *apiary*, he was very seldom stung by a bee.

a-plomb\ə-ˈpläm \N. poise. His nonchalance and *aplomb* in times of trouble always encouraged his followers.

a-poc-a-lyp-tic\ə-ˌpäk -ə-ˈlip -tik\ADJ. prophetic; pertaining to revelations. His *apocalyptic* remarks were dismissed by his audience as wild surmises.

a-poc-ry-phal\ə-ˈpäk -rə-fəl\ADJ. not genuine; sham. His *apocryphal* tears misled no one.

ap-o-gee\ˈap -ə-ˌ(ı)jē\N. highest point. When the moon in its orbit is furthest away from the earth, it is at its *apogee*.

a-po-plexy\ˈap-ə-ˌplek-sē \N. stroke; loss of consciousness followed by paralysis. He was crippled by an attack of *apoplexy*.

a-pos-tate\ə-ˈpäs -ˌtāt \N. one who abandons his religious faith or political beliefs. Because he switched from one party to another, his former friends shunned him as an *apostate*.

a-poth-e-cary\ə-ˈpäth -ə-ˌker -ē\N. druggist. In the *apothecaries'* weight, twelve ounces equal one pound.

ap-o-thegm\ˈap -ə-ˌthem \N. pithy, compact saying. Proverbs are *apothegms* that have become familiar sayings.

a-po-the-o-sis \ə-ˌpäth -ē-ˈō -səs\ N. deification; glorification. The *apotheosis* of a Roman emperor was designed to insure his eternal greatness.

ap-pall\ə-ˈpȯl\V. dismay; shock. We were *appalled* by the horrifying conditions in the city's jails.

ap-pa-ri-tion\ˌap -ə-ˈrish -ən\N. ghost; phantom. Hamlet was uncertain about the identity of the *apparition* that had appeared and spoken to him.

\ŋ\ sing   \ō\ go   \ȯ\ law   \ȯi\ boy   \th\ thin   \th\ the   \ü\ loot   \u̇\ foot
\y\ yet   \zh\ vision   \ä, k̲, ⁿ, œ, œ̄, ue, ue̅, ʸ\ *see* Pronunciation Symbols

ap-pease \ə-'pēz \ v. pacify; soothe. We have discovered that, when we try to *appease* our enemies, we encourage them to make additional demands.

ap-pel-la-tion\ap -ə-lā -shən\N. name; title. He was amazed when the witches hailed him with his correct *appellation*.

ap-pend\ə-'pend \ v. attach. I shall *append* this chart to my report.

ap-po-site\ap -ə-zət\ADJ. appropriate; fitting. He was always able to find the *apposite* phrase, the correct expression for every occasion.

ap-praise \ə-'prāz \ v. estimate value of. It is difficult to *appraise* the value of old paintings; it is easier to call them priceless. **ap-prais-al**\ə-'prā -zəl\N.

ap-pre-hend \ap -ri-hend \ v. arrest (a criminal); dread; perceive. The police will *apprehend* the culprit and convict him before long.

ap-pre-hen-sive \ap-ri-'hen(t) -siv\ ADJ. fearful; discerning. His *apprehensive* glances at the people who were walking in the street revealed his nervousness.

ap-prise\ə-'prīz \v. inform. When he was *apprised* of the dangerous weather conditions, he decided to postpone his trip.

ap-pro-ba-tion\,ap-rə-'bā-shən \N. approval. She looked for some sign of *approbation* from her parents.

ap-pro-pri-ate\ə-'prō-prē-,āt\v. acquire; take possession of for one's own use. The ranch owners *appropriated* the lands that had originally been set aside for the Indians' use.

ap-pur-te-nance\ə-'pərt -nən(t)s\ N. subordinate possession. He bought the estate and all its *appurtenances*.

ap-ro-pos\ap -rə-pō \PREP. with reference to; properly. I find your remarks *apropos* of the present situation timely and pertinent. also ADJ. and ADV.

ap-ti-tude\ap -tə-t(y)üd \N. fitness; talent. The counselor gave him an *aptitude* test before advising him about the career he should follow.

aq-ui-line \ak -wə-līn \ ADJ. curved, hooked. He can be recognized by his *aquiline* nose, curved like the beak of the eagle.

\ə\ **abut** \ᵊ\ **kitten, F table** \ər\ **further** \a\ **ash** \ā\ **ace** \ä\ **cot, cart**
\aù\ **out** \ch\ **chin** \e\ **bet** \ē\ **easy** \g\ **go** \i\ **hit** \ī\ **ice** \j\ **job**

ar-a-ble\är -ə-bəl\ADJ. fit for plowing. The land was no longer *arable;* erosion had removed the valuable topsoil.

ar-bi-ter\är -bət-ər\N. a person with power to decide a dispute; judge. As an *arbiter* in labor disputes, he has won the confidence of the workers and the employers.

ar-bi-trar-y\är -bə-ˌtrer -ē\ADJ. fixed or decided; despotic. Any *arbitrary* action on your part will be resented by the members of the board whom you do not consult.

ar-cade\är-kād \N. a covered passageway, usually lined with shops. The *arcade* was popular with shoppers because it gave them protection from the summer sun and the winter rain.

ar-cane\är-'kān\ADJ. secret; mysterious. What was *arcane* to us was clear to the psychologist.

ar-chae-ol-o-gy\är -kē-äl -ə-jē\N. study of artifacts and relics of early mankind. The professor of *archaeology* headed an expedition to the Gobi Desert in search of ancient ruins.

ar-cha-ic\är-kā -ik\ADJ. antiquated. "Methinks," "thee," and "thou" are *archaic* words which are no longer part of our normal vocabulary.

ar-che-type\är -ki-ˌtīp \N. prototype; primitive pattern. The Brooklyn Bridge was the *archetype* of the many spans that now connect Manhattan with Long Island and New Jersey.

ar-chi-pel-a-go\är -kə-ˌpel -ə-gō\N. group of closely located islands. When he looked at the map and saw the *archipelagoes* in the South Seas, he longed to visit them.

ar-chive\är -ˌkīv \N. public records; place where public records are kept. These documents should be part of the *archives* so that historians may be able to evaluate them in the future.

ar-dor\ärd -ər\N. heat; passion; zeal. His *ardor* was contagious; soon everyone was eagerly working.

ar-du-ous\ärj -(ə-)wəs\ADJ. hard; strenuous. His *arduous* efforts had sapped his energy.

ar-got\är -gət\N. slang. In the *argot* of the underworld, he "was taken for a ride."

\ŋ\ sing   \ō\ go   \ò\ law   \òi\ boy   \th\ thin   \th̲\ the   \ü\ loot   \u̇\ foot
\y\ yet   \zh\ vision   \à, k̲, ⁿ, œ, œ̄, ue, ue̅, ʸ\ *see* Pronunciation Symbols

aria\ˈär-ē-ə\ N. operatic solo. At her Metropolitan Opera audition, Marian Anderson sang an *aria* from *Norma*.

ar-id\ˈar-əd\ ADJ. dry; barren. The cactus has adapted to survive in an *arid* environment.

ar-ma-da\är-ˈmäd-ə\ N. fleet of warships. Queen Elizabeth's navy defeated the mighty *armada* that threatened the English coast.

ar-o-mat-ic\ar -ə-ˈmat -ik\ ADJ. fragrant. Medieval sailing vessels brought *aromatic* herbs from China to Europe. also N.

ar-raign\ə-ˈrān \ V. charge in court; indict. After his indictment by the Grand Jury, the accused man was *arraigned* in the County Criminal Court.

array\ə-ˈrā\ V. marshal; place in proper or desired order. His actions were bound to *array* public sentiment against him. also N.

array\ə-ˈrā\ V. clothe; adorn. She liked to watch her mother *array* herself in her finest clothes before going out for the evening. also N.

ar-rears\ə-ˈri(ə)rz\ N. being in debt. He was in *arrears* with his payments on the car.

ar-ro-gance\ar -ə-gən(t)s\ N. haughtiness. The *arrogance* of the nobility was resented by the middle class. **ar-ro-gant**\ˈar -ə-gənt\ ADJ.

ar-ro-gate\ˈar -ə-gāt \ V. claim without reasonable grounds. I am afraid that the manner in which he *arrogates* power to himself indicates that he is willing to ignore Constitutional limitations.

ar-roy-o \ə-ˈrȯi -ə\ N. gully. Until the heavy rains of the past spring, this *arroyo* had been a dry bed.

ar-tic-u-late\är-ˈtik-yə-lət\ ADJ. effective; distinct. Her *articulate* presentation of the advertising campaign impressed her employers. also V.

ar-ti-fact\ˈärt -ə-fakt \ N. product of primitive culture. Archaeologists debated the significance of the *artifacts* discovered in the ruins of Asia Minor and came to no conclusion.

ar-ti-fice\ˈärt -ə-fəs\ N. deception; trickery. The Trojan War proved to the Greeks that cunning and *artifice* were often more effective than military might.

---

ar-ti-san\\'ärt -ə-zən\ N. a manually skilled worker. Artists and *artisans* alike are necessary to the development of a culture.

as-cen-dan-cy\ə-'sen-dən-sē\ N. controlling influence. President Marcos failed to maintain his *ascendancy* over the Philippines.

as-cer-tain\as -ər-'tān \ v. find out for certain. Please *ascertain* his present address.

as-cet-ic\ə-'set -ik\ ADJ. practicing self-denial; austere. The cavalier could not understand the *ascetic* life led by the monks. also N.

as-cet-i-cism \ə-'set -ə-siz -əm\ N. doctrine of self-denial. We find *asceticism* carried on in many parts of the world.

as-cribe \ə-'skrīb \ v. refer; attribute; assign. I can *ascribe* no motive for his acts.

a-sep-tic\(ı)ā-'sep -tik\ ADJ. preventing putrefaction or blood poisoning by killing bacteria. Hospitals succeeded in lowering the mortality rate as soon as they introduced *aseptic* conditions.

ash-en\'ash -ən\ ADJ. ash-colored. His face was *ashen* with fear.

as-i-nine\'as -ᵊn-īn \ ADJ. stupid. Your *asinine* remarks prove that you have not given this problem any serious consideration.

a-skance\ə-'skan(t)s \ ADV. with a sideways or indirect look. Looking *askance* at her questioner, she displayed her scorn.

a-skew\ə-'skyü \ ADV. crookedly; slanted; at an angle. When he placed his hat *askew* upon his head, his observers laughed.

as-per-i-ty \a-'sper -ət-ē\ N. sharpness (of temper). These remarks, spoken with *asperity*, stung the boys to whom they had been directed.

as-per-sion \ə-'spər- zhən\ N. slanderous remark. Do not cast *aspersions* on his character.

as-pi-rant\'as -p(ə-)rənt\ N. seeker after position or status. Although I am an *aspirant* for public office, I am not willing to accept the dictates of the party bosses. also ADJ.

as-pi-ra-tion\as -pə-'rā -shən\ N. noble ambition. Man's *aspirations* should be as lofty as the stars.

---

as-sail \ə-ˈsā(ə)l \v. assault. He was *assailed* with questions after his lecture.

as-say \a-ˈsā \v. analyze; evaluate. When they *assayed* the ore, they found that they had discovered a very rich vein. **as-say** \as ͵-ā \N.

as-sess-ment \ə-ˈses-mənt \N. appraisal; estimation. I would like to have your *assessment* of the situation in South Africa.

as-sid-u-ous \ə-ˈsij -(ə-)wəs \ADJ. diligent. He worked *assiduously* at this task for weeks before he felt satisfied with his results. **as-si-du-i-ty** \as -ə-d(y)ü -ət-ē \N.

as-sim-i-late \ə-ˈsim -ə-͵lāt \v. absorb; cause to become homogeneous. The manner in which the United States was able to *assimilate* the hordes of immigrants during the nineteenth and the early part of the twentieth centuries will always be a source of pride. also N.

as-suage \ə-ˈswāj \v. ease; lessen (pain). Your messages of cheer should *assuage* his suffering. **as-suage-ment** \ə-ˈswāj-mənt \N.

as-ter-oid \ˈas -tə-͵ròid \N. small planet. *Asteroids* have become commonplace to the readers of interstellar travel stories in science fiction magazines.

a-stig-ma-tism \ə-ˈstig -mə-͵tiz -əm \N. eye defect which prevents proper focus. As soon as his parents discovered that the boy suffered from *astigmatism*, they took him to the optometrist for corrective glasses.

as-tral \ˈas -trəl \ADJ. relating to the stars. He was amazed at the number of *astral* bodies the new telescope revealed.

as-trin-gent \ə-ˈstrin -jənt \ADJ. binding; causing contraction. The *astringent* quality of the unsweetened lemon juice made swallowing difficult. also N.

as-tro-nom-i-cal \͵as-trə-ˈnäm-i-kəl \ADJ. enormously large or extensive. The government seems willing to spend *astronomical* sums on weapons development.

as-tute \ə-ˈst(y)üt \ADJ. wise; shrewd. That was a very *astute* observation. I shall heed it.

at-a-vism \ˈat -ə-͵viz -əm \N. resemblance to remote ancestors rather than to parents; deformity returning after passage of two or more generations. The doctors ascribed the child's deformity to an *atavism*.

ate-lier \at -ᵊl-yā \ N. workshop; studio. Stories of Bohemian life in Paris are full of tales of artists' starving or freezing in their *ateliers*.

a-the-is-tic \ā -thē-is -tik\ADJ. denying the existence of God. His *atheistic* remarks shocked the religious worshippers. **a-the-ist** \ā -thē-əst\

a-troc-i-ty \ə-träs -ət-ē\ N. brutal deed. In time of war, many *atrocities* are committed by invading armies.

at-ro-phy \a -trə-fē\ N. wasting away. Polio victims need physiotherapy to prevent the *atrophy* of affected limbs. also v.

at-ten-u-ate \ə-ten -yə-wāt \ V. make thin; weaken. By withdrawing their forces, the generals hoped to *attenuate* the enemy lines.

at-test \ə-test \V. testify, bear witness. Having served as a member of the Grand Jury, I can *attest* that our system of indicting individuals is in need of improvement.

at-tri-bute \a -trə-byüt \N. essential quality. His outstanding *attribute* was his kindness.

at-tri-tion \ə-trish -ən\N. gradual wearing down. They decided to wage a war of *attrition* rather than to rely on an all-out attack.

a-typ-i-cal \(ꞮꞮ)ā-tip -i-kəl\ADJ. not normal. You have taken an *atypical* case. It does not prove anything.

au-dac-i-ty \ȯ-das -ət-ē\ N. boldness. His *audacity* in this critical moment encouraged us.

au-dit \ȯd -ət\N. examination of accounts. When the bank examiners arrived to hold their annual *audit*, they discovered the embezzlements of the chief cashier. also v.

aug-ment \ȯg-ment \V. increase. How can we hope to *augment* our forces when our allies are deserting us?

au-gu-ry \ȯ -gyə-rē\N. omen; prophecy. He interpreted the departure of the birds as an *augury* of evil. **au-gur** \ȯ -gər\V, N.

au-re-ole \ȯr -ē-ōl \N. sun's corona; halo. Many medieval paintings depict saintly characters with *aureoles* around their heads.

\ŋ\ sing   \ō\ go   \ȯ\ law   \ȯi\ boy   \th\ thin   \<u>th</u>\ the   \ü\ loot   \u̇\ foot
\y\ yet   \zh\ vision   \à, <u>k</u>, ⁿ, œ, œ̄, ue, ūe̅, ʸ\ *see* Pronunciation Symbols

au-ro-ral\ə-'rōr -əl\ADJ. pertaining to the aurora borealis. The *auroral* display was particularly spectacular that evening. **au-ro-ra**\ə-'rōr -ə\N.

aus-pi-cious\ȯ-'spish -əs\ADJ. favoring success. With favorable weather conditions, it was an *auspicious* moment to set sail.

aus-tere\ȯ-'sti(ə)r \ADJ. strict, stern. His *austere* demeanor prevented us from engaging in our usual frivolous activities.

aus-ter-i-ty\ȯ-'ster -ət-ē\N. sternness; severity. The *austerity* and dignity of the court were maintained by the new justices.

au-then-ti-cate\ə-'thent -i‐kāt \V. prove genuine. An expert was needed to *authenticate* the original Van Gogh painting from its imitation.

au-thor-i-ta-tive\ə-'thär-ə-‐tāt-iv\ADJ. having the weight of authority; dictatorial. We accepted her analysis of the situation as *authoritative*.

au-to-crat\'ȯt -ə-‐krat \N. monarch with supreme power. The nobles tried to limit the powers of the *autocrat* without success. **au-toc-ra-cy**\ȯ-'täk -rə-sē\N.

au-tom-a-ton\ȯ-'täm -ət-ən\N. mechanism which imitates actions of humans. Long before science fiction readers became aware of robots, writers were presenting stories of *automatons* who could outperform men.

au-ton-o-mous\ȯ-'tän -ə-məs\ADJ. self-governing. This island is a colony; however, in most matters, it is *autonomous* and receives no orders from the mother country. **au-ton-o-my**\ȯ-'tän -ə-mē\N.

au-top-sy\'ȯ -‐täp -sē\N. examination of a dead body; post mortem. The medical examiner ordered an *autopsy* to determine the cause of death. also V.

aux-il-ia-ry\ȯg-'zil -yə-rē\ADJ. helper, additional or subsidiary. To prepare for the emergency, they built an *auxiliary* power station. also N.

av-a-rice\'av -(ə-)rəs\N. greediness for wealth. King Midas's *avarice* has been famous for centuries. **av-a-ri-cious**\av -ə-'rish -əs\ADJ.

\ə\ abut   \ᵊ\ kitten, F table   \ər\ further   \a\ ash   \ā\ ace   \ä\ cot, cart
\aù\ out   \ch\ chin   \e\ bet   \ē\ easy   \g\ go   \i\ hit   \ī\ ice   \j\ job

av-a-tar \ȧv -ə-ṭär \ N. incarnation. In Hindu mythology, the *avatar* of Vishnu is thoroughly detailed.

a-ver \ə-ˈvər \ V. state confidently. I wish to *aver* that I am certain of success.

a-verse \ə-ˈvərs \ADJ. reluctant. He was *averse* to revealing the sources of his information.

aver-sion \ə-ˈvər-zhən \ N. firm dislike. Their mutual *aversion* was so great that they refused to speak to one another.

avert \ə-ˈvərt \ V. prevent; turn away. She *averted* her eyes from the dead cat on the highway.

av-id \ȧv -əd\ADJ. greedy; eager for. He was *avid* for learning and read everything he could get. **a-vid-i-ty** \ə-vid -ət-ē\ N.

av-o-ca-tion \ȧv -ə-ˈkā -shən\ N. secondary or minor occupation. His hobby proved to be so fascinating and profitable that gradually he abandoned his regular occupation and concentrated on his *avocation*.

a-vow \ə-ˈvaủ \ V. declare openly. I must *avow* that I am innocent.

a-vun-cu-lar \ə-ˈvəŋ -kyə-lər\ADJ. like an uncle. *Avuncular* pride did not prevent him from noticing his nephew's shortcomings.

awe \ȯ \ N. solemn wonder. The tourists gazed with *awe* at the tremendous expanse of the Grand Canyon.

a-wry \ə-ˈrī \ ADV. distorted; crooked. He held his head *awry*, giving the impression that he had caught cold in his neck during the night. also ADJ.

ax-i-om \ȧk -sē-əm\N. self-evident truth requiring no proof. Before a student can begin to think along the lines of Euclidean geometry, he must accept certain principles or *axioms*.

az-ure \ȧzh -ər\ADJ. sky blue. *Azure* skies are indicative of good weather.

–b–

bab-ble\ˈbab -əl\ v. chatter idly. The little girl *babbled* about her doll. also N.

bac-cha-na-lian\ˌbak -ə-ˈnāl -yən\ ADJ. drunken. Emperor Nero attended the *bacchanalian* orgy.

bad-ger\ˈbaj -ər\ v. pester; annoy. She was forced to change her telephone number because she was *badgered* by obscene phone calls.

ba-di-nage\ˌbad-ᵊn-ˈäzh\ N. teasing conversation. Her friends at work greeted the news of her engagement with cheerful *badinage*.

baf-fle\ˈbaf -əl\ v. frustrate; perplex. The new code *baffled* the enemy agents. also N.

bag-a-telle\ˌbag-ə-ˈtel\ N. trifle. Trying to reassure Roxanne about his wound, Cyrano claimed it was a mere *bagatelle*.

bait\ˈbāt\ v. harass; tease. The soldiers *baited* the prisoners, terrorizing them.

bale-ful\ˈbā(ə)l -fəl\ ADJ. deadly; destructive. The drought was a *baleful* omen.

balk\ˈbȯk\ v. foil. When the warden learned that several inmates were planning to escape, he took steps to *balk* their attempt. also N.

bal-last\ˈbal-əst\ N. heavy substance used to add stability or weight. The ship was listing badly to one side; it was necessary to shift the *ballast* in the hold to get her back on an even keel. also V.

balm\ˈbä(l)m\ N. something that relieves pain. Friendship is the finest *balm* for the pangs of disappointed love.

balm-y\ˈbäm -ē\ ADJ. mild; fragrant. A *balmy* breeze refreshed us after the sultry blast.

ba-nal\bə-ˈnäl\ ADJ. hackneyed; commonplace; trite. His frequent use of clichés made his essay seem *banal*. **ba-nal-i-ty**\bə-ˈnal -ət-ē\ N.

ban-dy\ˈban-dē\ v. discuss lightly; exchange blows or words. The President refused to *bandy* words with the reporters at the press conference.

bane\ˈbān\ N. cause of ruin; poison. Lack of public transportation is the *bane* of urban life. **bane-ful**\bān-fəl\ ADJ.

\ə\ abut \ᵊ\ kitten, F table \ər\ further \a\ ash \ā\ ace \ä\ cot, cart
\au̇\ out \ch\ chin \e\ bet \ē\ easy \g\ go \i\ hit \ī\ ice \j\ job

bane-ful\\'bān -fəl\\ADJ. ruinous; poisonous. His *baneful* influence was feared by all.

ban-ter \\'bant -ər\ N. good-natured ridiculing. They resented his *banter* because they thought he was being sarcastic. also V.

barb \\'bärb \ N. sharp projection from fishhook, etc. The *barb* from the fishhook caught in his finger as he grabbed the fish. also V.

ba-roque\bə-'rōk \ADJ. highly ornate. They found the *baroque* architecture amusing.

bar-rage \bə-'räzh\ N. barrier laid down by artillery fire. The company was forced to retreat through the *barrage* of heavy cannons. also V.

bar-ris-ter \\'bar -ə-stər\ N. counselor-at-law. Galsworthy started as a *barrister*, but when he found the practice of law boring, turned to writing.

bar-ter-er \\'bärt -ər-ər\ N. trader. The *barterer* exchanged trinkets for the natives' furs. **bar-ter**\\'bärt -ər\V.

bask\ 'bask \V. luxuriate; take pleasure in warmth. *Basking* on the beach, she relaxed so completely that she fell asleep.

bas-soon \bə-'sün \ N. reed instrument of the woodwind family. In the orchestra, the *bassoon* is related to the oboe and the clarinet.

bas-tion\ 'bas-chən \N. fortress; defense. Once a *bastion* of democracy, under its new government the island became a dictatorship.

bate\\'bāt \V. let down; restrain. Until it was time to open the presents, the children had to *bate* their curiosity.

bat-ten\\'bat -ᵊn\V. grow fat; thrive upon others. We cannot accept a system where a favored few can *batten* in extreme comfort while others toil.

bau-ble\'bȯ -bəl\N. trinket; trifle. The child was delighted with the *bauble* she had won in the grab bag.

bawdy\ 'bȯd-ē \ADJ. indecent; obscene. She took offense at his *bawdy* remarks.

be-a-ti-fic\bē -ə-'tif -ik\ADJ. giving bliss; blissful. The *beatific* smile on the child's face made us very happy.

\ŋ\ sing \ō\ go \ȯ\ law · \ȯi\ boy \th\ thin \th\ the \ü\ loot \u̇\ foot
\y\ yet \zh\ vision \à, k̲, ⁿ, œ, œ̄, ue, ue̅, ʸ\ *see* Pronunciation Symbols

be·at·i·tude\bē-'at-ə-,t(y)üd\N. blessedness; state of bliss. Growing closer to God each day, the mystic achieved a state of indescribable *beatitude*.

be·di·zen\bi-dīz -ᵊn\V. dress with vulgar finery. The witch doctors were *bedizened* in all their gaudiest costumes.

be·drag·gle\bi-drag -əl\V. wet thoroughly. We were so *bedraggled* by the severe storm that we had to change into dry clothing. **be·drag·gled**\bi-drag -əld\ADJ.

be·guile\bi-gī(ə)l \V. delude; cheat; amuse. He *beguiled* himself during the long hours by playing solitaire.

be·he·moth\bi-'hē-məth\N. huge creature; something of monstrous size or power. Sportscasters nicknamed the linebacker "The *Behemoth*."

be·hold·en\bi-'hōl -dən\ADJ. obligated; indebted. Since I do not wish to be *beholden* to anyone, I cannot accept this favor.

be·hoove\bi-hüv \V. suited to; incumbent upon. In this time of crisis, it *behooves* all of us to remain calm and await the instructions of our superiors.

be·la·bor\bi-lā -bər\V. beat soundly; assail verbally. He was *belaboring* his opponent.

be·lat·ed\bi-lāt -əd\ADJ. delayed. He apologized for his *belated* note of condolence to the widow of his friend and explained that he had just learned of her husband's untimely death.

be·lea·guer\bi-lē -gər\V. besiege. As soon as the city was *beleaguered*, life became more subdued as the citizens began their long wait for outside assistance.

be·lie\bi-'lī\V. contradict; give a false impression. His coarse, hard-bitten exterior *belied* his inner sensitivity.

be·lit·tle\bi-lit -ᵊl\V. disparage; deprecate. Although I do not wish to *belittle* your contribution, I feel we must place it in its proper perspective.

bel·li·cose\'bel -i-ǩōs \ADJ. warlike. His *bellicose* disposition alienated his friends.

bel·lig·er·ent\bə-'lij(ə)-rənt\ADJ. quarrelsome. Whenever he had too much to drink, he became *belligerent* and tried to pick fights with strangers.

\ə\ abut \ᵊ\ kitten, F table \ər\ **further** \a\ **ash** \ā\ **ace** \ä\ **cot, cart**
\au̇\ **out** \ch\ **chin** \e\ **bet** \ē\ **easy** \g\ **go** \i\ **hit** \ī\ **ice** \j\ **job**

ben-e-dic-tion\ben -ə-dik -shən\N. blessing. The appearance of the sun after the many rainy days was like a *benediction*.

ben-e-fac-tor\ben -ə-fak -tər\N. gift, giver; patron. Scrooge later became Tiny Tim's *benefactor*.

ben-e-fi-ci-ary\ben -ə-fish -ē-er -ē\N. person entitled to benefits or proceeds of an insurance policy or will. You may change your *beneficiary* as often as you wish. also ADJ.

be-nev-o-lent\bə-nev(-ə) -lənt\ADJ. generous; charitable. His *benevolent* nature prevented him from refusing any beggar who accosted him.

be-night-ed\bi-nīt -əd\ADJ. overcome by darkness. In the *benighted* Middle Ages, intellectual curiosity was discouraged by the authorities.

be-nign\bi-nīn \ADJ. kindly; favorable; not malignant. The old man was well liked because of his *benign* attitude toward friend and stranger alike.

be-nig-ni-ty\bi-nig -nət-ē\N. state of being kind, benign, gracious. We have endowed our Creator with a *benignity* which permits forgiveness of our sins and transgressions.

ben-i-son\ben -ə-sən\N. blessing. Let us pray that the *benison* of peace once more shall prevail among the nations of the world.

be-rate\bi-rāt \v. scold strongly. He feared she would *berate* him for his forgetfulness.

be-reave-ment\bi-rēv -mənt\N. state of being deprived of something valuable or beloved. His friends gathered to console him upon his sudden *bereavement*.

be-reft\bi-reft \ADJ. deprived of; lacking. The foolish gambler soon found himself *bereft* of funds.

ber-serk\bə(r)-sərk \ADV. frenzied. Angered, he went *berserk* and began to wreck the room. also N.

be-smirch\bi-smərch \v. soil, defile. The scandalous remarks in the newspaper *besmirch* the reputations of every member of the society.

bes-tial\bes(h) -chəl\ADJ. beastlike; brutal. We must suppress our *bestial* desires and work for peaceful and civilized ends.

---

be-stow\bi-stō \v. confer. He wished to *bestow* great honors upon the hero.

be-troth\bi-träth \v. become engaged to marry. The announcement that they had become *betrothed* surprised their friends who had not suspected any romance. **be-troth-al** \bi-trōth -əl\N.

bevy\'bev-ē\N. large group. The movie actor was surrounded by a *bevy* of starlets.

bib-u-lous\'bib-yə-ləs\ADJ. inclined to drink; affected by alcohol; related to drinking. We could not help laughing at his *bibulous* farewells.

bi-cam-er-al\(')bī-'kam -(ə-)rəl\ADJ. two-chambered, as a legislative body. The United States Congress is a *bicameral* body.

bick-er\'bik-ər \v. quarrel. The children *bickered* morning, noon, and night, exasperating their parents.

bi-en-ni-al\(')bī-'en -ē-əl\ADJ. every two years. The plant bore *biennial* flowers, also N.

bi-fur-cate\(')bi-'fər -kət\ADJ. divided into two branches; forked. With a *bifurcate* branch and a piece of elastic rubber, he made a crude but effective slingshot.

big-ot-ry\big -ə-trē\N. stubborn intolerance. Brought up in a democratic atmosphere, the student was shocked by the *bigotry* and narrowness expressed by several of his classmates.

bil-ious\bil -yəs\ADJ. suffering from indigestion; irritable. His *bilious* temperament was apparent to all who heard him rant about his difficulties.

bilk\'bilk\v. swindle; cheat. The con man specialized in *bilking* insurance companies.

biv-ouac\biv(-ə) -wak \N. temporary encampment. While in *bivouac*, we spent the night in our sleeping bags under the stars. also V.

bi-zarre\bə-zär \ADJ. fantastic; violently contrasting. The plot of the novel was too *bizarre* to be believed.

blanch\'blanch \v. bleach; whiten. Although age had *blanched* his hair, he was still vigorous and energetic.

bland\bland \ADJ. soothing; mild. She used a *bland* ointment for her sunburn.

\ə\ abut	\ᵊ\ kitten, F table	\ər\ **further**	\a\ **ash**	\ā\ **ace**	\ä\ cot, cart
\aù\ **out**	\ch\ **chin**	\e\ **bet**	\ē\ **easy**	\g\ **go**	\i\ **hit** \ī\ **ice** \j\ **job**

blan·dish·ment \blan -dish-mənt\ N. flattery. Despite the salesperson's *blandishments,* the customer did not buy the outfit.

bla·sé \blä-zā \ ADJ. bored with pleasure or dissipation. Your *blasé* attitude gives your students an erroneous impression of the joys of scholarship.

blas·phe·mous \blas -fə-məs\ ADJ. profane; impious. The people in the room were shocked by his *blasphemous* language.

bla·tant \blāt -ᵊnt\ ADJ. loudly offensive. I regard your remarks as *blatant* and ill-mannered. **bla·tan·cy** \blāt -ᵊn-sē\ N.

bla·zon \blāz -ᵊn\ V. decorate with an heraldic coat of arms. *Blazoned* on his shield were the two lambs and the lion, the traditional coat of arms of his family. also N.

bleak \blēk \ ADJ. cold; cheerless. The Aleutian Islands are *bleak* military outposts.

blighted \blīt -əd\ ADJ. suffering from a disease; destroyed. The extent of the *blighted* areas could be seen only when viewed from the air. **blight** \blīt \ N.

blithe \blīth \ ADJ. gay; joyous. Shelley called the skylark a "*blithe* spirit" because of its happy song.

bloat·ed \blōt -əd\ ADJ. swollen or puffed as with water or air. The *bloated* corpse was taken from the river. **bloat** \blōt \ N, V.

blud·geon \bləj -ən\ N. club; heavy-headed weapon. His walking stick served him as a *bludgeon* on many occasions. also V.

blunder \ˈblən-dər\ N. error. The criminal's fatal *blunder* led to his capture. also V.

blurt \ˈblərt\ V. utter impulsively. Before she could stop him, he *blurted* out the news.

bode \bōd \ V. foreshadow; portend. The gloomy skies and the sulphurous odors from the mineral springs seemed to *bode* evil to those who settled in the area.

bo·gus \bō -gəs\ ADJ. counterfeit; not authentic. The police quickly found the distributors of the *bogus* twenty-dollar bills.

\ŋ\ **sing**   \ō\ **go**   \ȯ\ **law**   \ȯi\ **boy**   \th\ **thin**   \t̲h̲\ **the**   \ü\ **loot**   \u̇\ **foot**
\y\ **yet**   \zh\ **vision**   \ä, k̲, ⁿ, œ, œ̄, ue, ūe, ʸ\ *see* Pronunciation Symbols

bois·ter·ous\bói -st(ə-)rəs\ADJ. violent; rough; noisy. The unruly crowd became even more *boisterous* when he tried to quiet them.

bol·ster\bōl -stər\V. support; prop up. I do not intend to *bolster* your hopes with false reports of outside assistance; the truth is that we must face the enemy alone. also N.

bom·bas·tic \bäm¹bas -tik\ADJ. pompous; using inflated language. The orator spoke in a *bombastic* manner. **bom·bast**\bäm ‑bast \N.

boor·ish\bú(ə)r -ish\ADJ. rude; clownish. Your *boorish* remarks to the driver of the other car were not warranted by the situation and served merely to enrage him.

boun·ti·ful\baúnt -i-fəl\ADJ. generous; showing bounty. She distributed gifts in a *bountiful* and gracious manner.

bour·geois \bú(ə)rzh -wä \N. middle class. The French Revolution was inspired by the *bourgeois*. also ADJ.

bowd·ler·ize\bōd -lə‑rīz\V. expurgate. After the film editors had *bowdlerized* the language in the script, the motion picture's rating was changed from "R" to "PG."

brack·ish\brak -ish\ADJ. somewhat saline. He found the only wells in the area were *brackish;* drinking the water made him nauseated.

brag·ga·do·ci·o\brag -ə-dō-s(h)ē-ō \N. boasting. He was disliked because his manner was always full of *braggadocio*.

bra·va·do\brə¹väd-(ı)ō\N. swagger; assumed air of defiance. The *bravado* of the young criminal disappeared when he was confronted by the victims of his brutal attack.

bra·zen\brāz -ᵊn\ADJ. insolent. Her *brazen* contempt for authority angered the officials. also V.

breach\brēch \N. breaking of contract or duty; fissure; gap. They found a *breach* in the enemy's fortifications and penetrated their lines. also V.

breadth\'bretth\N. width; extent. We were impressed by the *breadth* of her knowledge.

bre·vi·a·ry \brē -v(y)ə-rē\ N. book containing the daily prayers. The religious sect demanded daily recitals of the *breviary* as well as formal Sabbath services.

\ə\ abut   \ᵊ\ kitten, F table   \ər\ further   \a\ ash   \ā\ ace   \ä\ cot, cart
\aú\ out   \ch\ chin   \e\ bet   \ē\ easy   \g\ go   \i\ hit   \ī\ ice   \j\ job

brev-i-ty \brev -ət-ē\ N. conciseness. *Brevity* is essential when you send a telegram or cablegram; you are charged for every word.

brin-dled \brin -dᵊld\ ADJ. tawny or grayish with streaks or spots. He was disappointed in the litter because the puppies were *brindled;* he had hoped for animals of a uniform color.

bris-tling \bris -(ə-)liŋ\ ADJ. rising like bristles; showing irritation. The dog stood there, *bristling* with anger. **bris-tle** \bris -əl\ N, V.

broach \brōch \ V. open up. He did not even try to *broach* the subject of poetry.

bro-cade \brō-kād \ N. rich, figured fabric. The sofa was covered with expensive *brocade.*

bro-chure \brō-shu̇(ə)r \ N. pamphlet. This *brochure* on farming was issued by the Department of Agriculture.

brooch \brōch \ N. ornamental clasp. She treasured the *brooch* because it was an heirloom.

brusque \brəsk \ ADJ. blunt; abrupt. She was offended by his *brusque* reply.

bu-col-ic \byü-käl -ik\ ADJ. rustic; pastoral. The meadow was the scene of *bucolic* gaiety.

buf-foon-er-y \⁽ᵗ⁾bə-fün -(ə-)rē\ N. clowning. Jimmy Durante's *buffoonery* was hilarious.

bug-a-boo \bəg -ə-bü \ N. bugbear; object of baseless terror. If we become frightened by such *bugaboos,* we are no wiser than the birds who fear scarecrows.

bul-lion \bu̇l -yən\ N. gold and silver in the form of bars. Much *bullion* is stored in the vaults at Fort Knox.

bul-wark \bu̇l -⁽ᵗ⁾wərk\ N. earthwork or other strong defense; person who defends. The navy is our principal *bulwark* against invasion.

bump-tious \bəm(p) -shəs\ ADJ. self-assertive. His classmates called him a show-off because of his *bumptious* airs.

bun-gle \bəŋ -gəl\ V. spoil by clumsy behavior. I was afraid you would *bungle* this assignment but I had no one else to send.

---

bu-reau-cra-cy \byù-rák -rə-sē\ N. government by bureaus. Many people fear that the constant introduction of federal agencies will create a government by *bureaucracy*.

bur-geon\'bər -jər.\V. grow forth; send out buds. In the spring, the plants that burgeon are a promise of the beauty that is to come.

bur-lesque\ᵗ bər-'lesk \V. give an imitation that ridicules. In his caricature, he *burlesqued* the mannerisms of his adversary. also N.

bur-ly\'bər-lē\ADJ. husky; muscular. The *burly* mover lifted the packing crate with ease.

bur-nish\'bər -nish\V. make shiny by rubbing; polish. The *burnished* metal reflected the lamplight. also N.

but-tress\bə -trəs\N. support or prop. The huge cathedral walls were supported by flying *buttresses*. also V.

bux-om\'bək -səm\ ADJ. plump; vigorous; jolly. The soldiers remembered the *buxom* nurse who had always been so pleasant to them.

—C—

ca·bal \kə-'bal \ N. small group of persons secretly united to promote their own interests. The *cabal* was defeated when their scheme was discovered. also V.

cache \kash \ N. hiding place. The detectives followed the suspect until he led them to the *cache* where he had stored his loot. also V.

ca·coph·o·ny \ka-'käf -ə-nē\ N. discord. Some people seem to enjoy the *cacophony* of an orchestra that is tuning up.

ca·dav·er \kə-'dav -ər\ N. corpse. In some states, it is illegal to dissect *cadavers*.

ca·dav·er·ous \kə-'dav -(ə-)rəs\ ADJ. like a corpse; pale. By his *cadaverous* appearance, we could see how the disease had ravaged him.

ca·jole \kə-'jōl \ V. coax; wheedle. I will not be *cajoled* into granting you your wish.

cal·i·ber \'kal -ə-bər\ N. ability; capacity. A man of such *caliber* should not be assigned such menial tasks.

cal·lig·ra·phy \kə-'lig -rə-fē\ N. beautiful writing; excellent penmanship. As we examine ancient manuscripts, we become impressed with the *calligraphy* of the scribes.

cal·lous \'kal -əs\ ADJ. hardened; unfeeling. He had worked in the hospital for so many years that he was *callous* to the suffering in the wards. **cal·lus** \'kal -əs\ N.

cal·low \'kal -ō\ ADJ. unfledged; youthful. In that youthful movement, the leaders were only a little less *callow* than their immature followers.

cal·o·rif·ic \kal -ə-'rif -ik\ ADJ. heat-producing. Coal is much more *calorific* than green wood.

ca·lum·ni·ate \kə-'ləm -nē-āt \ V. slander. Shakespeare wrote that love and friendship were subject to envious and *calumniating* time.

cal·um·ny \'kal -əm-nē\ N. malicious misrepresentation; slander. He could endure his financial failure, but he could not bear the *calumny* that his foes heaped upon him.

cam·e·o \'kam -ē-ō \ N. shell or jewel carved in relief. Tourists are advised not to purchase *cameos* from the street peddlers of Rome who sell poor specimens of the carver's art.

\ŋ\ sing \ō\ go \ȯ\ law \ȯi\ boy \th\ thin \th\ the \ü\ loot \u̇\ foot
\y\ yet \zh\ vision \à, ḵ, ⁿ, œ, œ̄, ue, ūe, ʸ\ *see* Pronunciation Symbols

ca-nard\kə-härd \N. unfounded rumor; exaggerated report. It is almost impossible to protect oneself from such a base *canard*.

can-dor\'kan -dər\N. frankness. The *candor* and simplicity of his speech impressed all. **can-did**\'kan -dəd\ADJ.

ca-nine\'kā-,nīn \ADJ. related to dogs; doglike. Some days the *canine* population of Berkeley seems almost to outnumber the human population.

can-ker\'kaŋ -kər\N. any ulcerous sore; any evil. Poverty is a *canker* in the body politic; it must be cured.

can-ny\'kan -ē\ADJ. shrewd; thrifty. The *canny* Scotsman was more than a match for the swindlers.

cant\'kant \N. jargon of thieves; pious phraseology. Many listeners were fooled by the *cant* and hypocrisy of his speech. also V.

can-tan-ker-ous\kan-'tan-k(ə)rəs\ADJ. ill humored; irritable. Constantly complaining about his treatment and refusing to cooperate with the hospital staff, he was a *cantankerous* patient.

can-ta-ta\kən-'tät -ə\N. story set to music, to be sung by a chorus. The choral society sang the new *cantata* composed by its leader.

can-ter\'kant -ər\N. slow gallop. Because the racehorse had outdistanced its competition so easily, the reporter wrote that the race was won in a *canter*. also V.

can-to\'kan -,tō \N. division of a long poem. In *The Man without a Country*, Philip Nolan is upset when he reads one of Sir Walter Scott's *cantos*.

can-vass\'kan -vəs\V. determine votes, etc. After *canvassing* the sentiments of his constituents, the congressman was confident that he represented the majority opinion of his district. also N.

ca-pa-cious \kə-pā -shəs\ ADJ. spacious. In the *capacious* areas of the railroad terminal, thousands of travelers lingered while waiting for their train.

ca-par-i-son \kə-par -ə-sən\ N. showy harness or ornamentation for a horse. The audience admired the *caparison* of the horses as they made their entrance into the circus ring. also V.

\ə\ abut \ᵊ\ kitten, F table \ər\ **further** \a\ **ash** \ā\ **ace** \ä\ cot, cart
\aủ\ **out** \ch\ **chin** \e\ bet \ē\ **easy** \g\ **go** \i\ hit \ī\ **ice** \j\ **job**

cap-il-lar-y \\'kap -ə-ˌler -ē\\ ADJ. having a very fine bore. The changes in surface tension of liquids in *capillary* vessels is of special interest to physicists. also N.

ca-pit-u-late \\kə-'pich -ə-ˌlāt \\ V. surrender. The enemy was warned to *capitulate* or face annihilation.

ca-price \\kə-'prēs \\ N. whim. Do not act on *caprice*. Study your problem.

ca-pri-cious \\kə-'prish -əs\\ ADJ. fickle; incalculable. The storm was *capricious* and changed course constantly.

cap-tion \\'kap -shən\\ N. title; chapter heading; text under illustration. I find the *captions* which accompany these cartoons very clever and humorous. also V.

cap-tious \\'kap -shəs\\ ADJ. faultfinding. His criticisms were always *captious* and frivolous, never offering constructive suggestions.

ca-rafe \\kə-'raf \\ N. glass water bottle; decanter. With each dinner, the patron receives a *carafe* of red or white wine.

car-at \\'kar -ət\\ N. unit of weight for precious stones; measure of fineness of gold. He gave her a three-*carat* diamond mounted in an eighteen-*carat* gold band.

car-cin-o-gen-ic \\kär-sin-ə-'jen-ik \\ ADJ. causing cancer. Many supposedly harmless substances have been revealed to be *carcinogenic*.

car-di-nal \\'kärd-nəl\\ ADJ. chief. If you want to increase your word power, the *cardinal* rule of vocabulary-building is to read.

ca-reen \\kə-'rēn \\ V. lurch; sway from side to side. The taxicab *careened* wildly as it rounded the corner.

car-i-ca-ture \\'kar -i-kə-ˌchù(ə)r \\ N. distortion; burlesque. The *caricatures* he drew always emphasized a personal weakness of the people he burlesqued. also V.

car-mine \\'kär -mən\\ N. rich red. *Carmine* in her lipstick made her lips appear black in the photographs.

car-nage \\'kär -nij\\ N. destruction of life. The *carnage* that can be caused by atomic warfare adds to the responsibilities of our statesmen.

car-nal \\'kärn -ᵊl\\ ADJ. fleshly. The public was more interested in *carnal* pleasures than in spiritual matters.

\ŋ\ **sing** \ō\ **go** \o\ **law** \òi\ **boy** \th\ **thin** \t̲h̲\ **the** \ü\ **loot** \ù\ **foot**
\y\ **yet**   \zh\ **vision**   \à, k̲, ⁿ, œ, œ̄, ue, ūe, ʸ\ *see* Pronunciation Symbols

car-niv-o-rous \kär-niv -(ə-)rəs\ ADJ. meat-eating. The lion is a *carnivorous* animal. **car-ni-vore**\kär -nə-vō(ə)r \N.

ca-rous-al\kə-raú -zəl\ N. drunken revel. The party degenerated into an ugly *carousal*.

carp-ing\kär -piŋ\ ADJ. finding fault. A *carping* critic disturbs sensitive people.

car-ri-on\kar -ē-ən\ N. rotting flesh of a dead body. Buzzards are nature's scavengers; they eat the *carrion* left behind by other predators.

carte blanche \kärt -blaⁿsh \ N. unlimited authority or freedom. Use your own discretion in this matter; I give you *carte blanche*.

car-tog-ra-pher\kär-täg -rə-fər\ N. maker of maps or charts. *Cartographers* are unable to provide accurate maps of legal boundaries in the Near East because of the unsettled political situation in that part of the world following the recent military actions.

cary-at-id \kar -ē-at -əd\ N. sculptured column of a female figure. The *caryatids* supporting the entablature reminded the onlooker of the columns he had seen in the Acropolis at Athens.

cas-cade \⁽¹⁾kas-kād\ N. small waterfall. We could not appreciate the beauty of the many *cascades* as we were forced to make detours around each of them. also V.

caste\kast \N. one of the hereditary classes in Hindu society. The differences created by the *caste* system in India must be eradicated if true democracy is to prevail in that country.

cas-ti-gate\kas -tə-gāt \V. punish. He decided to *castigate* the culprit personally.

ca-su-al-ty \kazh -əl-tē\ N. serious or fatal accident. The number of *casualties* on this holiday weekend was high.

ca-su-ist-ry \kazh -(ə-)wə-strē\ N. subtle or sophisticated reasoning resulting in minute distinctions. You are using *casuistry* to justify your obvious violation of decent behavior.

cat-a-clysm\kat -ə-kliz -əm\N. deluge; upheaval. A *cataclysm* such as the French Revolution affects all countries. **cat-a-clys-mic**\kat -ə-kliz -mik\ ADJ.

\ə\ abut　\ᵊ\ kitten, F table　\ər\ **further**　\a\ ash　\ā\ ace　\ä\ cot, cart
\aú\ out　\ch\ chin　\e\ bet　\ē\ easy　\g\ go　\i\ hit　\ī\ ice　\j\ job

cat-a-lyst \'kat -ᵊl-əst\ N. agent which brings about a chemical change while it remains unaffected and unchanged. Many chemical reactions cannot take place without the presence of a *catalyst*.

cat-a-pult \'kat -ə-ˌpəlt \ N. slingshot; a hurling machine. Airplanes are sometimes launched from battleships by *catapults*. also V.

cat-a-ract \'kat-ə-ˌrakt \ N. great waterfall; eye abnormality. She gazed with awe at the mighty *cataract* known as Niagara Falls.

ca-tas-tro-phe \kə-ˈtas -trə-(ˌ)fē\ N. calamity. The Johnstown flood was a *catastrophe*.

cat-e-chism \'kat -ə-ˌkiz -əm\ N. book for religious instruction; instruction by question and answer. He taught by engaging his pupils in a *catechism* until they gave him the correct answer.

ca-thar-sis \kə -ˈthär -səs\ N. purging or cleansing of any passage of the body. Aristotle maintained that tragedy created a *catharsis* by purging the soul of base concepts.

ca-thar-tic \kə-ˈthärt -ik\ N. purgative. Some drugs act as laxatives when taken in small doses but act as *cathartics* when taken in much larger doses. also ADJ.

cath-o-lic \kath -(ə-)lik\ ADJ. broadly sympathetic; liberal. He was extremely *catholic* in his reading tastes.

cau-cus \'kȯ -kəs\ N. private meeting of members of a party to select officers or determine policy. At the opening of Congress, the members of the Democratic Party held a *caucus* to elect the Majority Leader of the House and the Party Whip. also V.

caus-tic \'kȯ -stik\ ADJ. burning; sarcastically biting. The critic's *caustic* remarks angered the hapless actors who were the subjects of his sarcasm. also N.

cau-ter-ize \'kȯt -ə-ˌrīz \ V. burn with hot iron or caustic. In order to prevent infection, the doctor *cauterized* the wound.

cav-al-cade \'kav -əl-ˌkād \ N. procession; parade. As described by Chaucer, the *cavalcade* by Canterbury pilgrims was a motley group.

cav-il \'kav -əl\ V. make frivolous objections. I respect your sensible criticisms, but I dislike the way you *cavil* about unimportant details. also N.

cede \ sēd \ v. transfer; yield title to. I intend to *cede* this property to the city.

ce-ler-i-ty \ sə-ler -ət-ē\ N. speed; rapidity. Hamlet resented his mother's *celerity* in remarrying within a month after his father's death.

ce-les-tial \sə-les(h) -chəl\ ADJ. heavenly. He wrote about the music of "*celestial* spheres." also N.

cel-i-bate \ sel -ə-bət\ ADJ. unmarried; abstaining from sexual intercourse. He vowed to remain *celibate*. **cel-i-ba-cy** \ sel -ə-bə-sē\ N.

cen-sor \ sen(t) -sər\ N. overseer of morals; person who reads to eliminate inappropriate remarks. Soldiers dislike having their mail read by a *censor* but understand the need for this precaution. also v.

cen-so-ri-ous \sen-'sōr-ē-əs\ ADJ. critical. *Censorious* people delight in casting blame.

cen-sure \ sen -chər\ v. blame; criticize. He was *censured* for his ill-advised act. also N.

cen-taur \ sen -tȯ(ə)r \ N. mythical figure, half man and half horse. I was particularly impressed by the statue of the *centaur* in the Roman Hall of the museum.

cen-ti-grade \ sent -ə-grād \ ADJ. measure of temperature used widely in Europe. On the *centigrade* thermometer, the freezing point of water is zero degrees.

cen-trif-u-gal \sen-trif -yə-gəl\ ADJ. radiating; departing from the center. Many automatic drying machines remove excess moisture from clothing by *centrifugal* force. also N.

cen-trip-e-tal \sen-trip -ət-ᵊl\ADJ. tending toward the center. Does *centripetal* force or the force of gravity bring orbiting bodies to the earth's surface?

cen-tu-ri-on \sen-t(y)ùr -ē-ən\N. Roman army officer. Because he was in command of a company of one hundred soldiers, he was called a *centurion*.

ce-re-bral \sə-rē -brəl\ ADJ. pertaining to the brain or intellect. The content of philosophical works is *cerebral* in nature and requires much thought.

cer-e-bra-tion \ser -ə-brā -shən\N. thought. Mathematics problems sometimes require much *cerebration*. **cer-e-brate** \ser -ə-brāt \ V.

---

ces-sa-tion (se-sā -shən) N. stopping. The workers threatened a *cessation* of all activities if their demands were not met. **cease** (sēs) V.

ces-sion\\'sesh -ən\\ N. yielding to another; ceding. The *cession* of Alaska to the United States is discussed in this chapter.

chafe\\'chāf \\ V. warm by rubbing; make sore by rubbing. The collar *chafed* his neck. also N.

chaff\\'chaf\\ N. worthless products of an endeavor. When you separate the wheat from the chaff, be sure you throw out the *chaff*.

chaff-ing\\'chaf-iŋ\\ ADJ. bantering; joking. Sometimes his flippant and *chaffing* remarks annoy us.

cha-grin\\shə-grin \\ N. vexation; disappointment. His refusal to go with us filled us with *chagrin*. also V.

chal-ice\\chal -əs\\ N. goblet; consecrated cup. In a small room adjoining the cathedral, many ornately decorated *chalices* made by the most famous European goldsmiths were on display.

cha-me-leon\\kə-mēl -yən\\ N. lizard that changes color in different situations. Like the *chameleon*, he assumed the political thinking of every group he met.

champ\\'champ \\ V. chew noisily. His dining companions were amused by the way he *champed* his food.

cham-pi-on\\'cham-pē-ən\\ V. support militantly. Martin Luther King, Jr., won the Nobel Peace Prize because he *championed* the oppressed in their struggle for equality.

cha-ot-ic\\kā-ät -ik\\ ADJ. in utter disorder. He tried to bring order into the *chaotic* state of affairs. **cha-os**\\'kā-äs \\ N.

cha-ris-ma\\kə-riz -mə\\ N. divine gift; great popular charm or appeal of a political leader. Political commentators have deplored the importance of a candidate's *charisma* in these days of television campaigning.

char-la-tan \\'shär -lə-tən\\ N. quack; pretender to knowledge. Because he was unable to substantiate his claim that he had found a cure for the dread disease, he was called a *charlatan* by his colleagues.

char-y\\'cha(ə)r -ē\\ ADJ. cautiously watchful. She was *chary* of her favors.

\\ŋ\\ sing   \\ō\\ go   \\ȯ\\ law   \\ȯi\\ boy   \\th\\ thin   \\th\\ the   \\ü\\ loot   \\ù\\ foot
\\y\\ yet   \\zh\\ vision   \\à, k, ⁿ, œ, œ̄, ue, ūe, ʸ\\ *see* Pronunciation Symbols

chasm\\ˈkaz -əm\\N. abyss. They could not see the bottom of the *chasm*.

chas-sis\\ˈshas -ē\\N. framework and working parts of an automobile. Examining the car after the accident, the owner discovered that the body had been ruined but that the *chassis* was unharmed.

chaste\\chāst \\ADJ. pure. Her *chaste* and decorous garb was appropriately selected for the solemnity of the occasion. **chas-ti-ty** (ˈchas -tət-ē) N.

chas-tise\\(')chas -ˈtiz \\V. punish. I must *chastise* you for this offense.

chat-tel \\ˈchat'-ᵊl\\N. personal property. When he bought his furniture on the installment plan, he signed a *chattel* mortgage.

chau-vin-ist \\ˈshō -və-nəst\\N. blindly devoted patriot. A *chauvinist* cannot recognize any faults in his country, no matter how flagrant they may be.

check-er\\ˈchek-ər\\V. mark by changes in fortune. His long career was *checkered* by prosperity and failure. also N.

che-ru-bic\\chə-ˈrü-bik\\ADJ. angelic; innocent-looking. With her cheerful smile and rosy cheeks, she was a particularly *cherubic* child.

chi-ca-ner-y \\shik-ˈān -(ə-)rē\\N. trickery. Your deceitful tactics in this case are indications of *chicanery*.

chide\\chīd \\V. scold. Grandma began to *chide* Steven for his lying.

chi-me-ri-cal\\kī-ˈmer -i-kəl\\ADJ. fantastic; highly imaginative. Poe's *chimerical* stories are sometimes too morbid for reading in bed. **chi-me-ra**\\kī-ˈmir -ə\\N.

chi-ro-man-cy\\kī -rə-man(t) -sē\\N. art of telling fortunes by reading the hand; palmistry. The charlatans along the Midway claimed the ability to analyze character and predict the future by such means as handwriting analysis, phrenology and *chiromancy*.

chi-rop-o-dist\\kə-ˈräp -əd-əst\\N. one who treats disorders of the feet. The *chiropodist* treated the ingrown nail on the boy's foot.

cho-ler-ic\\ˈkäl -ə-rik\\ADJ. hot-tempered. His flushed, angry face indicated a *choleric* nature.

\\ə\\ abut \\ᵊ\\ kitten, F table \\ər\\ **further** \\a\\ **ash** \\ā\\ **ace** \\ä\\ cot, cart
\\aú\\ **out** \\ch\\ **chin** \\e\\ bet \\ē\\ **easy** \\g\\ go \\i\\ hit \\ī\\ **ice** \\j\\ **job**

cho-re-og-ra-phy \kōr -ē-äg -rə-fē\ N. art of dancing. Martha Graham introduced a form of *choreography* which seemed awkward and alien to those who had been brought up on classic ballet.

chron-ic\krän -ik\ADJ. long established as a disease. The doctors were able finally to attribute his *chronic* headaches and nausea to traces of formaldehyde gas in his apartment.

churl-ish\chər -lish\ADJ. boorish; rude. Dismayed by his *churlish* manners at the party, the girls vowed never to invite him again.

cil-i-at-ed\sil -ē-āt -əd\ADJ. having minute hairs. The paramecium is a *ciliated*, one-celled animal.

cir-clet\sər -klət\N. small ring; band. This tiny *circlet* is very costly because it is set with precious stones.

cir-cu-i-tous\sər ‐kyü -ət-əs\ ADJ. roundabout. Because of the traffic congestion on the main highways, he took a *circuitous* route. **cir-cuit** (sər′-kət) N, V.

cir-cum-lo-cu-tion\sər -kəm-lō-kyü -shən\N. indirect or roundabout expression. He was afraid to call a spade a spade and resorted to *circumlocution* to avoid direct reference to his subject.

cir-cum-scribe \sər -kəm-skrīb \ V. limit; confine. Although I do not wish to *circumscribe* your activities, I must insist that you complete this assignment before you start anything else.

cir-cum-spect \sər -kəm-spekt \ ADJ. prudent; cautious. Investigating before acting, he tried always to be *circumspect*.

cir-cum-vent\sər -kəm-vent \V. outwit; baffle. In order to *circumvent* the enemy, we will make two preliminary attacks in other sections before starting our major campaign.

cit-a-del\sit -əd-ᵊl\N. fortress. The *citadel* overlooked the city like a protecting angel.

cite (sīt) v. quote; commend. He could *cite* passages in the Bible from memory. **ci-ta-tion** \sī-tā -shən\N.

clair-voy-ant\kla(ə)r-voi -ənt\ADJ. having foresight. Cassandra's *clairvoyant* warning was not heeded by the Trojans. also N. **clair-voy-ance**\kla(ə)r-voi -ən(t)s\N.

\ŋ\ **sing**	\ō\ **go**	\ȯ\ **law**	\ȯi\ **boy**	\th\ **thin**	\<u>th</u>\ **the**	\ü\ **loot**	\u̇\ **foot**
\y\ **yet**	\zh\ **vision**	\à, k̲, ⁿ, œ, ōē, ue, ūē, ʸ\ *see* Pronunciation Symbols					

clam-ber\klam -(b)ər\v. climb by crawling. He *clambered* over the wall.

clan-des-tine \klan-des -tən\ADJ. secret. After avoiding their chaperon, the lovers had a *clandestine* meeting.

clar-i-on\klar -ē-ən\ADJ. shrill trumpetlike sound. We woke to the *clarion* call of the bugle. also N.

claus-tro-pho-bi-a\klò -strə-fō bē-ə\N. fear of being locked in. His fellow classmates laughed at his *claustrophobia* and often threatened to lock him in his room.

clav-i-cle\klav -i-kəl\N. collarbone. Even though he wore shoulder pads, the football player broke his *clavicle* during a practice scrimmage.

cleave \klēv \v. split asunder. The lightning *cleaves* the tree in two. **cleav-age**\klē -vij\N.

cleft\kleft \N. split. There was a *cleft* in the huge boulder. also ADJ.

clem-en-cy\klem -ən-sē\N. disposition to be lenient; mildness, as of the weather. The lawyer was pleased when the case was sent to Judge Smith's chambers because Smith was noted for his *clemency* toward first offenders.

cli-ché\kli-shā \N. phrase dulled in meaning by repetition. High school compositions are often marred by such *clichés* as "strong as an ox."

cli-mac-tic\klī-mak -tik\ADJ. relating to the highest point. When he reached the *climactic* portions of the book, he could not stop reading. **cli-max**\klī -maks \

clime\'klīm\N. region; climate. His doctor advised him to move to a milder *clime*.

clique\klēk \N. small exclusive group. He charged that a *clique* had assumed control of school affairs.

clois-ter\klòi stər\N. monastery or convent. The nuns lived in the *cloister*. also v.

clo-ven\'klō-vən\ADJ. split. Popular legends maintain that the devil has *cloven* hooves.

co-ad-ju-tor\kō -ə-jüt -ər\N. assistant; colleague. He was assigned as *coadjutor* of the bishop.

co-a-lesce\kō -ə-ləs \v. combine; fuse. The brooks *coalesce* into one large river.

---

cock-ade\kä-kād \N. decoration worn on hat. Members of that brigade can be recognized by the green and white *cockade* in their helmets.

cod-dle\'käd-əl\v. treat gently; pamper. Don't *coddle* the children so much; they need a taste of discipline.

cod-i-cil\käd -ə-səl\N. supplement to the body of a will. This *codicil* was drawn up five years after the writing of the original will.

co-erce\kō-ərs \v. force; repress. Do not *coerce* me into doing this; I hate force. **co-er-cion**\kō-ər -zhən\N.

co-eval\kō-'ē-vəl\ADJ. living at the same time as; contemporary. *Coeval* with the dinosaur, the pterodactyl flourished during the Mesozoic era.

cog\käg \N. tooth projecting from a wheel. On steep slopes, *cog* railways are frequently used to prevent slipping.

co-gent\kō -jənt\ADJ. convincing. He presented *cogent* arguments to the jury.

cog-i-tate\käj -ə-tāt \v. think over. *Cogitate* on this problem; the solution will come.

cog-nate\käg -nāt \ADJ. allied by blood; of the same or kindred nature. In the phrase "die a thousand deaths," the word "death" is a *cognate* object. also N.

cog-ni-zance\käg -nə-zən(t)s\N. knowledge. During the election campaign, the two candidates were kept in full *cognizance* of the international situation.

cog-no-men\käg-nō -mən\N. family name. He asked the court to change his *cognomen* to a more American-sounding name.

co-here\kō-hi(ə)r \v. stick together. Solids have a greater tendency to *cohere* than liquids.

co-he-sion \kō-hē -zhən\ N. force which keeps parts together. In order to preserve our *cohesion,* we must not let minor differences interfere with our major purposes.

co-hort\kō -hó(ə)rt \N. armed band. Caesar and his Roman *cohorts* conquered almost all of the known world.

co-in-ci-dent\kō-in(t) -səd-ənt\ADJ. occurring at the same time. Some people find the *coincident* events in Hardy's novels annoying.

---

col·an·der \ˈkəl -ən-dər\ N. utensil with perforated bottom used for straining. Before serving the spaghetti, place it in a *colander* to drain it.

col·lab·o·rate \kə-ˈlab -ə-ˌrāt \ V. work together. Two writers *collaborated* in preparing this book.

col·late \kə-ˈlāt \ V. examine in order to verify authenticity; arrange in order. They *collated* the newly found manuscripts to determine their age.

col·lat·er·al \kə-ˈlat -ə-rəl\ N. security given for loan. The sum you wish to borrow is so large that it must be secured by *collateral*.

col·la·tion \kə-ˈlā -shən\ N. a light meal. Tea sandwiches and cookies were offered at the *collation*.

col·lier \ˈkäl -yər\ N. worker in coal mine; ship carrying coal. The extended cold spell has prevented the *colliers* from delivering the coal to the docks as scheduled.

col·lo·qui·al \kə-ˈlō -kwē-əl\ ADJ. pertaining to conversational or common speech. Your use of *colloquial* expressions in a formal essay such as the one you have presented spoils the effect you hope to achieve.

col·lo·quy \ˈkäl -ə-kwē\ N. informal discussion. I enjoy our *colloquies*, but I sometimes wish that they could be made more formal and more searching.

col·lu·sion \kə-ˈlü -zhən\ N. conspiring in a fraudulent scheme. The swindlers were found guilty of *collusion*.

co·los·sal \kə-ˈläs -əl\ ADJ. huge. Radio City Music Hall has a *colossal* stage.

co·ma·tose \ˈkō -mə-ˌtōs \ ADJ. in a coma; extremely sleepy. The long-winded orator soon had his audience in a *comatose* state.

com·bus·ti·ble \kəm-ˈbəs -tə-bəl\ ADJ. easily burned. After the recent outbreak of fires in private homes, the fire commissioner ordered that all *combustible* materials be kept in safe containers. also N.

come·ly \ˈkəm -lē\ ADJ. attractive; aggreeable. I would rather have a *comely* wife than a rich one.

co·mes·ti·ble \kə-ˈmes -tə-bəl\ N. something fit to be eaten. The roast turkey and other *comestibles*, the wines, and the excellent service made this Thanksgiving dinner particularly memorable.

\ə\ abut	\ᵊ\ kitten, F table	\ər\ further	\a\ ash	\ā\ ace	\ä\ cot, cart
\au̇\ out	\ch\ chin	\e\ bet	\ē\ easy	\g\ go	\i\ hit \ī\ ice \j\ job

co·mi·ty\ˈkäm -ət-ē\ N. courtesy; civility. A spirit of *comity* should exist among nations.

com·man·deer \ˌkäm -ən-ˈdi(ə)r \ V. to draft for military purposes; take for public use. The policeman *commandeered* the first car that approached and ordered the driver to go to the nearest hospital.

com·men·su·rate \kə-ˈmen(t)s(-ə) -rət\ ADJ. equal in extent. Your reward will be *commensurate* with your effort.

com·mis·er·ate\kə-ˈmiz -ə-ˌrāt \ V. feel or express pity or sympathy for. Her friends *commiserated* with the widow.

com·mo·di·ous \kə-ˈmōd -ē-əs\ ADJ. spacious and comfortable. After sleeping in small roadside cabins, they found their hotel suite *commodious*.

com·mu·nal\kə-ˈmyün-ᵊl\ADJ. held in common; of a group of people. When they were divorced, they had trouble dividing their *communal* property.

com·pact\ˈkäm ˌpakt \ N. agreement; contract. The signers of the Mayflower *Compact* were establishing a form of government. **com·pact**\kəm-ˈpakt \ V, ADJ.

com·pat·i·ble \kəm-ˈpat -ə-bəl\ ADJ. harmonious; in harmony with. They were *compatible* neighbors, never quarreling over unimportant matters.

com·pen·di·um \kəm-ˈpen -dē-əm\ N. brief comprehensive summary. This text can serve as a *compendium* of the tremendous amount of new material being developed in this field.

com·pen·sa·tory\kəm-ˈpen(t)-sə-ˌtōr-ē\ADJ. making up for; repaying. Can a *compensatory* education program make up for the inadequate schooling he received in earlier years?

com·pi·la·tion \ˌkäm -pə-ˈlā -shən\ N. listing of statistical information in tabular or book form. The *compilation* of available scholarships serves a very valuable purpose.

com·pla·cent\kəm-ˈplās -ᵊnt\ADJ. self-satisfied. There was a *complacent* look on his face as he examined his paintings. **com·pla·cen·cy**\kəm-ˈplās -ᵊn-sē\N.

com·plai·sant\kəm-ˈplās -ᵊnt\ADJ. trying to please; obliging. The courtier obeyed the king's orders in a *complaisant* manner.

\ŋ\ sing   \ō\ go   \ò\ law   \òi\ boy   \th\ thin   \t͟h\ the   \ü\ loot   \u̇\ foot
\y\ yet   \zh\ vision   \à, k̲, ⁿ, œ, ōē, ue, ūē, ʳ\ *see* Pronunciation Symbols

com-ple-ment\\'käm -plə-mənt\\ N. that which completes. A predicate *complement* completes the meaning of the subject. also V.

com-pli-ant\\kəm-'plī -ənt\\ADJ. yielding. He was *compliant* and ready to conform to the pattern set by his friends.

com-plic-i-ty \\kəm-'plis -ət-ē\\ N. participation; involvement. You cannot keep your *complicity* in this affair secret very long; you would be wise to admit your involvement immediately.

com-port\\kəm-'pō(ə)rt \\V. bear one's self; behave. He *comported* himself with great dignity.

com-po-sure\\kəm-'pō-zhər\\N. mental calmness. Even the latest work crisis failed to shake her *composure*.

com-pre-hen-sive\\,käm-pri-'hen(t)-siv\\ADJ. thorough; inclusive. This book provides a *comprehensive* review of verbal and math skills for the SAT.

com-press\\kəm-'pres\\V. squeeze; contract. She *compressed* the package under her arm. **com-pres-sion** \\ kəm-'presh-ən\\N.

com-pro-mise\\'käm -prə-mīz \\V. adjust; endanger the interests or reputation of. Your presence at the scene of the dispute *compromises* our claim to neutrality in this matter. also N.

com-punc-tion\\kəm-'pəŋ(k) -shən\\N. remorse. The judge was especially severe in his sentencing because he felt that the criminal had shown no *compunction* for his heinous crime.

com-pute\\kəm-'pyüt \\V. reckon; calculate. He failed to *compute* the interest.

con-cat-e-nate\\kän-'kat -ə-ˌnāt \\V. link as in a chain. It is difficult to understand how these events could *concatenate* as they did without outside assistance. also ADJ.

con-cave\\kän-'kāv\\ADJ. hollow. The back-packers found partial shelter from the storm by huddling against the *concave* wall of the cliff.

con-cen-tric\\kən-'sen -trik\\ADJ. having a common center. The target was made of *concentric* circles.

\\ə\\ abut	\\ᵊ\\ kitten, F table	\\ər\\ **further**	\\a\\ **ash**	\\ā\\ **ace**	\\ä\\ **cot, cart**
\\aü\\ **out**	\\ch\\ **chin**	\\e\\ **bet**	\\ē\\ **easy**	\\g\\ **go**	\\i\\ **hit** \\ī\\ **ice** \\j\\ **job**

con-cep-tion\kən-'sep -shən\ N. beginning; forming of an idea. At the first *conception* of the work, he was consulted. **con-ceive**\kən-'sēv \ V.

con-ces-sion\kən-'sesh-ən\ N. an act of yielding. Before they could reach an agreement, both sides had to make certain *concessions*.

con-cil-i-ate\kən-'sil -ē-ͺāt \ V. pacify; win over. She tried to *conciliate* me with a gift. **con-cil-ia-to-ry**\kən-'sil -yə-ͺtōr -ē\ADJ.

con-cise\kən-'sīs \ADJ. brief and compact. The essay was *concise* and explicit.

con-clave\'kän -ͺklāv \ N. private meeting. He was present at all their *conclaves* as a sort of unofficial observer.

con-coct\kən-'käkt \V. prepare by combining; make up in concert. How did you ever *concoct* such a strange dish? **con-coc-tion**\kən-käk -shən\N.

con-com-i-tant\kən-'käm -ət-ənt\ N. that which accompanies. Culture is not always a *concomitant* of wealth. also ADJ.

con-cor-dat\kən-'kȯr -ͺdat \N. agreement, usually between the papal authority and the secular. One of the most famous of the agreements between a Pope and an emperor was the *Concordat* of Worms in 1122.

con-cur-rent\kən-'kər -ənt\ ADJ. happening at the same time. In America, the colonists were resisting the demands of the mother country; at the *concurrent* moment in France, the middle class was sowing the seeds of rebellion.

con-de-scend\kän -di-'send \ V. bestow courtesies with a superior air. The king *condescended* to grant an audience to the friends of the condemned man. **con-de-scen-sion** \kän -di-'sen -chən\N.

con-dign\kən-dīn \ADJ. adequate; deservedly severe. The public approved the *condign* punishment.

con-di-ment\'kän -də-mənt\ N. seasoning; spice. Spanish food is full of *condiments*.

con-dole \kən-dōl \ V. express sympathetic sorrow. His friends gathered to *condole* with him over his loss. **con-do-lence**\kən-dō -lən(t)s\N.

---

con-done\kən-'dōn \v. overlook; forgive. We cannot *condone* your recent criminal cooperation with the gamblers.

con-duit\'kän -ˌd(y)ü -ət\N. aqueduct; passageway for fluids. Water was brought to the army in the desert by an improvised *conduit* from the adjoining mountain.

con-fis-cate\'kän -fə-ˌskāt \v. seize; commandeer. The army *confiscated* all available supplies of uranium. also ADJ.

con-fla-gra-tion\ˌkän-flə-'grā-shən\N. great fire. In the *conflagration* that followed the 1906 earthquake, much of San Francisco was destroyed.

con-for-mi-ty\kən-'för -mət-ē\N. harmony; agreement. In *conformity* with our rules and regulations, I am calling a meeting of our organization.

con-geal\kən-'jē(ə)l \v. freeze, coagulate. His blood *congealed* in his veins as he saw the dread monster rush toward him.

con-gen-i-tal\kän-'jen -ə-t°l\ADJ. existing at birth. His *congenital* deformity disturbed his parents.

con-glom-er-a-tion\kən-ˌgläm -ə-'rā -shən\N. mass of material sticking together. In such a *conglomeration* of miscellaneous statistics, it was impossible to find a single area of analysis.

con-gru-ence\kən-'grü -ən(t)s\N. correspondence of parts; harmonious relationship. The student demonstrated the *congruence* of the two triangles by using the hypotenuse-arm theorem.

co-ni-fer\'kän -ə-fər\N. pine tree; cone-bearing tree. According to geologists, the *conifers* were the first plants to bear flowers.

con-jec-ture\kən-'jek -chər\N. surmise; guess. I will end all your *conjectures;* I admit I am guilty as charged. also V.

con-ju-gal\'kän -ji-gəl\ADJ. pertaining to marriage. Their dreams of *conjugal* bliss were shattered as soon as their temperaments clashed.

con-jure\'kän-jər\v. summon a devil; practice magic; imagine; invent. He *conjured* up an image of a reformed city and had the voters completely under his spell.

\ə\ abut   \°\ kitten, F table   \ər\ further   \a\ ash   \ā\ ace   \ä\ cot, cart
\aù\ out   \ch\ chin   \e\ bet   \ē\ easy   \g\ go   \i\ hit   \ī\ ice   \j\ job

con-niv-ance\kə-ˈnī -vən(t)s\N. pretense of ignorance of something wrong; assistance; permission to offend. With the *connivance* of his friends, he plotted to embarrass the teacher. **con-nive**\kə-ˈnīv \V.

con-nois-seur\ˌkän -ə-ˈsər \N. person competent to act as a judge of art, etc.; a lover of art. He had developed into a *connoisseur* of fine china.

con-no-ta-tion\ˌkän -ə-ˈtā -shən\ N. suggested or implied meaning of an expression. Foreigners frequently are unaware of the *connotations* of the words they use.

con-nu-bi-al\kə-ˈn(y)ü -bē-əl\ADJ. pertaining to marriage or the matrimonial state. In his telegram, he wished the newlyweds a lifetime of *connubial* bliss.

con-san-guin-i-ty \ˌkän -san -ˈgwin-ət-ē\ N. kinship. The lawsuit developed into a test of the *consanguinity* of the claimant to the estate.

con-sci-en-tious\ˌkän-chē-ˈen-chəs\ADJ. scrupulous; careful. A *conscientious* editor, she checked every definition for its accuracy.

con-se-crate\ˈkän(t) -sə-ˌkrāt \V. dedicate; sanctify. We shall *consecrate* our lives to this noble purpose. also ADJ.

con-sen-sus \kən-ˈsen(t) -səs\ N. general agreement. The *consensus* indicates that we are opposed to entering into this pact.

con-se-quen-tial\ˌkän(t)-sə-ˈkwen-chəl\ADJ. following as an effect; important; self-important. Convinced of his own importance, the actor strutted about the dressing room with a *consequential* air. **con-se-quence**\ˈkän(t)-sə-ˈkwen(t)s\N; **con-se-quent**\ˈkän(t)-sə-kwent\ADJ.

con-so-nance\ˈkän(t)-s(ə-)nən(t)s\N. harmony; agreement. Her agitation seemed out of *consonance* with her usual calm.

con-sort\kən-ˈsȯ(ə)rt \V. associate with. We frequently judge people by the company with whom they *consort*. **con-sort** \ˈkän -sȯ(ə)rt \N.

con-spic-u-ous\kən-ˈspik-yə-wəs\ADJ. easily seen; noticeable; striking. Janet was *conspicuous* both for her red hair and for her height.

con-spir-a-cy \kən-'spir-ə-sē\ N. treacherous plot. Brutus and Cassius joined in the *conspiracy* to kill Julius Caesar.

con-stit-u-ent \kən-'stich-(ə-)wənt\ N. supporter. The congressman received hundreds of letters from angry *constituents* after the Equal Rights Amendment failed to pass.

con-straint \kən-'stränt \N. compulsion; repression of feelings. There was a feeling of *constraint* in the room because no one dared to criticize the speaker. **con-strain** \kən-'strän \V.

con-strue \kən-'strü \V. explain; interpret. If I *construe* your remarks correctly, you disagree with the theory already advanced.

con-sum-mate \kən-'səm -ət\ ADJ. complete. I have never seen anyone who makes as many stupid errors as you do; you must be a *consummate* idiot. **con-sum-mate** \'kän(t) -sə-māt \V.

con-tam-i-nate \kən-'tam -ə-nāt \ V. pollute. The sewage system of the city so *contaminated* the water that swimming was forbidden.

con-ten-tious \kən-'ten -chəs\ ADJ. quarrelsome. We heard loud and *contentious* noises in the next room.

con-text \'kän -tekst \ N. writings preceding and following the passage quoted. Because these lines are taken out of *context*, they do not convey the message the author intended.

con-tig-u-ous \kən-'tig -yə-wəs\ ADJ. adjacent to; touching upon. The two countries are *contiguous* for a few miles; then they are separated by the gulf.

con-ti-nence \'känt -ᵊn-ən(t)s\ N. self-restraint; sexual chastity. He vowed to lead a life of *continence*. **con-ti-nent** \'känt -ᵊn-ənt\ ADJ.

con-tin-gent \kən-'tin -jənt\ ADJ. conditional. The continuation of this contract is *contingent* on the quality of your first output. **con-tin-gen-cy** \kən-'tin -jən-sē\ N.

con-tor-tion \kən-'tȯr -shən\ N. twisting; distortion. As the effects of the opiate wore away, the *contortions* of the patient became more violent and demonstrated how much pain he was enduring. **con-tort** \kən-'tȯ(ə)rt \V.

\ə\ **abut**   \ᵊ\ **kitten, F table**   \ər\ **further**   \a\ **ash**   \ā\ **ace**   \ä\ **cot, cart**
\au̇\ **out**   \ch\ **chin**   \e\ **bet**   \ē\ **easy**   \g\ **go**   \i\ **hit**   \ī\ **ice**   \j\ **job**

con-tra-band \ˈkän -trə-ˌband \ ADJ. illegal trade; smuggling. The Coast Guard tries to prevent traffic in *contraband* goods. also N.

con-tra-vene \ˌkän -trə-ˈvēn \ V. contradict; infringe on. I will not attempt to *contravene* your argument for it does not affect the situation.

con-trite \ˈkän -ˌtrīt \ ADJ. penitent. Her *contrite* tears did not influence the judge when he imposed sentence. **con-tri-tion**\kən-ˈtrish -ən\N.

con-tro-vert \ˈkän -trə-ˌvərt \ V. oppose with arguments; contradict. To *controvert* your theory will require much time but it is essential that we disprove it.

con-tu-ma-cious \ˌkän -t(y)ə-ˈmā -shəs\ ADJ. disobedient; resisting authority. The *contumacious* mob shouted defiantly at the police. **con-tu-ma-cy**\kən-ˈt(y)ü -mə-sē\N.

con-tume-ly\kən-ˈt(y)ü -mə-lē\ N. scornful insolence; insult. The "proud man's *contumely*" is distasteful to Hamlet.

con-tu-sion\kən-ˈt(y)ü -zhən\N. bruise. He was treated for *contusions* and abrasions.

co-nun-drum\kə-ˈnən-drəm \N. riddle; difficult problem. During the long car ride, she invented *conundrums* to entertain the children.

con-vene\kən-ˈvēn \ V. assemble. Because much needed legislation had to be enacted, the governor ordered the legislature to *convene* in special session by January 15.

con-ver-sant\kən-ˈvərs -ᵊnt\ADJ. familiar with. The lawyer is *conversant* with all the evidence.

con-vey-ance\kən-ˈvā -ən(t)s\ N. vehicle; transfer. During the transit strike, commuters used various kinds of *conveyances*.

con-vic-tion\kən-ˈvik-shən\N. strongly held belief. Nothing could shake his *conviction* that she was innocent. (secondary meaning)

con-viv-ial \kən-ˈviv -yəl\ ADJ. festive; gay; characterized by joviality. The *convivial* celebrators of the victory sang their college songs.

con-voke \kən-ˈvōk \ V. call together. Congress was *convoked* at the outbreak of the emergency. **con-vo-ca-tion** \ˌkän -və-ˈkā -shən\N.

---

con-vo-lut-ed \ˈkän -və-ˌlüt -əd\ ADJ. coiled around; involved; intricate. His argument was so *convoluted* that few of us could follow it intelligently.

co-pi-ous\ˈkō-pē-əs\ADJ. plentiful. He had *copious* reasons for rejecting the proposal.

co-quette\kō-ˈket \N. flirt. Because she refused to give him any answer to his proposal of marriage, he called her a *coquette*. also v.

cor-dial\ˈkȯr-jəl\ADJ. gracious; heartfelt. Our hosts greeted us at the airport with a *cordial* and a hearty hug.

cor-don \ˈkȯrd -ᵊn\ N. extended line of men or fortifications to prevent access or egress. The police *cordon* was so tight that the criminals could not leave the area. also v.

cor-nice\ˈkȯr -nəs\N. projecting molding on building (usually above columns). Because the *cornice* stones had been loosened by the storms, the police closed the building until repairs could be made. also v.

cor-ol-lary\ˈkȯr-ə-ˌler-ē\N. consequence; accompaniment. Brotherly love is a complex emotion, with sibling rivalry its natural *corollary.*

cor-po-re-al\kȯr ˈpȯr -ē-əl\ADJ. bodily; material. He was not a churchgoer; he was interested only in *corporeal* matters.

cor-pu-lent\ˈkȯr -pyə-lənt\ADJ. very fat. The *corpulent* man resolved to reduce. **cor-pu-lence** \ˈkȯr -pyə-lən(t)s\ N.

cor-re-la-tion\kȯr -ə-ˈlā -shən\N. mutual relationship. He sought to determine the *correlation* that existed between ability in algebra and ability to interpret reading exercises.

cor-rob-o-rate\kə-ˈräb -ə-ˌrāt \V. confirm. Unless we find a witness to *corroborate* your evidence, it will not stand up in court.

cor-ro-sive \kə-ˈrō -siv\ ADJ. eating away by chemicals or disease. Stainless steel is able to withstand the effects of *corrosive* chemicals.

cor-ru-gat-ed\ˈkȯr-ə-ˌgāt-əd\ADJ. wrinkled; ridged. She wished she could smooth away the wrinkles from his *corrugated* brow.

\ə\ abut	\ᵊ\ kitten, F table	\ər\ further	\a\ ash	\ā\ ace	\ä\ cot, cart
\aů\ out	\ch\ chin	\e\ bet	\ē\ easy	\g\ go	\i\ hit	\ī\ ice	\j\ job

cor-sair \ kȯr -ˌsa(ə)r \ N. pirate; pirate ship. The *corsairs*, preying on shipping in the Mediterranean, were often inspired by racial and religious hatreds as well as by the desire for money and booty.

cor-tege\ kȯr-ˈtezh \ N. procession. The funeral *cortege* proceeded slowly down the avenue.

cor-us-cate \ ˈkȯr -ə-ˌskāt \ V. glitter; scintillate. His wit is the kind that *coruscates* and startles all his listeners.

cos-mic \ ˈkäz -mik\ ADJ. pertaining to the universe; vast. *Cosmic* rays derive their name from the fact that they bombard the earth's atmosphere from outer space. **cosmos**\ˈkäz -məs\N.

co-te-rie\ ˈkōt -ə-(ˌ)rē\ N. group that meets socially; select circle. After his book had been published, he was invited to join the literary *coterie* that lunched daily at the hotel.

coun-te-nance\ ˈkaȯnt-ᵊn-ən(t)s \V. approve; tolerate. He refused to *countenance* such rude behavior on their part.

coun-ter-mand\ˈkaȯnt -ər-ˌmand \V. cancel; revoke. The general *countermanded* the orders issued in his absence. also N.

coun-ter-part\ ˈkaȯnt -ər-ˌpärt \ N. a thing that completes another; things very much alike. Night and day are *counterparts*.

coup\ˈkü \ N. highly successful action or sudden attack. As the news of his *coup* spread throughout Wall Street, his fellow brokers dropped by to congratulate him.

cou-ple\ˈkəp-əl\V. join; unite. The Flying Karamazovs *couple* expert juggling and amateur joking in their night-club act.

cou-ri-er\ˈkȯr-ē-ər\N. messenger. The publisher sent a special *courier* to pick up the manuscript.

cov-e-nant\ˈkəv -(ə-)nənt\N. agreement. We must comply with the terms of the *convenant*. also V.

co-vert\kō -(ˌ)vərt\ADJ. secret; hidden; implied. He could understand the *covert* threat in the letter. also N.

cov-et-ous\ˈkəv -ət-əs\ADJ. avaricious; eagerly desirous of. The child was *covetous* by nature and wanted to take the toys belonging to his classmates. **cov-et**\ˈkəv -ət\V.

\ŋ\ **sing**   \ō\ **go**   \ȯ\ **law**   \ȯi\ **boy**   \th\ **thin**   \t͟h\ **the**   \ü\ **loot**   \u̇\ **foot**
\y\ **yet**   \zh\ **vision**   \à, k̲, ⁿ, œ, œ̄, ue, ue̅, ʳ\ *see* Pronunciation Symbols

cow-er \ˈkau̇(-ə)r\ v. shrink quivering, as from fear. The frightened child *cowered* in the corner of the room.

coy \ˈkȯi\ ADJ. shy; modest; coquettish. She was *coy* in her answers to his offer.

coz-en \ˈkəz -ᵊn\ v. cheat; hoodwink; swindle. He was the kind of individual who would *cozen* his friends in a cheap card game but remain eminently ethical in all his business dealings.

crab-bed \ˈkrab -əd\ ADJ. sour; peevish. The *crabbed* old man was avoided by the children because he scolded them when they made noise.

crass \ˈkras\ ADJ. very unrefined; grossly insensible. The philosophers deplored the *crass* commercialism.

cra-ven \ˈkrā-vən\ ADJ. cowardly. His *craven* behavior in this critical period was criticized.

cre-dence \ˈkrēd -ᵊn(t)s\ N. belief. Do not place any *credence* in his promises.

cre-do \ˈkrēd -(ˌ)ō\ N. creed. I believe we may best describe his *credo* by saying that it approximates the Golden Rule.

cre-du-li-ty \kri-ˈd(y)ü -lət-ē\ N. belief on slight evidence. The witch doctor took advantage of the *credulity* of the superstitious natives. **cred-u-lous** \ˈkrej -ə-ləs\ ADJ.

creed \ˈkrēd\ N. system of religious or ethical beliefs. In any loyal American's *creed*, love of democracy must be emphasized.

cre-scen-do \krə-ˈshen -(ˌ)dō\ N. increase in the volume of sound in a musical passage. The overture suddenly changed from a quiet pastoral theme to a *crescendo* featured by blaring trumpets and clashing cymbals. also ADJ, ADV.

crest-fall-en \ˈkrest -fȯ -lən\ ADJ. dejected; dispirited. We were surprised at his reaction to the failure of his project; instead of being *crestfallen*, he was busily engaged in planning new activities.

crev-ice \ˈkrev -əs\ N. crack; fissure. The mountain climbers found footholds in the tiny *crevices* in the mountainside.

cringe \ˈkrinj\ v. shrink back, as if in fear. The dog *cringed*, expecting a blow.

cri-te-ri-on\krī-tir -ē-ən\ N. standard used in judging. What *criterion* did you use when you selected this essay as the prizewinner?

crone \'krōn \ N. hag. The toothless *crone* frightened us when she smiled.

crotch-et-y \'kräch -ət-ē\ ADJ. eccentric; whimsical. Although he was reputed to be a *crotchety* old gentleman, I found his ideas substantially sound and sensible.

crux\'krəks \ N. crucial point. This is the *crux* of the entire problem.

crypt \'kript \ N. secret recess or vault, usually used for burial. Until recently, only bodies of rulers and leading statesmen were interred in this *crypt*.

cryp-tic\'krip -tik\ADJ. mysterious; hidden; secret. His *cryptic* remarks could not be interpreted.

cu-bi-cle\'kyü -bi-kəl\N. small chamber used for sleeping. After his many hours of intensive study in the library, he retired to his *cubicle*.

cui-sine \kwi-zēn \ N. style of cooking. French *cuisine* is noted for its use of sauces and wines.

cul-de-sac\'kəl -di-ṣak \ N. blind alley; trap. The soldiers were unaware that they were marching into a *cul-de-sac* when they entered the canyon.

cu-li-nar-y \'kəl -ə-ner -ē\ADJ. relating to cooking. Many chefs attribute their *culinary* skill to the wise use of spices.

cull\'kəl \ V. pick out; reject. Every month the farmer *culls* the nonlaying hens from his flock and sells them to the local butcher. also N.

cul-mi-na-tion \kəl -mə-nā -shən\ N. attainment of highest point. His inauguration as President of the United States marked the *culmination* of his political career.

cul-pa-ble\'kəl -pə-bəl\ADJ. deserving blame. Corrupt politicians who condone the activities of the gamblers are equally *culpable*.

cul-vert \'kəl -vərt\ N. artificial channel for water. If we build a *culvert* under the road at this point, we will reduce the possibility of the road's being flooded during the rainy season.

\ŋ\ **sing**   \ō\ **go**   \ȯ\ **law**   \ȯi\ **boy**   \th\ **thin**   \t̲h̲\ **the**   \ü\ **loot**   \u̇\ **foot**
\y\ **yet**   \zh\ **vision**   \ä, k, ⁿ, œ, œ̅, ue, u̅e̅, \ *see* Pronunciation Symbols

cum·ber·some\ 'kəm-bər-səm \ADJ. heavy; hard to manage. He was burdened down with *cumbersome* parcels.

cu·pid·i·ty\kyü-'pid -ət-ē\N. greed. The defeated people could not satisfy the *cupidity* of the conquerors, who demanded excessive tribute.

cu·ra·tor\ 'kyü(ə)r-āt-ər\N.superintendent; manager. The members of the board of trustees of the museum expected the new *curator* to plan events and exhibitions which would make the museum more popular.

cur·mud·geon\₍ₗ₎kər-'məj-ən\N.churlish, miserly individual. Although he was regarded by many as a *curmudgeon*, a few of us were aware of the many kindnesses and acts of charity he secretly performed.

cur·ry\'kər -ē\v. dress; treat leather; seek favor. The courtier *curried* favors of the king.

cur·sive\'kər -siv\ADJ. flowing, running. In normal writing we run our letters together in *cursive* form; in printing, we separate the letters. also N.

cur·so·ry\'kərs -(-ə)-rē\ADJ. casual; hastily done. A *cursory* examination of the ruins indicates the possibility of arson; a more extensive study should be undertaken.

cur·tail\₍ₗ₎kər-'tā(ə)l \ v. shorten; reduce. During a coal shortage, we must *curtail* our use of this vital commodity.

cyn·ic\'sin -ik\ N. one who is skeptical or distrustful of human motives. A *cynic* at all times, he was suspicious of all altruistic actions of others.**cyn·i·cal**\'sin -i-kəl\ADJ.

cy·no·sure\'sī -nə-shù(ə)r \N. the object of general attention. As soon as the movie star entered the room, she became the *cynosure* of all eyes.

\ə\ abut	\ᵊ\ kitten, F table	\ər\ further	\a\ ash	\ā\ ace	\ä\ cot, cart
\aů\ out	\ch\ chin	\e\ bet	\ē\ easy	\g\ go	\i\ hit	\ī\ ice	\j\ job

–d–

da-is\ˈdā -əs\ N. raised platform for guests of honor. When he approached the *dais*, he was greeted by cheers from the people who had come to honor him.

dal-ly \ˈdal -ē\ V. trifle with; procrastinate. Laertes told Ophelia that Hamlet could only *dally* with her affections.

dank\ˈdaŋk \ ADJ. damp. The walls of the dungeon were *dank* and slimy.

dap-pled\ˈdap-əld\ADJ. spotted. The sunlight filtering through the screens created a *dappled* effect on the wall.

das-tard \ˈdas -tərd\ N. coward. This sneak attack is the work of a *dastard*. **das-tard-ly**\ˈdas -tərd-lē\ADJ.

daub\ˈdȯb\ V. smear (as with paint). From the way he *daubed* his paint on the canvas, I could tell he knew nothing of oils. also N.

daunt\ˈdȯnt \ V. intimidate. Your threats cannot *daunt* me.

daunt-less\ˈdȯnt -ləs\ADJ. bold. Despite the dangerous nature of the undertaking, the *dauntless* soldier volunteered for the assignment.

daw-dle \ˈdȯd -ᵊl\ V. loiter; waste time. Inasmuch as we must meet a deadline, do not *dawdle* over this work.

dead-lock\ˈded-ˌläk \ N. standstill; stalemate. The negotiations had reached a *deadlock*. also V.

dead-pan \ˈded-ˌpan \ADJ. wooden; impassive. We wanted to see how long he could maintain his *deadpan* expression.

dearth\ˈdərth \ N. scarcity. The *dearth* of skilled labor compelled the employers to open trade schools.

de-ba-cle \di-ˈbäk -əl\ N. breaking up; downfall. This *debacle* in the government can only result in anarchy.

de-base\di-ˈbās \ V. reduce to lower state. Do not *debase* yourself by becoming maudlin.

de-bauch\di-ˈbȯch \ V. corrupt; make intemperate. A vicious newspaper can *debauch* public ideals. **de-bauch-er-y** \di-ˈbȯch -(ə-)rē\N.

de-bil-i-tate \di-ˈbil -ə-ˌtāt \ V. weaken; enfeeble. Overindulgence *debilitates* character as well as physical stamina.

deb-o-nair\deb -ə-ˈna(ə)r \ADJ. friendly; aiming to please. The *debonair* youth was liked by all who met him, because of his cheerful and obliging manner.

\ŋ\ sing \ō\ go \ȯ\ law \ȯi\ boy \th\ thin \th\ the \ü\ loot \u̇\ foot
\y\ yet \zh\ vision \ə, k̲, ⁿ, œ, œ̄, ue, ue̅, ʳ\ *see* Pronunciation Symbols

deb-u-tante\deb -yü-tänt \N. young woman making formal entrance into society. As a *debutante*, she was often mentioned in the society columns of the newspapers.

dec-a-dence\dek -əd-ən(t)s\N. decay. The moral *decadence* of the people was reflected in the lewd literature of the period.

de-cant\di-'kant \V. pour off gently. Be sure to *decant* this wine before serving it.

de-cap-i-tate\di-'kap-ə-ˌtāt\V. behead. They did not hang Lady Jane Grey; they *decapitated* her.

de-cid-u-ous \di-'sij -ə-wəs\ ADJ. falling off as of leaves. The oak is a *deciduous* tree.

dec-i-mate\des -ə-ˌmāt \V. kill, usually one out of ten. We do more to *decimate* our population in automobile accidents than we do in war.

de-ci-pher\di-'sī-fər\V. decode. I could not *decipher* the doctor's handwriting.

de-cliv-i-ty \di-'kliv -ət-ē\ N. downward slope. The children loved to ski down the *declivity*.

dé-col-le-té\ˌdā-ˌkäl -ə-'tā \ADJ. having a low-necked dress. Current fashion decrees that evening gowns be *décolleté* this season; bare shoulders are again the vogue.

de-com-po-si-tion\(ˌ)dē-ˌkäm-pə-'zish-ən\N. decay. Despite the body's advanced state of *decomposition*, the police were able to identify the murdered man. **de-com-pose**\ˌdē-kəm-'pōz\V.

dec-o-rous\dek -ə-rəs\ADJ. proper. Her *decorous* behavior was praised by her teachers. **de-co-rum**\di-'kōr -əm\N.

de-coy\dē -kói \N. lure or bait. The wild ducks were not fooled by the *decoy*. **de-coy**\di-'kói \V.

de-crep-it\di-'krep -ət\ADJ. worn out by age. The *decrepit* car blocked traffic on the highway.

de-crep-i-tude\di-'krep -ə-ˌt(y)üd \N. state of collapse caused by illness or old age. I was unprepared for the state of *decrepitude* in which I had found my old friend; he seemed to have aged twenty years in six months.

de-cry \di-'krī \V. disparage. Do not attempt to increase your stature by *decrying* the efforts of your opponents.

\ə\ abut　\ə\ kitten, F table　\ər\ further　\a\ ash　\ā\ ace　\ä\ cot, cart
\aü\ out　\ch\ chin　\e\ bet　\ē\ easy　\g\ go　\i\ hit　\ī\ ice　\j\ job

de·duc·i·ble\di-'d(y)ü -sə-bəl\ADJ. derived by reasoning. If we accept your premise, your conclusions are easily *deducible*.

de·fal·cate \di-'fal -kāt \ v. misuse money held in trust. Legislation was passed to punish brokers who *defalcated* their clients' funds.

def·a·ma·tion \def -ə-'mā -shən\ N. harming a person's reputation. Such *defamation* of character may result in a slander suit.

de·fault\di-'fölt\ N. failure to do. As a result of her husband's failure to appear in court, she was granted a divorce by *default*. also v.

de·feat·ist\di-'fēt -əst\ADJ. attitude of one who is ready to accept defeat as a natural outcome. If you maintain your *defeatist* attitude, you will never succeed. also N.

de·fec·tion\di-'fek -shən\N. desertion. The children, who had made him an idol, were hurt most by his *defection* from our cause.

def·er·ence\def -(ə-)rən(t)s\N. courteous regard for another's wish. In *deference* to his desires, the employers granted him a holiday.

de·file\di-'fī(ə)l\ v. pollute; profane. The hoodlums *defiled* the church with their scurrilous writing.

de·fin·i·tive\di-'fin -ət-iv\ADJ. final; complete. Carl Sandburg's *Abraham Lincoln* may be regarded as the *definitive* work on the life of the Great Emancipator.

de·flect\di-'flekt\ v. turn aside. His life was saved when his cigarette case *deflected* the bullet.

de·fray\di-'frā\v. pay the costs of. Her employer offered to *defray* the costs of her postgraduate education.

deft\ 'deft \ADJ. neat; skillful. The *deft* waiter uncorked the champagne without spilling a drop.

de·funct\di-'fəŋ(k)t\ ADJ. dead; no longer in use or existence. The lawyers sought to examine the books of the *defunct* corporation.

de·grad·ed\di-'grād -əd\ADJ. lowered in rank; debased. The *degraded* wretch spoke only of his past glories and honors.

---

de-i-fy\\'dē-ə-,fī\\ v. turn into a god; idolize. Admire the rock star all you want; just don't *deify* him.

deign\\dān\\ v. condescend. He felt that he would debase himself if he *deigned* to answer his critics.

de-lec-ta-ble\\di-'lek-tə-bəl\\ADJ. delightful; delicious. We thanked our host for a most *delectable* meal.

de-lete\\di-'lēt\\ v. erase, strike out. If you *delete* this paragraph, the composition will have more appeal.

del-e-te-ri-ous\\del -ə-'tir -ē-əs\\ADJ. harmful. Workers in nuclear research must avoid the *deleterious* effects of radioactive substances.

de-lin-e-a-tion \\di-lin -ē-'ā -shən\\ N. portrayal. He is a powerful storyteller, but he is weakest in his *delineation* of character.

del-i-ques-cent\\del -i-'kwes -ᵊnt\\ADJ. capable of absorbing moisture from the air and becoming liquid. Since this powder is extremely *deliquescent*, it must be kept in a hermetically sealed container until it is used.

de-lir-i-um \\di-'lir -ē-əm\\ N. mental disorder marked by confusion. The drunkard in his *delirium* saw strange animals.

de-lude\\di-'lüd\\ v. deceive. Do not *delude* yourself into believing that he will relent.

de-lu-sion\\di-'lü -zhən\\N. false belief; hallucination. This scheme is a snare and a *delusion*.

de-lu-sive \\di-'lü -siv\\ADJ. deceptive; raising vain hopes. Do not raise your hopes on the basis of his *delusive* promises.

dem-a-gogue\\dem -ə-,gäg\\N. person who appeals to people's prejudice; false leader of people. He was accused of being a *demagogue* because he made promises which aroused futile hopes in his listeners.

de-mean\\di-'mēn\\ v. degrade; humiliate. He felt that he would *demean* himself if he replied to the scurrilous letter.

de-mean-or\\di-'mē -nər\\N. behavior; bearing. His sober *demeanor* quieted the noisy revelers.

de-ment-ed\\di-'ment-əd\\ADJ. insane. She became increasingly *demented* and had to be hospitalized.

\\ə\\ abut \\ᵊ\\ kitten, F table \\ər\\ **further** \\a\\ **ash** \\ā\\ **ace** \\ä\\ cot, cart
\\aú\\ out \\ch\\ **chin** \\e\\ bet \\ē\\ **easy** \\g\\ **go** \\i\\ hit \\ī\\ ice \\j\\ **job**

de-mise\di-ˈmīz\ N. death. Upon the *demise* of the dictator, a bitter dispute about succession to power developed. also v.

de-mo-li-tion\dem -ə-ˈlish -ən\N. destruction. One of the major aims of the air force was the complete *demolition* of all means of transportation by bombing of rail lines and terminals.

de-mo-ni-ac \di-ˈmō-nē-ˌak\ ADJ. fiendish. The Spanish Inquisition devised many *demoniac* means of torture. **de-mon**\dē -mən\N.

de-mot-ic \di-ˈmät -ik\ ADJ. pertaining to the people. He lamented the passing of aristocratic society and maintained that a *demotic* society would lower the nation's standards.

de-mur\di-ˈmər\ V. delay; object. To *demur* at this time will only worsen the already serious situation; now is the time for action. also N.

de-mure \di-ˈmyu̇(ə)r\ ADJ. grave; serious; coy. She was *demure* and reserved.

den-i-grate\ˈden -i-ˌgrāt\ V. blacken. All attempts to *denigrate* the character of our late President have failed; the people still love him and cherish his memory.

den-i-zen\ˈden -ə-zən\N. inhabitant of. Ghosts are *denizens* of the land of the dead who return to earth.

de-no-ta-tion\dē -nō-ˈtā -shən\N. meaning; distinguishing by name. A dictionary will always give us the *denotation* of a word; frequently, it will also give us its connotation.

de-noue-ment\dā -ˌnü -ˈmän\ N. outcome; final development of the plot of a play. The play was childishly written; the *denouement* was obvious to sophisticated theatergoers as early as the middle of the first act.

de-pict\di-ˈpikt\ V. portray. In this book, the author *depicts* the slave owners as kind and benevolent masters.

dep-i-late\ˈdep -ə-ˌlāt\ V. remove hair. Many women *depilate* their legs.

de-plete\di-ˈplēt\ V. reduce; exhaust. We must wait until we *deplete* our present inventory before we order replacements.

\ŋ\ sing	\ō\ go	\o�section\ law	\oi\ boy	\th\ thin	\th\ the	\ü\ loot	\u̇\ foot
\y\ yet	\zh\ vision	\a̱, k̲, ⁿ, œ, œ̄, ue, ūe, ʸ\ *see* Pronunciation Symbols

de-ploy\di-'plói\ v. move troops so that the battle line is extended at the expense of depth. The general ordered the battalion to *deploy* in order to meet the offensive of the enemy.

de-pose\di-'pōz\ v. dethrone; remove from office. The army attempted to *depose* the king and set up a military government.

de-po-si-tion\dep -ə-'zish -ən\ N. testimony under oath. He made his *deposition* in the judge's chamber.

de-prav-i-ty\di-'prav -ət-ē\ N. corruption; wickedness. The *depravity* of his behavior shocked all.

dep-re-cate\'dep -ri-kāt\ v. disapprove regretfully. I must *deprecate* your attitude and hope that you will change your mind.

dep-re-ca-to-ry\'dep -ri-kə-tōr -ē\ ADJ. disapproving. Your *deprecatory* criticism has offended the author.

de-pre-ci-ate\di-'prē -shē-āt\ v. lessen in value. If you neglect this property, it will *depreciate*.

dep-re-da-tion\dep -rə-'dā -shən\ N. plundering. After the *depredations* of the invaders, the people were penniless.

de-range\di-'rānj\ v. make insane. He was mentally *deranged*.

der-e-lict\'der -ə-.likt\ ADJ. abandoned. The *derelict* craft was a menace to navigation. also N.

de-ride\di-'rīd\ v. scoff at. The people *derided* his grandiose schemes.

de-ri-sion\di-'rizh -ən\ N. ridicule. They greeted his proposal with *derision* and refused to consider it seriously.

de-riv-a-tive\di-'riv -ət-iv\ ADJ. unoriginal; derived from another source. Although her early poetry was clearly *derivative* in nature, the critics thought she had promise and eventually would find her own voice.

der-ma-tol-o-gist\der -mə-'täl -ə-jəst\ N. one who studies the skin and its disease. I advise you to consult a *dermatologist* about your acne.

de-rog-a-to-ry \di-'räg -ə-.tōr -ē\ ADJ. expressing a low opinion. I resent your *derogatory* remarks.

---

des-cant\ˈdes-ˌkant\ v. discuss fully. He was willing to *descant* upon any topic of conversation, even when he knew very little about the subject under discussion, also N.

de-scry\di-ˈskrī\ v. catch sight of. In the distance, we could barely *descry* the enemy vessels.

des-e-crate\ˈdes-i-ˌkrāt\ v. profane; violate the sanctity of. The soldiers *desecrated* the temple.

des-ic-cate\ˈdes-i-ˌkāt\ v. dry up. A tour of this smokehouse will give you an idea of how the pioneers used to *desiccate* food in order to preserve it.

de-sid-er-a-tum\di-ˌsid-ə-ˈrät-əm\ N. that which is desired. Our first *desideratum* must be the establishment of peace; we can then attempt to remove the causes of the present conflict.

de-spi-ca-ble\di-ˈspik-ə-bəl\ ADJ. contemptible. Your *despicable* remarks call for no reply.

de-spise\di-ˈspīz\ v. scorn. I *despise* your attempts at a reconciliation at this time.

de-spoil\di-ˈspói(ə)l\ v. plunder. If you do not yield, I am afraid the enemy will *despoil* the buildings.

de-spon-dent\di-ˈspän-dənt\ ADJ. depressed; gloomy. To the dismay of his parents, he became more and more *despondent* every day. **de-spon-den-cy**\di-ˈspän-dən-sē\N.

des-po-tism\ˈdes-pə-ˌtiz-əm\N. tyranny. The people rebelled against the *despotism* of the king.

des-ti-tute\ˈdes-tə-ˌt(y)üt\ ADJ. extremely poor. The illness left the family *destitute*.

des-ul-to-ry\ˈdes-el-ˌtōr-ē\ADJ. aimless; jumping around. The animals' *desultory* behavior indicated that they had no awareness of their predicament.

de-ter-gent\di-ˈtər-jənt\N. cleansing agent. Many new *detergents* have replaced soap.

de-ter-mi-nate\di-ˈtərm-(ə-)nət\ADJ. having a fixed order of procedure; invariable. At the royal wedding, the procession of the nobles followed a *determinate* order of precedence.

\ŋ\ sing   \ō\ go   \ò\ law   \òi\ boy   \th\ thin   \t͟h\ the   \ü\ loot   \u̇\ foot
\y\ yet   \zh\ vision   \à, k̲, ⁿ, œ, œ̄, ue, ūe, ʸ\ see Pronunciation Symbols

det-o-na-tion \det -ᵊn-ā -shən\ N. explosion. The *detonation* could be heard miles away.

de-trac-tion \di-ˈtrak -shən\ N. slandering; aspersion. He is offended by your frequent *detractions* of his ability as a leader.

det-ri-ment \ˈde -trə-mənt\ N. harm; damage. Your acceptance of his support will ultimately prove to be a *detriment* rather than an aid to your cause.

de-vi-ate \ˈdē -vē-āt\ V. turn away from. Do not *deviate* from the truth. **de-vi-ate** (dē -vē-ət) ADJ.

de-vi-ous \ˈdē -vē-əs\ ADJ. going astray; erratic. Your *devious* behavior in this matter puzzles me since you are usually direct and straightforward.

de-void \di-ˈvoid\ ADJ. lacking. He was *devoid* of any personal desire for gain in his endeavor to secure improvement in the community.

de-volve \di-ˈvälv\ V. deputize; pass to others. It *devolved* upon us, the survivors, to arrange peace terms with the enemy.

de-vout \di-ˈvaut\ ADJ. pious. The *devout* man prayed daily.

dex-ter-ous \ˈdek -st(ə-)rəs\ ADJ. skillful. The magician was so *dexterous* that we could not follow him as he performed his tricks.

di-a-bol-i-cal \dī -ə-ˈbäl -i-kəl\ ADJ. devilish. This scheme is so *diabolical* that I must reject it.

di-a-dem \ˈdī -ə-dem\ N. crown. The king's *diadem* was on display at the museum.

di-a-lec-tic \dī -ə-ˈlek -tik\ N. art of debate. I am not skilled in *dialectic* and, therefore, cannot answer your arguments as forcefully as I wish.

di-aph-a-nous \dī-ˈaf -ə-nəs\ ADJ. sheer; transparent. They admired her *diaphanous* and colorful dress.

di-a-tribe \ˈdī -ə-trīb\ N. bitter scolding; invective. During the lengthy *diatribe* delivered by his opponent he remained calm and self-controlled.

di-chot-o-my \dī-ˈkät -ə-mē\ N. branching into two parts. The *dichotomy* of our legislative system provides us with many safeguards.

dic-tum \ˈdik -təm\ N. authoritative and weighty statement. He repeated the statement as though it were the *dictum* of the most expert worker in the group.

\ə\ abut \ᵊ\ kitten, F table \ər\ further \a\ ash \ā\ ace \ä\ cot, cart
\aú\ out \ch\ chin \e\ bet \ē\ easy \g\ go \i\ hit \ī\ ice \j\ job

di-dac-tic\dī-'dak -tik\ ADJ. teaching; instructional. The *didactic* qualities of his poetry overshadow its literary qualities; the lesson he teaches is more memorable than the lines.

dif-fi-dence \'dif -əd-ən(t)s\ N. shyness. You must overcome your *diffidence* if you intend to become a salesperson.

dif-fu-sion \dif-'yü -zhən\ N. wordiness; spreading in all directions like a gas. Your composition suffers from a *diffusion* of ideas; try to be more compact. **dif-fuse**\dif-'yüs\ ADJ.\dif-'yüz\V.

di-gres-sive \dī-'gres -iv\ ADJ. wandering away from the subject. His book was marred by his many *digressive* remarks.

di-lap-i-da-tion \də-,lap -ə-'dā -shən\ N. ruin because of neglect. We felt that the *dilapidation* of the building could be corrected by several coats of paint.

di-late\dī-'lāt\ V. expand. In the dark, the pupils of your eyes *dilate*.

dil-a-to-ry\'dil -ə-,tōr -ē\ADJ. delaying. Your *dilatory* tactics may compel me to cancel the contract.

di-lem-ma\də-'lem -ə\ N. problem; choice of two unsatisfactory alternatives. In this *dilemma*, he knew no one to whom he could turn for advice.

dil-et-tante \'dil -ə-tänt\ N. aimless follower of the arts; amateur; dabbler. He was not serious in his painting; he was rather a *dilettante*.

dim-i-nu-tion\dim -ə-'n(y)ü -shən\N. lessening; reduction in size. The blockaders hoped to achieve victory as soon as the *diminution* of the enemy's supplies became serious.

dint\'dint\ N. means; effort. By *dint* of much hard work, the volunteers were able to place the raging forest fire under control. also V.

dip-so-ma-ni-ac \dip-sə-'mā -nē-,ak\ N. one who has a strong craving for intoxicating liquor. The picture *The Lost Weekend* was an excellent portrayal of the struggles of the *dipsomaniac*.

dire\'dī(ə)r\ ADJ. disastrous. People ignored his *dire* predictions of an approaching depression.

dirge\'dərj\ N. lament with music. The funeral *dirge* stirred us to tears.

---

dis·a·buse\dis -ə-'byüz\ v. correct a false impression; undeceive. I will attempt to *disabuse* you of your impression of my client's guilt; I know he is innocent.

dis·ar·ray\ˌdis-ə-'rā\ N. a disorderly or untidy state. After the New Year's party, the once orderly house was in total *disarray.*

dis·a·vow·al\ˌdis -ə-'vaú(-ə)l\ N. denial; disclaiming. His *disavowal* of his part in the conspiracy was not believed by the jury.

dis·burse\dis-'bərs\v. pay out. When you *disburse* money on the company's behalf, be sure to get a receipt.

dis·cern·i·ble\dis-'ər -nə-bəl\ ADJ. distinguishable; perceivable. The ships in the harbor were not *discernible* in the fog.

dis·cern·ing\dis-'ər -niŋ\ADJ. mentally quick and observant; having insight. Because he was considered the most *discerning* member of the firm, he was assigned the most difficult cases.

dis·claim\dis-'klām\ v. disown; renounce claim to. If I grant you this privilege, will you *disclaim* all other rights?

dis·close\dis-'klōz\v. reveal. Although competitors offered him bribes, he refused to *disclose* any information about his company's forthcoming product. **dis·clo·sure**\dis-'klō-zhər\N.

dis·com·fit\dis-'kəm(p) -fət\v. put to rout; defeat; disconcert. This ruse will *discomfit* the enemy. **dis·com·fi·ture**\dis-'kəm(p) -fə-ˌchù(ə)r\ N.

dis·con·cert\ˌdis -kən-'sərt\ v. confuse; upset; embarrass. The lawyer was *disconcerted* by the evidence produced by his adversary.

dis·con·so·late\dis-'kän(t) -s(ə-)lət\ADJ. sad. The death of his wife left him *disconsolate.*

dis·cor·dant\dis-'kórd -ᵊnt\ ADJ. inharmonious; conflicting. He tried to unite the *discordant* factions.

dis·count\'dis-ˌkaúnt\v. disregard. Be prepared to *discount* what he has to say about his ex-wife. (secondary meaning)

---

dis-cred-it \(')dis-'kred-ət\ v. defame; destroy confidence in; disbelieve. The campaign was highly negative in tone; each candidate tried to *discredit* the other.

dis-crep-an-cy \dis-'krep-ən-sē\ N. lack of consistency; difference. The police noticed some *discrepancies* in his description of the crime and did not believe him.

dis-crete \dis-'krēt\ ADJ. separate; unconnected. The universe is composed of *discrete* bodies.

dis-cre-tion \dis-'kresh -ən\ N. prudence; ability to adjust actions to circumstances. Use your *discretion* in this matter.

dis-crim-i-nat-ing \dis-'krim-ə-nāt-iŋ\ ADJ. able to see differences. They feared he was not sufficiently *discriminating* to judge complex works of modern art. (secondary meaning) **dis-crim-i-na-tion** \dis-,krim-ə-'nā-shən\ N; **dis-crim-i-nate** \dis-'krim-ə-nāt\ v.

dis-cur-sive \dis-'kər -siv\ ADJ. digressing; rambling. They were annoyed and bored by his *discursive* remarks.

dis-dain \dis-'dān\ v. treat with scorn or contempt. You make enemies of all you *disdain*. also N.

dis-grun-tle \dis-'grənt -ᵊl\ v. make discontented. The passengers were *disgruntled* by the numerous delays.

dis-ha-bille \dis -ə-'bē(ə)l \ N. in a state of undress. Because he was certain that he would have no visitors, he lounged around the house in a state of *dishabille,* wearing only his pajamas and a pair of old bedroom slippers.

dis-heart-ened \(')dis-'härt-ᵊnd\ ADJ. lacking courage and hope. His failure to pass the bar exam *disheartened* him.

di-shev-eled \dish-'ev -əld\ ADJ. untidy. Your *disheveled* appearance will hurt your chances in this interview.

dis-in-gen-u-ous \dis -ᵊn-'jen -yə-wəs\ ADJ. not naive; sophisticated. Although he was young, his remarks indicated that he was *disingenuous.*

dis-in-ter-est-ed \(ᵗ)dis -'in-trəst-əd\ ADJ. unprejudiced. The only *disinterested* person in the room was the judge.

dis-joint-ed \(ᵗ)dis-'jöint -əd\ ADJ. disconnected. His remarks were so *disjointed* that we could not follow his reasoning.

---

dis·mem·ber \⁽ʰ⁾dis-'mem-bər\ v. cut into small parts. When the Austrian Empire was *dismembered*, several new countries were established.

dis·par·age \dis-'par-ij\ v. belittle. Do not *disparage* anyone's contribution; these little gifts add up to large sums.

dis·pa·rate \dis-'par-ət\ ADJ. basically different; unrelated. It is difficult, if not impossible, to organize these *disparate* elements into a coherent whole.

dis·par·i·ty \dis-'par-ət-ē\ N. difference; condition of inequality. The *disparity* in their ages made no difference at all.

dis·pas·sion·ate \⁽ʰ⁾dis-'pash-(ə-)nət\ ADJ. calm; impartial. In a *dispassionate* analysis of the problem, he carefully examined the causes of the conflict and proceeded to suggest suitable remedies.

dis·per·sion \dis-'pər-zhən\ N. scattering. The *dispersion* of this group throughout the world may be explained by their expulsion from their homeland.

dis·pir·it·ed \⁽ʰ⁾dis-'pir-ət-əd\ ADJ. lacking in spirit. The coach used all the tricks at his command to buoy up the enthusiasm of his team, which had become *dispirited* at the loss of the star player.

dis·pu·ta·tious \dis-pyə-'tā-shəs\ ADJ. argumentative; fond of argument. People avoided discussing contemporary problems with him because of his *disputatious* manner.

dis·qui·si·tion \dis-kwə-'zish-ən\ N. a formal systematic inquiry; an explanation of the results of a formal inquiry. In his *disquisition*, he outlined the steps he had taken in reaching his conclusions.

dis·sec·tion \dis-'ek-shən\ N. analysis; cutting apart in order to examine. The *dissection* of frogs in the laboratory is particularly unpleasant to some students.

dis·sem·ble \dis-'em-bəl\ v. disguise; pretend. Even though you are trying to *dissemble* your motive in joining this group, we can see through your pretense.

dis·sem·i·nate \dis-'em-ə-ˌnāt\ v. scatter (like seeds). The invention of the radio has helped propagandists to *disseminate* their favorite doctrines very easily.

dis-sent\dis-'ent\v. disagree. In the recent Supreme Court decision, Justice Marshall *dissented* from the majority opinion. also N.

dis-ser-ta-tion\dis -ər-'tā -shən\N. formal essay. In order to earn a graduate degree from many of our universities, a candidate is frequently required to prepare a *dissertation* on some scholarly subject.

dis-sim-u-late \(ı)dis-'im -yə-ˌlāt\ v. pretend; conceal by feigning. She tried to *dissimulate* her grief by her gay attitude.

dis-si-pate\dis -ə-ˌpāt\ v. squander. The young man quickly *dissipated* his inheritance.

dis-so-lute \dis -ə-ˌlüt\ ADJ. loose in morals. The *dissolute* life led by these people is indeed shocking.

dis-so-nance\dis -ə-nən(t)s\N. discord. Some contemporary musicians deliberately use *dissonance* to achieve certain effects.

dis-suade\dis-'wād\ v. advise against. He could not *dissuade* his friend from joining the conspirators.

dis-sua-sion\dis-'wā -zhən\N. advice against. All his powers of *dissuasion* were useless.

dis-tend \dis-'tend\ v. expand; swell out. I can tell when he is under stress by the way the veins *distend* on his forehead.

dis-tor-tion\dis-'tȯr -shən\N. twisting out of shape. It is difficult to believe the newspaper accounts of this event because of the *distortions* and exaggerations written by the reporters.

dis-trait\di-'strā\ ADJ. absentminded. Because of his personal problems, the professor often appeared *distrait* and unconcerned about routine.

dis-traught\dis-'trȯt\ ADJ. upset; distracted by anxiety. The *distraught* parents searched the ravine for their lost child.

di-ur-nal \dī-'ərn -ᵊl\ ADJ. daily. A farmer cannot neglect his *diurnal* tasks at any time; cows, for example, must be milked regularly.

di-va\dē -və\N. operatic singer; prima donna. Although world famous as a *diva*, she did not indulge in fits of temperament.

di-verge\də-'vərj\ v. vary; go in different directions from the same point. The spokes of the wheel *diverge* from the hub.

di-vers\dī-vərz\ ADJ. several; differing. We could hear *divers* opinions of his ability.

di-verse\dī-vərs\ ADJ. differing in some characteristics; various. There are *diverse* ways of approaching the problem.

di-ver-si-ty\də-'vər-sət-ē\ N. variety; dissimilitude. The *diversity* of colleges in this country indicates that many levels of ability are being cared for.

di-vest\dī-'vest\ v. strip; deprive. He was *divested* of his power to act.

div-i-na-tion\div-ə-'nā-shən\ N. foreseeing the future with aid of magic. I base my opinions not on any special gift of *divination* but on the laws of probability.

di-vulge\də-'vəlj\ v. reveal. I will not tell you this news because I am sure you will *divulge* it prematurely.

doc-ile\däs-əl\ADJ. obedient; easily managed. As *docile* as he seems today, that old lion was once a ferocious, snarling beast.

dock-et\däk-ət\N. program as for trial; book where such entries are made. The case of Smith vs. Jones was entered in the *docket* for July 15. also v.

doc-u-ment\'däk-yə-,ment\v. provide written evidence. She kept all the receipts from her business trip in order to *document* her expenses for the firm. also N.

dod-der-ing\däd-(ə-)riŋ\ADJ. shaky; infirm from old age. Although he is not as yet a *doddering* and senile old man, his ideas and opinions no longer can merit the respect we gave them years ago.

doff\däf\v. take off. He *doffed* his hat to the lady.

dog-ger-el\'dòg-(ə-)rəl\N. poor verse. Although we find occasional snatches of genuine poetry in his work, most of his writing is mere *doggerel*.

dog-mat-ic\dòg-'mat-ik\ADJ. positive; arbitrary. Do not be so *dogmatic* about that statement; it can be easily refuted.

\ə\ abut	\ᵊ\ kitten, F table	\ər\ further	\a\ ash	\ā\ ace	\ä\ cot, cart
\aú\ out	\ch\ chin	\e\ bet	\ē\ easy	\g\ go	\i\ hit	\ī\ ice	\j\ job

dol-drums\\'dōl-drəmz\\ N. blues; listlessness; slack period. Once the excitement of meeting her deadline was over, she found herself in the *doldrums.*

do-lor-ous\\dō -lə-rəs\\ ADJ. sorrowful. He found the *dolorous* lamentations of the bereaved family emotionally disturbing and he left as quickly as he could.

dolt\\dōlt\\ N. stupid person. I thought I was talking to a mature audience; instead, I find myself addressing a pack of *dolts* and idiots.

do-mi-cile\\däm -ə-ˌsīl\\ N. home. Although his legal *domicile* was in New York City, his work kept him away from his residence for many years. also V.

dor-mant \\'dȯr -mənt\\ ADJ. sleeping; lethargic; torpid. Sometimes *dormant* talents in our friends surprise those of us who never realized how gifted our acquaintances really are. **dor-man-cy**\\'dȯr -mən-sē\\N.

dor-sal\\dȯr -səl\\ADJ. relating to the back of an animal. A shark may be identified by its *dorsal* fin, which projects above the surface of the ocean. also N.

dot-age\\dōt -ij\\N. senility. In his *dotage,* the old man bored us with long tales of events in his childhood.

dough-ty\\daut -ē\\ADJ. courageous. Many folk tales have sprung about this *doughty* pioneer who opened up the New World for his followers.

dour\\'daủ(ə)r\\ ADJ. sullen; stubborn. The man was *dour* and taciturn.

douse\\'daủs\\V. plunge into water; drench; extinguish. They *doused* each other with hoses and water balloons.

dowdy\\'daủd-ē\\ADJ. slovenly; untidy. She tried to change her *dowdy* image by buying a new fashionable wardrobe.

dreg\\dreg\\ N. sediment; worthless residue. The *dregs* of society may be observed in this slum area of the city.

droll\\drōl\\ ADJ. queer and amusing. He was a popular guest because his *droll* anecdotes were always amusing. also N.

drone\\'drōn\\N. idle person; male bee. Content to let his wife support him, the would-be writer was in reality nothing but a *drone.*

---

drone\ \'drōn\ v. talk dully; buzz or murmur like a bee. On a gorgeous day, who wants to be stuck in a classroom listening to the teacher *drone*.

dross\ \'dräs\ N. waste matter; worthless impurities. Many methods have been devised to separate the valuable metal from the *dross*.

drudg-ery\ \'drəj -(ə-)rē\ N. menial work. Cinderella's fairy godmother rescued her from a life of *drudgery*.

du-bi-ous\ \'d(y)ü -bē-əs\ ADJ. doubtful. He has the *dubious* distinction of being the lowest man in his class.

du-en-na \d(y)ü-'en -ə\ N. attendant of young female; chaperone. Their romance could not flourish because of the presence of her *duenna*.

dul-cet\ \'dəl -sət\ ADJ. sweet sounding. The *dulcet* sounds of the birds at dawn were soon drowned out by the roar of traffic passing our motel.

du-plic-i-ty\ \d(y)ü-'plis -ət-ē\ N. double-dealing; hypocrisy. People were shocked and dismayed when they learned of his *duplicity* in this affair for he had always seemed honest and straightforward.

du-ress\ \d(y)ü-'res\ N. forcible restraint, especially unlawfully. The hostages were held under *duress* until the prisoners' demands were met.

dwin-dle\ \'dwin-dəl\ v. shrink; reduce. They spent so much money that their funds *dwindled* to nothing.

dy-nam-ic \dī-'nam -ik\ ADJ. active; efficient. A *dynamic* government is necessary to meet the demands of a changing society. also N.

dys-pep-tic\ \dis-'pep-tik\ ADJ. suffering from indigestion. All the talk about rich food made him feel *dyspeptic*. **dys-pep-sia**\ \dis-'pep-shə\ N.

\ə\ abut	\ᵊ\ kitten, F table	\ər\ **further**	\a\ ash	\ā\ ace	\ä\ cot, cart
\au̇\ **out**	\ch\ **chin**	\e\ bet	\ē\ **easy**	\g\ **go**	\i\ **hit**　\ī\ **ice**　\j\ **job**

—e—

earth-y\ˈər -thē\ ADJ. unrefined; coarse. His *earthy* remarks often embarrassed the women in his audience.

e-bul-lient \i-ˈbùl -yənt\ ADJ. showing excitement; overflowing with enthusiasm. His *ebullient* nature could not be repressed; he was always laughing and gay. **e-bul-li-ence**\i-ˈbul -yən(t)s\ N.

ec-cen-tric-i-ty\ek -ˌsen -ˈtris -ət-ē\ N. oddity; idiosyncrasy. Some of his friends tried to account for his rudeness to strangers as the *eccentricity* of genius. **ec-cen-tric**\ik-ˈsen -trik\ ADJ., N.

ec-cle-si-as-tic \ik-ˌlē -ze-ˈas -tik\ ADJ. pertaining to the church. The minister donned his *ecclesiastic* garb and walked to the pulpit. also N.

é-clat\ā-ˈklä \ N. brilliance; glory. To the delight of his audience, he completed his task with *éclat* and consummate ease.

e-clec-ti-cism\e-ˈklek -tə-ˌsiz -əm\ N. selection of elements from various sets of opinions or systems. The *eclecticism* of the group was demonstrated by their adoption of principles and practices of many forms of government.

eclipse\i-ˈklips \ V. darken; extinguish; surpass. The new stock market high *eclipsed* the previous record set in 1989.

ec-sta-sy \ˈek -stə-sē\ N. rapture; joy; any overpowering emotion. The announcement that the war had ended brought on an *ecstasy* of joy that resulted in many uncontrolled celebrations.

ed-i-fy\ˈed -ə-ˌfī \ V. instruct; correct morally. Although his purpose was to *edify* and not to entertain his audience, many of his listeners were amused and not enlightened.

e-duce\i-ˈd(y)üs \ V. draw forth; elicit. He could not *educe* a principle that would encompass all the data.

ee-rie\ˈi(ə)r -ē\ ADJ. weird. In that *eerie* setting, it was easy to believe in ghosts and other supernatural beings.

ef-face\i-ˈfās\ V. rub out. The coin had been handled so many times that its date had been *effaced*.

ef-fec-tu-al \i-ˈfek -chə(-wə)l\ ADJ. efficient. If we are to succeed in this endeavor, we must seek *effectual* means of securing our goals.

ef-fem-i-nate \ə-¹fem -ə-nət\ ADJ. having womanly traits. His voice was high-pitched and *effeminate*. also N.

ef-fer-vesce \ef-ər-¹ves \ V. bubble over; show excitement. Some of us cannot stand the way she *effervesces* over trifles.

ef-fete \e-¹fēt\ ADJ. worn out; exhausted; barren. The literature of the age reflected the *effete* condition of the writers; no new ideas were forthcoming.

ef-fi-ca-cy \¹ef -i-kə-sē\ N. power to produce desired effect. The *efficacy* of this drug depends on the regularity of the dosage.

ef-fi-gy \¹ef -ə-jē\ N. dummy. The mob showed its irritation by hanging the judge in *effigy*.

ef-flu-vi-um \e-¹flü -vē-əm\ N. noxious smell. Air pollution has become a serious problem in our major cities; the *effluvium* and the poisons in the air are hazards to life.

ef-fron-ter-y \i-¹frənt -ə-rē\ N. shameless boldness. He had the *effrontery* to insult the guest.

ef-fu-sion \i-¹fyü -zhən\ N. pouring forth. The critics objected to his literary *effusion* because it was too flowery.

ef-fu-sive \i-¹fyü -siv\ ADJ. pouring forth; gushing. Her *effusive* manner of greeting her friends finally began to irritate them.

e-go-ism \¹ē -gə-₁wiz -əm\ N. excessive interest in one's self; belief that one should be interested in one's self rather than in others. His *egoism* prevented him from seeing the needs of his colleagues.

e-go-tism \¹ē-gə-₁tiz -əm\ N. conceit; vanity. We found his *egotism* unwarranted and irritating.

e-gre-gious \i-¹grē -jəs\ ADJ. gross; shocking. He was an *egregious* liar.

e-gress \¹ē -₁gres\ N. exit. Barnum's sign "To the *Egress*" fooled many people who thought they were going to see an animal and instead found themselves in the street. **e-gress** \ē-¹gres\ V.

e-jac-u-la-tion \i-jak -yə-¹lā -shən\ N. exclamation. He could not repress an *ejaculation* of surprise when he heard the news.

\ə\ abut   \ᵊ\ kitten, F table   \ər\ further   \a\ ash   \ā\ ace   \ä\ cot, cart
\aů\ out   \ch\ chin   \e\ bet   \ē\ easy   \g\ go   \i\ hit   \ī\ ice   \j\ job

elab-o-ra-tion \i-ˌlab-ə-'rā-shən\ N. addition of details; intricacy. Tell what happened simply, without any *elaboration*. **elab-o-rate** \i-'lab-ə-ˌrāt\ V.

e-la-tion \i-'lā -shən\ N. a rise in spirits; exaltation. She felt no *elation* at finding the purse.

el-e-gi-a-cal \ˌel -ə-'jī -ə-kəl\ ADJ. like an elegy; mournful. The essay on the lost crew was *elegiacal* in mood. **el-e-gy** \'el -ə-jē\ N.

e-lic-it \i-'lis -ət\ V. draw out by discussion. The detectives tried to *elicit* where he had hidden his loot.

elix-ir \i-'lik-sər\ N. cure-all; something invigorating. The news of her chance to go abroad acted on her like an *elixir*.

el-o-quence \'el-ə-kwən(t)s\ N. expressiveness; persuasive speech. The crowds were stirred by Martin Luther King's *eloquence*.

e-lu-ci-date \i-'lü -sə-ˌdāt\ V. explain; enlighten. He was called upon to *elucidate* the disputed points in his article.

e-lu-sive \ē-'lü -siv\ ADJ. evasive; baffling; hard to grasp. His *elusive* dreams of wealth were costly to those of his friends who supported him financially.

elu-so-ry \e-'lüs(ə)rē\ ADJ. tending to deceive expectations; elusive. He argued that the project was an *elusory* one and would bring disappointment to all.

ely-sian \i-'lizh-ən\ ADJ. relating to paradise; blissful. An afternoon sail on the bay was for her an *elysian* journey.

e-ma-ci-ate \i-'mā -shē-ˌāt\ V. to make thin and wasted. He was wan and *ematiated* after his long period of starvation.

em-a-nate \'em -ə-ˌnāt\ V. issue forth. A strong odor of sulphur *emanated* from the spring.

e-man-ci-pate \i-'man(t) -sə-ˌpāt\ V. set free. At first, the attempts of the Abolitionists to *emancipate* the slaves were unpopular in New England as well as in the South.

em-bark \im-'bärk\ V. commence; go on a boat or airplane; begin a journey. In devoting herself to the study of gorillas, Dian Fossey *embarked* on a course of action that was to cost her her life.

---

em·bed\im-'bed\ v. enclose; place in something. Tales of actual historical figures like King Alfred have become *embedded* in legends.

em·bel·lish \im-'bel -ish\ v. adorn. His handwriting was *embellished* with flourishes.

em·bez·zle·ment\im-'bez -əl-mənt\ N. stealing. The bank teller confessed his *embezzlement* of the funds.

em·bla·zon\im-'blāz -ᵊn\ v. deck in brilliant colors. *Emblazoned* on his shield was his family coat of arms.

em·broil\im-'broi(ə)l\ v. throw into confusion; involve in strife; entangle. He became *embroiled* in the heated discussion when he tried to arbitrate the dispute.

em·bry·on·ic \ˌem -brē-'än -ik\ ADJ. undeveloped; rudimentary. The evil of class and race hatred must be eliminated while it is still in an *embryonic* state; otherwise, it may grow to dangerous proportions.

e·mend\ē-'mend\ v. correct; correct by a critic. The critic *emended* the book by selecting the passages which he thought most appropriate to the text.

e·men·da·tion\ē -ˌmen -'dā -shən\ N. correction of errors; improvement. Please initial all the *emendations* you have made in this contract.

e·mer·i·tus\i-'mer -ət-əs\ ADJ. retired but retained in an honorary capacity. As professor *emeritus,* he retained all his honors without having to meet the obligations of daily assignments. also N.

e·met·ic\i-'met -ik\N. substance causing vomiting. The use of an *emetic* like mustard is useful in cases of poisoning.

em·i·nent\'em -ə-nənt\ADJ. high; lofty. After his appointment to this *eminent* position, he seldom had time for his former friends.

em·is·sary \'em-ə-ˌser-ē\ N. agent; messenger. The Secretary of State was sent as the President's special *emissary* to the conference on disarmament.

e·mol·lient\i-'mäl -yənt\N. soothing or softening remedy. He applied an *emollient* to the inflamed area. Also ADJ.

em·pir·i·cal\im-'pir -i-kəl\ADJ. based on experience. He distrusted hunches and intuitive flashes; he placed his reliance entirely on *empirical* data.

\ə\ abut \ᵊ\ kitten, F table \ər\ further \a\ ash \ā\ ace \ä\ cot, cart \au\ out \ch\ chin \e\ bet \ē\ easy \g\ go \i\ hit \ī\ ice \j\ job

em-u-late\\'em -yə-ˌlāt \\ v. rival; imitate. As long as our political leaders *emulate* the virtues of the great leaders of this country, we shall flourish.

en-am-or \\in-'am -ər\\ v. overwhelmed by love. Narcissus was *enamored* of his own beauty.

en-clave\\'en -ˌklāv \\ N. territory enclosed within an alien land. The Vatican is an independent *enclave* in Italy.

en-co-mi-um \\en-'kō -mē-əm\\ N. praise; eulogy. He was sickened by the *encomiums* and panegyrics expressed by speakers who had previously been among the first to vilify the man they were now honoring.

en-com-pass\\in-'kəm -pəs\\v. surround. Although we were *encompassed* by enemy forces, we were cheerful for we were well stocked and could withstand a siege until our allies joined us.

en-croach-ment\\in-'krōch -mənt\\N. gradual intrusion. The *encroachment* of the factories upon the neighborhood lowered the value of the real estate.

en-cum-ber\\in-'kəm -bər\\v. burden. Some people *encumber* themselves with too much luggage when they take short trips.

en-dear-ment \\in-'di(ə)r -mənt\\ N. fond statement. Your gifts and *endearments* cannot make me forget your earlier insolence.

en-dem-ic\\en-'dem -ik\\ ADJ. prevailing among a specific group of people or in a specific area or country. This disease is *endemic* in this part of the world; more than 80 percent of the population are at one time or another affected by it.

en-dive\\'en -ˌdīv\\ N. species of leafy plant used in salads. The salad contained *endive* in addition to the ingredients usually used.

en-dorse\\in-'dȯ(ə)rs\\v. approve; support. Everyone waited to see which one of the rival candidates for the city council the mayor would *endorse*. (secondary meaning) **en-dorse-ment**\\in-'dȯr-smənt\\N.

en-due\\in-'d(y)ü \\ v. provide with some quality; endow. He was *endued* with a lion's courage.

\\ŋ\\ **sing**   \\ō\\ **go**   \\ȯ\\ **law**   \\ȯi\\ **boy**   \\th\\ **thin**   \\t͟h\\ **the**   \\ü\\ **loot**   \\ u̇\\ **foot**
\\y\\ **yet**   \\zh\\ **vision**   \\à, k̲, ⁿ, œ, œ̄, ue, ūe, ʳ\\ *see* Pronunciation Symbols

en-er-gize\'en -ər-ˌjīz \ v. invigorate; make forceful and active. We shall have to re-*energize* our activities by getting new members to carry on.

e-ner-vate\'en -ər-ˌvāt \ v. weaken. The hot days of August are *enervating*. **e-ner-vate**\i-'nər -vət\ADJ.

en-gen-der\in-'jen -dər\ v. cause; produce. This editorial will *engender* racial intolerance unless it is denounced.

en-grossed\in-'grōst \ ADJ. occupied fully. John was so *engrossed* in his studies that he did not hear his mother call. **en-gross**\in-'grōs \ v.

en-hance\in-'han(t)s\ v. advance; improve. Your chances for promotion in this department will be *enhanced* if you take some more courses in evening school.

e-nig-ma\i-'nig -mə\ N. puzzle. Despite all attempts to decipher the code, it remained an *enigma*.

e-nig-mat-ic\ˌen -ₒig -'mat -ik\ADJ. obscure; puzzling. Many have sought to fathom the *enigmatic* smile of the *Mona Lisa*.

en-join\in-'jȯin \ v. command; order; forbid. The owners of the company asked the court to *enjoin* the union from picketing the plant.

en-mi-ty\'en-mət-ē\ N. ill will; hatred. At Camp David, President Carter labored to bring an end to the *enmity* that prevented the peaceful coexistence of Egypt and Israel.

en-nui\än -'wē\ N. boredom. The monotonous routine of hospital life induced a feeling of *ennui* which made him moody and irritable.

e-nor-mi-ty\i-'nȯr -mət-ē\N. hugeness (in a bad sense). He did not realize the *enormity* of his crime until he saw what suffering he had caused.

en-rap-ture \in-'rap -chər\ v. please intensely. The audience was *enraptured* by the freshness of the voices and the excellent orchestration.

en-sconce\in-'skän(t)s \ v. settle comfortably. The parents thought that their children were *ensconced* safely in the private school and decided to leave for Europe.

en-sue \in-'sü \ v. follow. The evils that *ensued* were the direct result of the miscalculations of the leaders.

\ə\ abut	\ᵊ\ kitten, F table	\ər\ **further**	\a\ **ash**	\ā\ **ace**	\ä\ cot, cart
\aů\ **out**	\ch\ **chin**	\e\ **bet**	\ē\ **easy**	\g\ **go**	\i\ **hit**	\ī\ **ice**	\j\ **job**

en-thrall\in-'thról\ v. capture; enslave. From the moment he saw her picture, he was *enthralled* by her beauty.

en-tice\in-'tīs\ v. lure; attract; tempt. She always tried to *entice* her baby brother into mischief.

en-ti-ty\'en(t) -ət-ē\ N. real being. As soon as the Charter was adopted, the United Nations became an *entity* and had to be considered as a factor in world diplomacy.

en-to-mol-o-gy\ent -ə-'mäl -ə-jē\ N. study of insects. I found *entomology* the least interesting part of my course in biology; studying insects bored me.

en-trance\in-'tran(t)s\ v. put under a spell; carry away with emotion. Shafts of sunlight on a wall could *entrance* her and leave her spellbound.

en-treat\in-'trēt\ v. plead; ask earnestly. She *entreated* her father to let her stay out till midnight.

en-trée\'än -ˌtrā\ N. entrance. Because of his wealth and social position, he had *entrée* into the most exclusive circles.

en-tre-pre-neur\ˌäⁿn -trə-p(r)ə-'nər\ N. businessman; contractor. Opponents of our present tax program argue that it discourages *entrepreneurs* from trying new fields of business activity.

en-vi-ron\in-'vī -rən\ v. enclose; surround. In medieval days, Paris was *environed* by a wall. **en-vi-rons**\in-'vī -rənz\ N.

e-phem-er-al\i-'fem(-ə) -rəl\ ADJ. short-lived; fleeting. The mayfly is an *ephemeral* creature. also N.

ep-ic\'ep-ik\ N. long heroic poem, novel, or similar work of art. Kurosawa's film *Seven Samurai* is an epic portraying the struggle of seven warriors to destroy a band of robbers.

ep-ic\'ep-ik\ ADJ. unusually great in size or extent; heroic; impressive. The task of renovating the decrepit subway system was one of truly *epic* dimensions: it would cost millions of dollars and involve thousands of laborers working night and day.

---

ep·i·cure\\ep -i‚kyū(ə)r \ N. connoisseur of food and drink. *Epicures* frequent this restaurant because it features exotic wines and dishes.

ep·i·cu·re·an \‚ep -i-kyū-'rē-ən\ N. person who devotes himself to pleasures of the senses, especially to food. This restaurant is famous for its menu, which can cater to the most exotic whim of the *epicurean*. also ADJ.

ep·i·gram\‚ep -ə‚gram \ N. witty thought or saying, usually short. Poor Richard's *epigrams* made Benjamin Franklin famous.

ep·i·logue \‚ep -ə‚lòg\ N. short speech at conclusion of dramatic work. The audience was so disappointed in the play that many did not remain to hear the *epilogue*.

ep·i·taph\‚ep -ə‚taf \ N. inscription in memory of a dead person. In his will, he dictated the *epitaph* he wanted placed on his tombstone.

ep·i·thet\ 'ep -ə-‚thet \N. descriptive word or phrase. Homer's writings featured the use of such *epithets* as "rosy-fingered dawn."

e·pit·o·me\i-'pit -ə-mē\N. summary; concise abstract. This final book is the *epitome* of all his previous books. **e·pit·o·mize**\i-'pit -ə‚mīz \ V.

ep·och\‚ep -ək\N. period of time. The glacial *epoch* lasted for thousands of years.

eq·ua·ble\‚ek -wə-bəl\ADJ. tranquil; steady; uniform. After the hot summers and cold winters of New England, he found the climate of the West Indies *equable* and pleasant.

e·qua·nim·i·ty \‚ē -kwə-'nim -ət-ē\ N. calmness of temperament. In his later years, he could look upon the foolishness of the world with *equanimity* and humor.

e·ques·tri·an\i-'kwes -trē-ən\N. rider on horseback. These paths in the park are reserved for *equestrians* and their steeds. also ADJ.

equi·lib·ri·um \‚ē-kwə-'lib-rē-əm \N. balance. After the divorce, he needed some time to regain his *equilibrium*.

e·qui·nox\‚ē -kwə‚näks \ N. period of equal days and nights; the beginning of Spring and Autumn. The vernal *equinox* is usually marked by heavy rainstorms.

\ə\ **abut** \ᵊ\ **kitten, F table** \ər\ **further** \a\ **ash** \ā\ **ace** \ä\ **cot, cart**
\aù\ **out** \ch\ **chin** \e\ **bet** \ē\ **easy** \g\ **go** \i\ **hit** \ī\ **ice** \j\ **job**

equi-poise\'ek-wə-ˌpȯiz\ N. balance; balancing force; equilibrium. The high wire acrobat used his pole as an *equipoise* to overcome the swaying caused by the wind.

eq-ui-ta-ble\ek -wət-ə-bəl\ADJ. fair; impartial. I am seeking an *equitable* solution to this dispute, one which will be fair and acceptable to both sides.

eq-ui-ty \'ek -wət-ē\ N. fairness; justice. Our courts guarantee *equity* to all.

e-quiv-o-cal \i-'kwiv -ə-kəl\ ADJ. doubtful; ambiguous. Macbeth was misled by the *equivocal* statements of the witches.

e-quiv-o-cate \i-'kwiv -əˌkāt\ V. lie; mislead; attempt to conceal the truth. The audience saw through his attempts to *equivocate* on the subject under discussion and ridiculed his remarks.

e-rode\i-'rōd\ V. eat away. The limestone was *eroded* by the dripping water.

e-rot-ic\i-'rät -ik\ ADJ. pertaining to passionate love. The *erotic* passages in this novel should be removed as they are merely pornographic.

er-rant\'er -ənt\ADJ. wandering. Many a charming tale has been written about the knights-*errant* who helped the weak and punished the guilty during the Age of Chivalry.

er-rat-ic\ir-'at-ik\ADJ. odd; unpredictable. Investors become anxious when the stock market appears *erratic*.

er-ro-ne-ous\ir-'ō-nē-əs\ADJ. mistaken; wrong. I thought my answer was correct, but it was *erroneous*.

er-u-dite\'er -(y)əˌdīt\ ADJ. learned; scholarly. His *erudite* writing was difficult to read because of the many allusions which were unfamiliar to most readers.

er-u-di-tion \ˌer -(y)ə-'dish -ən\ N. high degree of knowledge and learning. Although they respected his *erudition,* the populace refused to listen to his words of caution and turned to less learned leaders.

es-ca-pade \'es -kə-ˌpād \ N. prank; flighty conduct. The headmaster could not regard this latest *escapade* as a boyish joke and expelled the young man.

es-chew\is(h)-'chü\ V. avoid. He tried to *eschew* all display of temper.

---

es-o-ter-ic \es -ə-ter -ik\ ADJ. known only to the chosen few. Those students who had access to his *esoteric* discussions were impressed by the scope of his thinking.

es-pi-o-nage \es -pē-ə-näzh \ N. spying. In order to maintain its power, the government developed a system of *espionage* which penetrated every household.

es-pouse \is-'paůz\ v. adopt; support. She was always ready to *espouse* a worthy cause.

es-prit de corps \is-prēd -ə-kō(ə)r \ N. comradeship; spirit. West Point cadets are proud of their *esprit de corps*.

es-trange \is-'tränj\ v. alienate. The wife was *estranged* from her husband and sought a divorce.

e-the-re-al \i-'thir -ē-əl\ ADJ. light; heavenly; fine. Visitors were impressed by her *ethereal* beauty, her delicate charm.

eth-nic \eth -nik\ ADJ. relating to races. Intolerance between *ethnic* groups is deplorable and usually is based on lack of information. also N.

eth-nol-o-gy \eth-'näl -ə-jē\ N. study of man. Sociology is one aspect of the science of *ethnology*.

et-y-mol-o-gy \et -ə-'mäl -ə-jē\ N. study of derivation, structure and development of words. To the student of *etymology*, the dictionary is a tremendous source of information.

eu-gen-ic \yů-'jen -ik\ ADJ. pertaining to the improvement of race. It is easier to apply *eugenic* principles to the raising of racehorses or prize cattle than to the development of human beings. **eu-gen-ics** \yů-jen -iks\ N.

eu-lo-gis-tic \yü -lə-'jis -tik\ ADJ. praising. To everyone's surprise, the speech was *eulogistic* rather than critical in tone.

eu-lo-gy \'yü -lə-jē\ N. praise. All the *eulogies* of his friends could not remove the sting of the calumny heaped upon him by his enemies.

eu-phe-mism \'yü -fə-miz -əm\ N. mild expression in place of an unpleasant one. The expression "He passed away" is a *euphemism* for "He died."

eu-pho-ni-ous \yů-'fō -nē-əs\ ADJ. pleasing in sound. Italian and Spanish are *euphonious* languages and therefore easily sung.

---

eu-tha-na-sia\ ‚yü-thə-'nā-zh(ē-)ə\ N. mercy killing. Many people support *euthanasia* for terminally ill patients who wish to die.

ev-a-nes-cent\ev -ə-'nes -ᵊnt\ ADJ. fleeting; vanishing. For a brief moment, the entire skyline was bathed in an orange-red hue in the *evanescent* rays of the sunset.

e-va-sive \i-'vā-siv\ ADJ. not frank; eluding. Your *evasive* answers convinced the judge that you were withholding important evidence. **e-vade**\i-'vād\ V.

e-vince\i-'vin(t)s\ V. show clearly. When he tried to answer the questions, he *evinced* his ignorance of the subject matter.

e-vis-cer-ate\i-'vis -ə‚rāt\ V. disembowel; remove entrails. The medicine man *eviscerated* the animal and offered the entrails to the angry gods.

e-voke\i-'vōk\ V. call forth. He *evoked* much criticism by his hostile manner.

ex-ac-er-bate\ig-'zas -ər‚bāt\ V. worsen; embitter. This latest arrest will *exacerbate* the already existing discontent of the people and enrage them.

ex-ac-tion\ig-'zak -shən\N. exorbitant demand; extortion. The colonies rebelled against the *exactions* of the mother country.

ex-alt\ig-'zȯlt\V. raise in rank or dignity; praise. The actor Alec Guiness was *exalted* to the rank of knighthood by the queen.

ex-as-per-ate \ig-'zas -pə‚rāt\ V. vex. Johnny often *exasperates* his mother with his pranks.

ex-che-quer \'eks -‚chek -ər\ N. treasury. He had been Chancellor of the *Exchequer* before his promotion to the high office he now holds.

ex-ci-sion \ik-'sizh -ən\ N. act of cutting away. With the *excision* of the dead and dying limbs of this tree, you have not only improved its appearance but you have enhanced its chances of bearing fruit. **ex-cise**\ik-'sīz\ V.

ex-co-ri-ate\ek-'skōr -ē‚āt\ V. flay; abrade. These shoes are so ill-fitting that they will *excoriate* the feet and create blisters.

ex-cul-pate\'ek -₍ı₎skəl‚pāt\ V. clear from blame. He was *exculpated* of the crime when the real criminal confessed.

ex-e-cra-ble\ˈek -si-krə-bəl\ADJ. very bad. The anecdote was in *execrable* taste.

ex-e-crate\ˈek -sə-ˌkrāt\ V. curse; express abhorrence for. The world *execrates* the memory of Hitler and hopes that genocide will never again be the policy of any nation.

ex-e-cute\ˈek-si-ˌkyüt\v. put into effect; carry out. The choreographer wanted to see how well she could *execute* a pirouette. (secondary meaning) **ex-e-cu-tion**\ˌek-si-ˈkyü-shən\N.

ex-e-ge-sis \ek -sə-ˈjē -səs\ N. explanation, especially of Biblical passages. I can follow your *exegesis* of this passage to a limited degree; some of your reasoning eludes me.

ex-em-pla-ry\ig-ˈzem -plə-rē\ADJ. serving as a model; outstanding. Her *exemplary* behavior was praised at Commencement.

ex-haus-tive\ig-ˈzȯ-stiv\ADJ. thorough; comprehensive. We have made an *exhaustive* study of all published SAT tests and are happy to share our research with you.

ex-hort\ig-ˈzȯr(ə)rt\ V. urge. The evangelist will *exhort* all sinners in his audience to reform.

ex-hume\igz-ˈ(y)üm\V. dig out of the ground; remove from a grave. Because of the rumor that he had been poisoned, his body was *exhumed* in order that an autopsy might be performed.

ex-i-gen-cy\ˈek -sə-jən-sē\N. urgent situation. In this *exigency*, we must look for aid from our allies.

ex-ig-u-ous\ig-ˈzig -yə-wəs\ADJ. small; minute. Grass grew there, an *exiguous* outcropping among the rocks.

ex-o-dus \ˈek -səd-əs\ N. departure. The *exodus* from the hot and stuffy city was particularly noticeable on Friday evenings.

ex of-fi-ci-o\ek -sə-ˈfish -ē-ō\ ADJ. by virtue of one's office. The Mayor was *ex officio* chairman of the committee that decided the annual tax rate. also ADV.

ex-on-er-ate\ig-ˈzän -ə-ˌrāt\ V. acquit; exculpate. I am sure this letter will *exonerate* you.

ex-or-bi-tant\ig-ˈzȯr -bət-ənt\ADJ. excessive. The people grumbled at his *exorbitant* prices but paid them because he had a monopoly.

| \ə\ **abut** | \ᵊ\ **kitten, F table** | \ər\ **further** | \a\ **ash** | \ā\ **ace** | \ä\ **cot, cart** |
| \aů\ **out** | \ch\ **chin** | \e\ **bet** | \ē\ **easy** | \g\ **go** | \i\ **hit** | \ī\ **ice** | \j\ **job** |

ex-or-cise\ˈek ˌsȯr ˌsīz\ v. drive out evil spirits. By incantation and prayer, the medicine man sought to *exorcise* the evil spirits which had taken possession of the young warrior.

ex-ot-ic\igˈzät -ik\ADJ. not native; strange. Because of his *exotic* headdress, he was followed in the streets by small children who laughed at his strange appearance. also N.

ex-pa-ti-ate\ek-ˈspā -shē͵ āt\ v. talk at length. At this time, please give us a brief resumé of your work; we shall permit you to *expatiate* later.

ex-pa-tri-ate\ek-ˈspā -trē͵ āt\ N. exile; someone who has withdrawn from his native land. Henry James was an American *expatriate* who settled in England. also V, ADJ.

ex-pe-di-en-cy\ik-ˈspēd -ē-ən-sē\N. that which is advisable or practical. He was guided by *expediency* rather than by ethical considerations.

ex-pe-di-tious-ly\ˌek -spə-ˈdish -əs-lē\ADV. rapidly and efficiently. Please adjust this matter as *expeditiously* as possible as it is delaying important work.

ex-per-tise\ˌek-(ˌ)spər-ˈtēz\N. specialized knowledge; expert skill. Although she was knowledgeable in a number of fields, she was hired for her particular *expertise* in computer programming.

ex-pi-ate\ˈek -spē͵ āt\ v. make amends for (a sin). He tried to *expiate* his crimes by a full confession to the authorities.

ex-ple-tive\ˈek -splət-iv\N. interjection; profane oath. The sergeant's remarks were filled with *expletives* which reflected on the intelligence and character of the new recruits. also ADJ.

ex-plic-it\ik-ˈsplis -ət\ADJ. definite; open. Your remarks are *explicit;* no one can misinterpret them.

ex-ploit\ˈek-ˌsplȯit\N. deed or action, particularly a brave deed. Raoul Wallenberg was noted for his *exploits* in rescuing Jews from Hitler's forces.

ex-ploit\ ik-ˈsplȯit\v. make use of, sometimes unjustly. Cesar Chavez fought attempts to *exploit* migrant farmworkers in California. **ex-ploi-ta-tion**\ˌek-ˌsplȯi-ˈtā-shən\N.

\ŋ\ **sing**   \ō\ **go**   \ȯ\ **law**   \ȯi\ **boy**   \th\ **thin**   \t̲h̲\ **the**   \ü\ **loot**   \u̇\ **foot**
\y\ **yet**   \zh\ **vision**   \à, k̲, ⁿ, œ, œ̄, ue, ūe, ʸ\ *see* Pronunciation Symbols

ex-pos-tu-la-tion\ik-ˌspäs -chəˈlā -shən\ N. remonstrance. Despite the teacher's scoldings and *expostulations*, the class remained unruly.

ex-punge\ikˈspənj\ V. cancel; remove. If you behave, I will *expunge* this notation from your record.

ex-pur-gate\ek -spərˌgāt\ V. clean; remove offensive parts of a book. The editors felt that certain passages in the book had to be *expurgated* before it could be used in this classroom.

ex-tant\ek -stənt\ ADJ. still in existence. Although the authorities suppressed the book, many copies are *extant* and may be purchased at exorbitant prices.

ex-tem-po-ra-ne-ous \ₒek-ˌstem-pə-ˈrā -nē -əs\ ADJ. not planned; impromptu. Because his *extemporaneous* remarks were misinterpreted, he decided to write all his speeches in advance.

ex-ten-u-ate \ikˈsten -yə-ˌwāt\ V. weaken; mitigate. It is easier for us to *extenuate* our own shortcomings than those of others.

ex-tir-pate\ek -stərˌpāt\ V. root up. We must *extirpate* and destroy this monstrous philosophy.

ex-tol\ikˈstōl\ V. praise; glorify. The astronauts were *extolled* as the pioneers of the Space Age.

ex-tort\ik-ˈstȯ(ə)rt\ V. wring from; get money by threats, etc. The blackmailer *extorted* money from his victim.

ex-tra-di-tion\ₑek -strəˈdish -ən\ N. surrender of prisoner by one state to another. The lawyers opposed the *extradition* of their client on the grounds that for more than five years he had been a model citizen.

ex-tra-ne-ous\ekˈstrā -nē -əs\ ADJ. not essential; external. Do not pad your paper with *extraneous* matters; stick to essential items only.

ex-tra-vert \ek -strəˌvərt\ N. person interested mostly in external objects and actions. A good salesman is usually an *extravert*, who likes to mingle with people. also **ex-tro-vert.**

ex-tri-cate \ek -strəˌkāt\ V. free; disentangle. He found that he could not *extricate* himself from the trap.

---

ex-trin-sic \ek-ˈstrin-zik\ ADJ. external; not inherent; foreign. Do not be fooled by *extrinsic* causes. We must look for the intrinsic reason.

ex-trude \ik-ˈstrüd\ v. force or push out. Much pressure is required to *extrude* these plastics.

ex-u-ber-ant \ig-ˈzü-b(ə-)rənt\ ADJ. abundant; effusive; lavish. His speeches were famous for his *exuberant* language and vivid imagery.

ex-ude \ig-ˈzüd\ v. discharge; give forth. The maple syrup is obtained from the sap that *exudes* from the trees in early spring. **ex-u-da-tion** \ek-s(y)ù-ˈdā-shən\ N.

ex-ult \ig-ˈzəlt\ v. rejoice. We *exulted* when our team won the victory.

—f—

fab·ri·cate\\'fab -ri؛kāt \ v. build; lie. If we pre*fabricate* the buildings in this project, we can reduce the cost considerably.

fa·cade\\fə-'säd \N. front of the building. The *facade* of the church has often been photographed by tourists.

fac·et \\'fas -ət\ N. small plane surface (of a gem); a side. The stonecutter decided to improve the rough diamond by providing it with several *facets*.

fa·ce·tious\\fə-'sē -shəs\ADJ. humorous; jocular. Your *facetious* remarks are not appropriate at this serious moment.

fac·ile \\'fas -əl\ ADJ. easy; expert. Because he was a *facile* speaker, he never refused a request to address an organization.

fa·cil·i·tate \\fə-'sil -ə-؛tāt \ v. make less difficult. He tried to *facilitate* matters at home by getting a part-time job.

fac·tion\\'fak -shən\N. party; clique; dissension. The quarrels and bickering of the two small *factions* within the club disturbed the majority of the members.

fac·tious\\'fak -shəs\ADJ. inclined to form factions; causing dissension. Your statement is *factious* and will upset the harmony that now exists.

fac·ti·tious \\fak-'tish -əs\ ADJ. artificial; sham. Hollywood actresses often create *factitious* tears by using glycerine.

fac·to·tum \\fak-'tōt -əm\ N. handyman; person who does all kinds of work. Although we had hired him as a messenger, we soon began to use him as a *factotum* around the office.

fac·ul·ty \\'fak-əl-tē\N. mental or bodily power; teaching staff. As he grew old, he feared he might lose his *faculties* and become useless to his employer.

fal·la·cious\\fə-'lā -shəs\ADJ. misleading. Your reasoning must be *fallacious* because it leads to a ridiculous answer.

fal·li·ble\\'fal -ə-bəl\ADJ. liable to err. I know I am *fallible*, but I feel confident that I am right this time.

fal·low\\'fal -(؛)ō \ADJ. plowed but not sowed; uncultivated. Farmers have learned that it is advisable to permit land to lie *fallow* every few years. also N., V.

fal·ter\\'fȯl-tər\v. hesitate. When told to dive off the high board, she did not *falter*, but proceeded at once.

\ə\ abut	\ᵊ\ kitten, F table	\ər\ further	\a\ ash	\ā\ ace	\ä\ cot, cart
\aů\ out	\ch\ chin	\e\ bet	\ē\ easy	\g\ go	\i\ hit	\ī\ ice	\j\ job

fa·nat·i·cism\fə-'nat -ə-ˌsiz -əm\N. excessive zeal. The leader of the group was held responsible even though he could not control the *fanaticism* of his followers.

fan·cied \'fan(t) -sēd\ ADJ. imagined; unreal. You are resenting *fancied* insults. No one has ever said such things about you.

fan·ci·er \'fan(t) -sē-ər\ N. breeder or dealer of animals. The dog *fancier* exhibited his prize collie at the annual Kennel Club show.

fan·ci·ful\'fan(t) -si-fəl\ADJ. whimsical; visionary. This is a *fanciful* scheme because it does not consider the facts.

fan·fare \'fan ˌfa(ə)r\ N. call by bugles or trumpets. The exposition was opened with a *fanfare* of trumpets and the firing of a cannon.

fan·tas·tic\fan-'tas -tik\ADJ. unreal; grotesque; whimsical. Your fears are *fantastic* because no such animal as you have described exists.

farce\'färs\N. broad comedy; mockery. Nothing went right; the entire interview degenerated into a *farce*. **far·ci·cal**\'fär-si-kəl\ADJ.

fas·tid·i·ous\fa-'stid -ē-əs\ADJ. difficult to please; squeamish. The waitresses disliked serving him dinner because of his very *fastidious* taste.

fa·tal·ism\'fāt -ᵊl-ˌiz -əm\N. belief that events are determined by forces beyond one's control. With *fatalism*, he accepted the hardships that beset him. **fa·tal·is·tic**\ˌfāt -ᵊl-'is -tik\ADJ.

fath·om\'fath-əm\v. comprehend; investigate. I find his motives impossible to *fathom*.

fat·u·ous\'fach -(ə-)wəs\ADJ. foolish; inane. He is far too intelligent to utter such *fatuous* remarks.

fau·na\'fȯn -ə\N. animals of a period or region. The scientist could visualize the *fauna* of the period by examining the skeletal remains and the fossils.

faux pas\fō -ˌpä \ N. an error or slip (in manners or behavior). Your tactless remarks during dinner were a *faux pas*.

fawn\'fȯn \ v. court favor by cringing and flattering. He *fawned* over his boss in an attempt to gain approval.

---

fe-al-ty\\'fē(-ə)l -tē\\N. loyalty; faithfulness. The feudal lord demanded *fealty* of his vassals.

fea-si-ble\\'fē -zə-bəl\\ADJ. practical. This is an entirely *feasible* proposal. I suggest we adopt it.

fe-brile\\'feb ˌrīl \\ADJ. feverish. In his *febrile* condition, he was subject to nightmares and hallucinations.

fe-cun-di-ty \\fiˈkən -dət-ē\\ N. fertility; fruitfulness. The *fecundity* of his mind is illustrated by the many vivid images in his poems.

feign\\'fān \\ v. pretend. Lady Macbeth *feigned* illness in the courtyard.

feint\\'fānt \\ N. trick; shift; sham blow. The boxer was fooled by his opponent's *feint* and dropped his guard. also v.

fe-lic-i-tous\\fiˈlis -ət-əs\\ADJ. apt; suitably expressed; well chosen. He was famous for his *felicitous* remarks and was called upon to serve as master-of-ceremonies at many a banquet.

fell\\'fel \\ ADJ. cruel; deadly. Henley writes of the "*fell* clutch of circumstance" in his poem "Invictus." also N, V.

fel-on\\'fel-ən \\N. person convicted of a grave crime. A convicted *felon* loses the right to vote.

fer-ment\\'fər ˌment \\ N. agitation; commotion. The entire country was in a state of *ferment*. **fer-ment**\\fər⁽ʳ⁾-ment \\ v.

fer-ret\\'fer -ət\\v. drive or hunt out of hiding. He *ferreted* out their secret. also N.

fer-vent\\'fər -vənt\\ADJ. ardent; hot. He felt that the *fervent* praise was excessive and somewhat undeserved.

fer-vid \\'fər -vəd\\ ADJ. ardent. His *fervid* enthusiasm inspired all of us to undertake the dangerous mission.

fer-vor\\'fər -vər\\N. glowing ardor. Their kiss was full of the *fervor* of first love.

fes-ter\\'fes -tər\\v. generate pus. When his finger began to *fester*, the doctor lanced it and removed the splinter which had caused the pus to form. also N.

fes-tive\\'fes-tiv\\ADJ. joyous; celebratory. Their wedding in the park was a *festive* occasion.

fete\\'fāt\\ v. honor at a festival. The returning hero was *feted* at a community supper and dance. also N.

fet-id\\'fet -əd\\ ADJ. malodorous. The neglected wound became *fetid*.

fe-tish\\'fet -ish\\ N. object supposed to possess magical powers; an object of special devotion. The native wore a *fetish* around his neck to ward off evil spirits.

fet-ter\\'fet -ər\\ v. shackle. The prisoner was *fettered* to the wall. also N.

fi-as-co\\fē-'äs -₍ı₎kō\\ N. total failure. Our ambitious venture ended in a *fiasco*.

fi-at\\'fē -ət\\ N. command. I cannot accept government by *fiat;* I feel that I must be consulted.

fick-le\\'fik -əl\\ ADJ. changeable; faithless. He discovered she was *fickle*.

fic-ti-tious\\fik-'tish -əs\\ ADJ. imaginary. Although this book purports to be a biography of George Washington, many of the incidents are *fictitious*.

fi-del-i-ty\\fə-'del -ət-ē\\ N. loyalty. A dog's *fidelity* to its owner is one of the reasons why that animal is a favorite household pet.

fi-du-ci-ar-y\\fe-'d(y)ü -shē-₋er -ē\\ ADJ. pertaining to a position of trust. In his will, he stipulated that the bank act in a *fiduciary* capacity and manage his estate until his children became of age. also N.

fig-ment\\'fig -mənt\\ N. invention; imaginary thing. That incident is a *figment* of your imagination.

filch\\'filch\\ v. steal. The boys *filched* apples from the fruit stand.

fil-i-al\\'fil -ē-əl\\ ADJ. pertaining to a son or daughter. Many children forget their *filial* obligations and disregard the wishes of their parents.

fi-na-le\\fə-'nal -ē\\ N. conclusion. It is not until we reach the *finale* of this play that we can understand the author's message.

fi-nesse\\fə-'nes \\ N. delicate skill. The *finesse* and adroitness of the surgeon impressed the observers in the operating room. also v.

\\ŋ\\ sing   \\ō\\ go   \\ȯ\\ law   \\ȯi\\ boy   \\th\\ thin   \\t͟h\\ the   \\ü\\ loot   \\u̇\\ foot
\\y\\ yet   \\zh\\ vision   \\ȧ, k̲, ⁿ, œ, œ̄, ue, ūe, ʸ\\ *see* Pronunciation Symbols

fin-ick-y\\'fin -i-kē\\ADJ. too particular; fussy. The old lady was *finicky* about her food.

fi-nite\\'fī -nīt \\ ADJ. limited. It is difficult for humanity with its *finite* existence to grasp the infinite.

fire-brand\\'fī(ə)r-,brand \\N. hothead; troublemaker. The police tried to keep track of all the local *firebrands* when the President came to town.

fis-sure\\'fish -ər\\ N. crevice. The mountain climbers secured footholds in tiny *fissures* in the rock. also V.

fit-ful\\'fit -fəl\\ADJ. spasmodic; intermittent. After several *fitful* attempts, he decided to postpone the start of the project until he felt more energetic.

flac-cid\\'flak -səd\\ADJ. flabby. His sedentary life had left him with *flaccid* muscles.

fla-gel-late\\'flaj -ə-,lāt \\ V. flog; whip. The Romans used to *flagellate* criminals with a whip that had three knotted strands. **fla-gel-late**\\'flaj -ə-lət\\ADJ, N.

flag-ging\\'flag -iŋ\\ADJ. weak; drooping. The encouraging cheers of the crowd lifted the team's *flagging* spirits.

fla-grant\\'flā -grənt\\ADJ. conspicuously wicked. We cannot condone such *flagrant* violations of the rules.

flail \\'flā(ə)l \\ V. thresh grain by hand; strike or slap. In medieval times, warriors *flailed* their foe with a metal ball attached to a handle. also N.

flair\\'fla(ə)r \\ N. talent. He has an uncanny *flair* for discovering new artists before the public has become aware of their existence.

flam-boy-ant \\flam-'bòi -ənt\\ ADJ. ornate. Modern architecture has discarded the *flamboyant* trimming on buildings and emphasizes simplicity of line.

flaunt\\'flònt \\ V. display ostentatiously. She is not one of those actresses who *flaunt* their physical charms; she can act.

flay\\'flā \\ V. strip off skin; plunder. The criminal was condemned to be *flayed* alive.

fleck\\'flek \\ V. spot. Her cheeks, *flecked* with tears, were testimony to the hours of weeping. also N.

\\ə\\ abut   \\ᵊ\\ kitten, F table   \\ər\\ **further**   \\a\\ **ash**   \\ā\\ **ace**   \\ä\\ **cot, cart**
\\aú\\ **out**   \\ch\\ **chin**   \\e\\ **bet**   \\ē\\ **easy**   \\g\\ **go**   \\i\\ **hit**   \\ī\\ **ice**   \\j\\ **job**

fledg-ling\\'flej -liŋ\\ADJ. inexperienced. While it is necessary to provide these *fledgling* poets with an opportunity to present their work, it is not essential that we admire everything they write. also N.

fleece\\'flēs\\N. wool coat of a sheep. They shear sheep of their *fleece,* which they then comb into separate strands of wool.

fleece\\'flēs\\V. rob; plunder. The tricksters *fleeced* him of his inheritance.

flick\\'flik\\N. light stroke as with a whip. The horse needed no encouragement; only one *flick* of the whip was all the jockey had to apply to get the animal to run at top speed. also V.

flinch\\'flinch\\V. hesitate; shrink. He did not *flinch* in the face of danger but fought back bravely.

flip-pan-cy\\'flip -ən-sē\\N. trifling gaiety. Your *flippancy* at this serious moment is offensive.

floe\\'flō\\N. mass of floating ice. The ship made slow progress as it battered its way through the ice *floes.*

flo-ra\\'flŏr -ə\\N. plants of a region or era. Because she was a botanist, she spent most of her time studying the *flora* of the desert.

flor-id\\'flŏr -əd\\ADJ. flowery; ruddy. His complexion was even more *florid* than usual because of his anger.

flo-til-la\\flō-'til -ə\\N. small fleet. It is always an exciting and interesting moment when the fishing *flotilla* returns to port.

flot-sam\\'flät -səm\\N. drifting wreckage. Beachcombers eke out a living by salvaging the *flotsam* and jetsam of the sea.

flout\\'flaut\\V. reject; mock. The headstrong youth *flouted* all authority; he refused to be curbed.

fluc-tu-a-tion\\ˌflək -chə-'wā -shən\\N. wavering. Meteorologists watch the *fluctuations* of the barometer in order to predict the weather.

flu-en-cy\\'flü -ən-sē\\N. smoothness of speech. He spoke French with *fluency* and ease.

flus-ter\\'fləs -tər\\V. confuse. The teacher's sudden question *flustered* him and he stammered his reply. also N.

\\ŋ\\ sing   \\ō\\ go   \\ȯ\\ law   \\ȯi\\ boy   \\th\\ thin   \\th̠\\ the   \\ü\\ loot   \\u̇\\ foot
\\y\\ yet   \\zh\\ vision   \\à, k̠, ⁿ, œ, œ̄, ue, ūe, ʸ\\ *see* Pronunciation Symbols

flut-ed\'flüt -əd\ADJ. having vertical parallel grooves (as in a pillar). All that remained of the ancient building were the *fluted* columns.

flux\'fləks\ N. flowing series of changes. While conditions are in such a state of *flux*, I do not wish to commit myself too deeply in this affair. also V.

foi-ble\'fȯi -bəl\N. weakness; slight fault. We can overlook the *foibles* of our friends.

foil\'fȯi(ə)l\N. contrast. In "Star Wars," dark, evil Darth Vader is a perfect *foil* for fair-haired, naive Luke Skywalker.

foil\'fȯi(ə)l\v. defeat; frustrate. In the end, Skywalker is able to *foil* Vader's diabolical schemes.

foist\'fȯist\ V. insert improperly; palm off. I will not permit you to *foist* such ridiculous ideas upon the membership of this group.

fo-ment\fō-ment\ V. stir up; instigate. This report will *foment* dissension in the club.

fool-har-dy\'fül -ˌhärd -ē\ADJ. rash. Don't be *foolhardy*. Get the advice of experienced people before undertaking this venture.

fop-pish\'fäp -ish\ADJ. vain about dress and appearance. He tried to imitate the *foppish* manner of the young men of the court.

for-ay\'fȯr -ˌā\ N. raid. The company staged a midnight *foray* against the enemy outpost. also V.

for-bear-ance\fȯr-'bar -ən(t)s\N. patience. We must use *forbearance* in dealing with him because he is still weak from his illness.

fore-bod-ing\fōr-'bōd-iŋ\ N. premonition of evil. Caesar ridiculed his wife's *forebodings* about the Ides of March. also ADJ.

fo-ren-sic\fə-'ren(t) -sik\ADJ. suitable to debate or courts of law. In his best *forensic* manner, the lawyer addressed the jury. also N.

fore-sight\'fō(ə)r-ˌsīt\N. ability to foresee future happenings; prudence. A wise investor, she had the *foresight* to buy land just before the current real estate boom.

---

for·mal·i·ty \fȯr-'mal-ət-ē\ N. adherence to established rules or procedures. Signing this is a mere *formality*; it does not obligate you in any way.

for·mi·da·ble \'fȯr -məd-ə-bəl\ ADJ. menacing; threatening. We must not treat the battle lightly for we are facing a *formidable* foe.

forte \'fō(ə)rt\ N. strong point or special talent. I am not eager to play this rather serious role, for my *forte* is comedy.

for·ti·tude \'fȯrt -ə-ˌt(y)üd\ N. bravery; courage. He was awarded the medal for his *fortitude* in the battle.

for·tu·i·tous \fȯr-'t(y)ü -ət-əs\ ADJ. accidental; by chance. There is no connection between these two events; their timing is entirely *fortuitous*.

fos·ter \'fȯs -tər\ V. rear; encourage. According to the legend, Romulus and Remus were *fostered* by a she-wolf. also ADJ.

fra·cas \'frāk -əs\ N. brawl, melee. The military police stopped the *fracas* in the bar and arrested the belligerents.

frac·tious \'frak -shəs\ ADJ. unruly. The *fractious* horse unseated its rider.

frail·ty \'frā(-ə)l -tē\ N. weakness. Hamlet says, "*Frailty,* thy name is woman."

fran·chise \'fran -ˌchīz\ N. right granted by authority. The city issued a *franchise* to the company to operate surface transit lines on the streets for ninety-nine years. also V.

fran·tic \'frant -ik\ ADJ. wild. At the time of the collision, many people became *frantic* with fear.

fraud·u·lent \'frȯ -jə-lənt\ ADJ. cheating; deceitful. The government seeks to prevent *fraudulent* and misleading advertising.

fraught \'frȯt\ ADJ. filled. Since this enterprise is *fraught* with danger, I will ask for volunteers who are willing to assume the risks.

fray \'frā\ N. brawl. The three musketeers were in the thick of the *fray.* also V.

free·boo·ter \'frē -ˌbüt -ər\ N. buccaneer. This town is a rather dangerous place to visit as it is frequented by pirates, *freebooters,* and other plunderers.

\ŋ\ sing   \ō\ go   \ȯ\ law   \ȯi\ boy   \th\ thin   \t̲h̲\ the   \ü\ loot   \u̇\ foot
\y\ yet   \zh\ vision   \ä, k̲, ⁿ, œ, œ̄, ue, ūe, '\ *see* Pronunciation Symbols

fre·net·ic\fri-'net -ik\ADJ. frenzied; frantic. His *frenetic* activities convinced us that he had no organized plan of operation.

fren·zied\'fren -zēd\ADJ. madly excited. As soon as they smelled smoke, the *frenzied* animals milled about in their cages.

fres·co\'fres -(ˌ)kō\N. painting on plaster (usually fresh). The cathedral is visited by many tourists who wish to admire the *frescoes* by Giotto.

fret\'fret\V. to be annoyed or vexed. To *fret* over your poor grades is foolish; instead, decide to work harder in the future.

fric·tion\'frik -shən\N. clash in opinion; rubbing against. At this time when harmony is essential, we cannot afford to have any *friction* in our group.

frieze\'frēz\N. ornamental band on a wall. The *frieze* of the church was adorned with sculpture.

frig·id\'frij -əd\ADJ. intensely cold. Alaska is in the *frigid* zone.

frit·ter\'frit -ər\V. waste. He could not apply himself to any task and *frittered* away his time in idle conversation.

fri·vol·i·ty\friv-'äl-ət-ē\N. lack of seriousness. We were distressed by his *frivolity* during the recent grave crisis. **friv·o·lous**\'friv-(ə-)ləs\ADJ.

frol·ic·some\'fräl -ik-səm\ADJ. prankish; gay. The *frolicsome* puppy tried to lick the face of its master.

fruc·ti·fy\'frək -təˌfī\V. bear fruit. This tree should *fructify* in three years.

fru·gal·i·ty\frü-'gal -ət-ē\N. thrift. In these difficult days, we must live with *frugality*.

fru·i·tion\frü-'ish -ən\N. bearing of fruit; fulfillment; realization. This building marks the *fruition* of all our aspirations and years of hard work.

frus·trate\'frəs ˌtrāt\V. thwart; defeat. We must *frustrate* this dictator's plan to seize control of the government.

ful·crum\'ful -krəm\N. support on which a lever rests. If we use this stone as a *fulcrum* and the crowbar as a lever, we may be able to move this boulder.

\ə\ abut   \ᵊ\ kitten, F table   \ər\ further   \a\ ash   \ā\ ace   \ä\ cot, cart
\aù\ out   \ch\ chin   \e\ bet   \ē\ easy   \g\ go   \i\ hit   \ī\ ice   \j\ job

ful·mi·nate\\'fül -mə͵nāt\\ v. thunder; explode. The people against whom he *fulminated* were innocent of any wrongdoing.

ful·some\\'fül -səm\\ ADJ. disgustingly excessive. His *fulsome* praise of the dictator annoyed his listeners.

func·tion·ar·y \\'fəŋ(k) -shə͵ner -ē\\ N. official. As his case was transferred from one *functionary* to another, he began to despair of ever reaching a settlement.

fu·ne·re·al \\fyù-'nir -ē-əl\\ ADJ. sad; solemn. I fail to understand why there is such a *funereal* atmosphere; we have lost a battle, not a war.

fu·ror\\'fyù(ə)r ͵ó(ə)r \\ N. frenzy; great excitement. The story of his embezzlement of the funds created a *furor* on the Stock Exchange.

fur·tive\\'fərt -iv\\ADJ. stealthy. The boy took a *furtive* look at his classmate's test paper.

fu·sion\\'fyü -zhən\\N. union; coalition. The opponents of the political party in power organized a *fusion* of disgruntled groups and became an important element in the election.

fu·tile\\ 'fyüt-əl\\ADJ. ineffective; fruitless. Why waste your time on *futile* pursuits?

—g—

gad-fly\ˈgad ˌflī\ N. animal-biting fly; an irritating person. Like a *gadfly*, he irritated all the guests at the hotel; within forty-eight hours, everyone regarded him as an annoying busybody.

gain-say\gān-ˈsā\ V. deny. He could not *gainsay* the truth of the report.

gait\ˈgāt\ N. manner of walking or running; speed. The lame man walked with an uneven *gait*.

gal-axy\ˈgal -ək-sē\ N. the Milky Way; any collection of brilliant personalities. The deaths of such famous actors as Clark Gable, Gary Cooper and Spencer Tracy demonstrate that the *galaxy* of Hollywood superstars is rapidly disappearing.

gall\ˈgȯl\ N. bitterness; nerve. The knowledge of his failure filled him with *gall*.

gall\ˈgȯl\ V. annoy; chafe. Their taunts *galled* him.

gal-le-on\ˈgal -ē-ən\ N. large sailing ship. The Spaniards pinned their hopes on the *galleon*, the large warship; the British, on the smaller and faster pinnace.

gal-va-nize\ˈgal -və-ˌniz\ V. stimulate by shock; stir up. The entire nation was *galvanized* into strong military activity by the news of the attack on Pearl Harbor.

gam-bit\ˈgam -bət\ N. opening in chess in which a piece is sacrificed. The player was afraid to accept his opponent's *gambit* because he feared a trap which as yet he could not see.

gam-bol\ˈgam -bəl\ V. skip; leap playfully. Watching children *gamboling* in the park is a pleasant experience. also N.

game-ly\ˈgām-lē\ ADV. in a plucky manner. Because he had fought *gamely* against a much superior boxer, the crowd gave him a standing ovation when he left the arena.

game-ster\ˈgām -stər\ N. gambler. An inveterate *gamester*, he was willing to wager on the outcome of any event, even one which involved the behavior of insects.

gam-ut\ˈgam -ət\ N. entire range. In this performance, the leading lady was able to demonstrate the complete *gamut* of her acting ability.

---

gape\\'gāp \ v. open widely. The huge pit *gaped* before him; if he stumbled, he would fall in. also N.

gar-ble \gär -bəl\ mix up; change meaning by distortion. Because the report was *garbled* it confused many readers who were not familiar with the facts. also N.

gar-goyle \gär ˌgȯil \ N. waterspout carved in grotesque figures on building. The *gargoyles* adorning the Cathedral of Notre Dame in Paris are amusing in their grotesqueness.

gar-ish \ga(ə)r -ish\ ADJ. gaudy. She wore a *garish* rhinestone necklace.

gar-ner\gär -nər\ v. gather; store up. He hoped to *garner* the world's literature in one library. also N.

gar-nish\'gär -nish\ v. decorate. Parsley was used to *garnish* the boiled potato. also N.

gar-ru-li-ty \gə-'rü -lət-ē\ N. talkativeness. The man who married a mute wife asked the doctor to make him deaf because of his wife's *garrulity* after her cure.

gar-ru-lous \'gar -ə-ləs\ ADJ. loquacious; wordy. Many members avoided the company of the *garrulous* old gentleman because his constant chatter on trivial matters bored them.

gas-tron-o-my\ga-'strän -ə-mē\ N. science of preparing and serving good food. One of the by-products of his trip to Europe was his interest in *gastronomy;* he enjoyed preparing and serving foreign dishes to his friends.

gauche \gōsh\ ADJ. clumsy; boorish. Such remarks are *gauche* and out of place; you should apologize for making them.

gaunt\'gȯnt\ ADJ. lean and angular; barren. His once round face looked surprisingly *gaunt* after he had lost weight.

gaunt-let \gȯnt -lət\ N. leather glove. Now that we have been challenged, we must take up the *gauntlet* and meet our adversary fearlessly.

ga-zette\gə-'zet \ N. official periodical publication. He read the *gazettes* regularly for the announcement of his promotion.

\ŋ\ sing   \ō\ go   \ȯ\ law   \ȯi\ boy   \th\ thin   \t͟h\ the   \ü\ loot   \u̇\ foot
\y\ yet   \zh\ vision   \à, k̲, ⁿ, œ, œ̄, ue, ūe, ʸ\ *see* Pronunciation Symbols

ge-ne-al-o-gy \jē -nē-äl -ə-jē\ N. record of descent; lineage. He was proud of his *genealogy* and constantly referred to the achievements of his ancestors.

gen-er-al-i-ty \jen -ə-ral -ət-ē\ N. vague statement. This report is filled with *generalities;* you must be more specific in your statements.

ge-ner-ic \jə-her -ik\ ADJ. characteristic of a class or species. You have made the mistake of thinking that his behavior is *generic;* actually, very few of his group behave the way he does. also N.

ge-ni-al-i-ty \jē -nē-al -ət-ē\ N. cheerfulness; kindliness; sympathy. This restaurant is famous and popular because of the *geniality* of the proprietor who tries to make everyone happy.

gen-re \zhän -rə\ N. style of art illustrating scenes of common life. His painting of fisher folk at their daily tasks is an excellent illustration of *genre* art.

gen-teel \jen-tē(ə)l\ ADJ. well-bred; elegant. We are looking for a man with a *genteel* appearance who can inspire confidence by his cultivated manner.

gen-til-i-ty \jen-til -ət-ē\ N. those of gentle birth; refinement. Her family was proud of its *gentility*.

gen-try \jen -trē\ N. people of standing; class of people just below nobility. The local *gentry* did not welcome the visits of the summer tourists and tried to ignore their presence in the community.

gen-u-flect \jen -yə₋flekt\ V. bend the knee as in worship. A proud democrat, he refused to *genuflect* to any man.

ger-mane \₍ᵢ₎jər-ʹmān\ ADJ. pertinent; bearing upon the case at hand. The lawyer objected that the testimony being offered was not *germane* to the case at hand.

ger-mi-nal \jərm -nəl\ ADJ. pertaining to a germ; creative. Such an idea is *germinal;* I am certain that it will influence thinkers and philosophers for many generations.

ger-mi-nate \jər -mə₋nāt\ V. cause to sprout; sprout. After the seeds *germinate* and develop their permanent leaves, the plants may be removed from the cold frames and transplanted to the garden.

\ə\ abut	\ᵊ\ kitten, F table	\ər\ further	\a\ ash	\ā\ ace	\ä\ cot, cart
\aů\ out	\ch\ chin	\e\ bet	\ē\ easy	\g\ go	\i\ hit	\ī\ ice	\j\ job

ger-ry-man-der \ˌjer -ē-ˈman -dər\ v. change voting district lines in order to favor a political party. The illogical pattern of the map of this congressional district is proof that the State Legislature *gerrymandered* this area in order to favor the majority party. also N.

ges-tate \ˈjes ˌtāt \ v. evolve, as in prenatal growth. While this scheme was being *gestated* by the conspirators, they maintained complete silence about their intentions.

ges-tic-u-la-tion \je-ˌstik -yə-ˈlā -shən\ N. motion; gesture. Operatic performers are trained to make exaggerated *gesticulations* because of the large auditoriums in which they appear.

ghast-ly \ˈgast -lē\ ADJ. horrible. The murdered man was a *ghastly* sight.

gib-ber \ˈjib -ər\ v. speak foolishly. The demented man *gibbered* incoherently.

gib-bet \ˈjib -ət\ N. gallows. The bodies of the highwaymen were left dangling from the *gibbet* as a warning to other would-be transgressors. also v.

gibe \ˈjīb \ v. mock. As you *gibe* at their superstitious beliefs, do you realize that you, too, are guilty of similarly foolish thoughts?

gig \ˈgig \ N. two-wheeled carriage. As they drove down the street in their new *gig*, drawn by the dappled mare, they were cheered by the people who recognized them.

gin-ger-ly \ ˈjin-jər-lē\ ADV. very carefully. To separate egg whites, first crack the egg *gingerly*. also ADJ.

gist \ˈjist \ N. essence. She was asked to give the *gist* of the essay in two sentences.

glaze \ˈglāz \ v. cover with a thin and shiny surface. The freezing rain *glazed* the streets and made driving hazardous. also N.

glean \ˈglēn\ v. gather leavings. After the crops had been harvested by the machines, the peasants were permitted to *glean* the wheat left in the fields. **glean-ings** \glē′-niŋz\ N.

glib \ˈglib \ ADJ. fluent. He is a *glib* speaker.

gloam-ing \ˈglō -miŋ\ N. twilight. The snow began to fall in the *gloaming* and continued all through the night.

\ŋ\ **sing**   \ō\ **go**   \ȯ\ **law**   \ȯi\ **boy**   \th\ **thin**   \t͟h\ **the**   \ü\ **loot**   \u̇\ **foot**
\y\ **yet**   \zh\ **vision**   \à, k̲, ⁿ, œ, œ̄, ue, ūe, ʸ\ *see* Pronunciation Symbols

gloat\\'glōt\\ V. express evil satisfaction; view malevolently. As you *gloat* over your ill-gotten wealth, do you think of the many victims you have defrauded? also N.

glos-sa-ry\\'gläs -(ə-)rē\\N. brief explanation of words used in the text. I have found the *glossary* in this book very useful; it has eliminated many trips to the dictionary.

glos-sy\\'gläs -ē\\ADJ. smooth and shining. I want this photograph printed on *glossy* paper. also N.

glower\\'glaù(-ə)r\\V. scowl. The angry boy *glowered* at his father.

glut\\'glət\\ V. overstock; fill to excess. The manufacturers *glutted* the market and could not find purchasers for the many articles they had produced. also N.

glu-ti-nous \\'glüt -nəs\\ ADJ. sticky; viscous. Molasses is a *glutinous* substance.

glut-ton-ous\\'glət -nəs\\ADJ. greedy for food. The *gluttonous* boy ate all the cookies.

gnarled\\'här(-ə)ld\\ ADJ. twisted. The *gnarled* oak tree had been a landmark for years and was mentioned in several deeds.

gnome\\'nōm\\ N. dwarf; underground spirit. In medieval mythology, *gnomes* were the special guardians and inhabitants of subterranean mines.

goad\\'gōd\\ V. urge on. He was *goaded* by his friends until he yielded to their wishes. also N.

gorge\\'gȯ(ə)rj\\V. stuff oneself. The gluttonous guest *gorged* himself with food as though he had not eaten for days. also N.

gor-y\\'gō(ə)r -ē\\ADJ. bloody. The audience shuddered as they listened to the details of the *gory* massacre.

gos-sa-mer \\'gäs -ə-mər\\ ADJ. sheer; like cobwebs. Nylon can be woven into *gossamer* or thick fabrics. also N.

gouge\\'gaùj\\ V. tear out. In that fight, all the rules were forgotten; the adversaries bit, kicked, and tried to *gouge* each other's eyes out. also N.

gour-mand\\'gu̇(ə)r -ˌmänd \\ N. epicure; person who takes excessive pleasure in food and drink. The *gourmand* liked the French cuisine.

---

gour-met\\'gu̇(ə)r ͵mā\ N. connoisseur of food and drink. The *gourmet* stated that this was the best onion soup he had ever tasted.

gra-na-ry\\'grān -(ə-)rē\ N. storehouse for grain. We have reason to be thankful, for our crops were good and our *granaries* are full.

gran-dil-o-quent\gran-dil -ə-kwənt\ ADJ. pompous; bombastic; using high-sounding language. The politician could never speak simply; he was always *grandiloquent*.

gran-di-ose\\'gran -dē-͵ōs\ ADJ. imposing; impressive. His *grandiose* manner impressed those who met him for the first time.

gran-u-late\\'gran -yə͵lāt\ V. form into grains. Sugar that has been *granulated* dissolves more readily than lump sugar. **gran-ule**\\'gran -yü(ə)l\(ʹ\)\N.

graph-ic\\'graf -ik\ADJ. pertaining to the art of delineating; vividly described. I was particularly impressed by the *graphic* presentation of the story. also N.

gra-tis\\'grat -əs\ ADV. free. The company offered to give one package *gratis* to every purchaser of one of their products. also ADJ.

gra-tu-i-tous\grə-'t(y)ü -ət-əs\ ADJ. given freely; unwarranted. I resent your *gratuitous* remarks because no one asked for them.

gra-tu-i-ty\grə-'t(y)ü -ət-ē\ N. tip. Many service employees rely more on *gratuities* than on salaries for their livelihood.

gre-gar-i-ous\gri-'gar -ē-əs\ADJ. sociable. He was not *gregarious* and preferred to be alone most of the time.

gri-mace\\'grim -əs\ N. a facial distortion to show feeling such as pain, disgust, etc. Even though he remained silent, his *grimace* indicated his displeasure. also V.

gris-ly\\'griz -lē\ ADJ. ghastly. She shuddered at the *grisly* sight.

gro-tesque\grō-'tesk\ADJ. fantastic; comically hideous. On Halloween people enjoy wearing *grotesque* costumes.

grot-to\\'grät -͵(ı)ō\N. small cavern. The Blue *Grotto* in Capri can be entered only by small boats rowed by natives through a natural opening in the rocks.

---

grov-el \\'gräv -əl\\ v. crawl or creep on ground; remain prostrate. Even though we have been defeated, we do not have to *grovel* before our conquerors.

grudg-ing\\'grəj-iŋ'\\ADJ. unwilling; reluctant; stingy. We received only *grudging* support from the mayor despite his earlier promises of aid.

gru-el \\'grü -əl\\ N. liquid food made by boiling oatmeal, etc., in milk or water. Our daily allotment of *gruel* made the meal not only monotonous but also unpalatable.

gru-el-ing\\'grü -ə-liŋ\\ADJ. exhausting. The marathon is a *grueling* race.

grue-some \\'grü -səm\\ ADJ. grisly. People screamed when his *gruesome* appearance was flashed on the screen.

gruff\\grəf \\ ADJ. rough-mannered. Although he was blunt and *gruff* with most people, he was always gentle with children.

guf-faw\\(ₒ)gə-'fó \\ N. boisterous laughter. The loud *guffaws* that came from the closed room indicated that the members of the committee had not yet settled down to serious business. also v.

guile \\'gī(ə)l\\ N. deceit; duplicity. He achieved his high position by *guile* and treachery.

guile-less\\gī(ə)l-ləs\\ADJ. without deceit. He is naive, simple, and *guileless;* he cannot be guilty of fraud.

guise \\gīz\\ N. appearance; costume. In the *guise* of a plumber, the detective investigated the murder case.

gull-ible\\gəl -ə-bəl\\ADJ. easily deceived. He preyed upon *gullible* people who believed his stories of easy wealth.

gus-ta-to-ry\\'gəs -tə-ˌtōr -ē\\ADJ. affecting the sense of taste. This food has great *gustatory* appeal because of the spices it contains.

gus-to \\'gəs -(ₒ)tō\\ N. enjoyment; enthusiasm. He accepted the assignment with such *gusto* that I feel he would have been satisfied with a smaller salary.

gus-ty\\gəs -tē\\ADJ. windy. The *gusty* weather made sailing precarious.

gut-tur-al \\gət -ə-rəl\\ ADJ. pertaining to the throat. *Guttural* sounds are produced in the throat or in the back of the tongue and palate.

\\ə\\ abut   \\ᵊ\\ kitten, F table   \\ər\\ further   \\a\\ ash   \\ā\\ ace   \\ä\\ cot, cart
\\aú\\ out   \\ch\\ chin   \\e\\ bet   \\ē\\ easy   \\g\\ go   \\i\\ hit   \\ī\\ ice   \\j\\ job

–h–

hack-les\\'hak -əls\\ N. hairs on back and neck of a dog. The dog's *hackles* rose and he began to growl as the sound of footsteps grew louder. also V.

hack-neyed \\'hak -nēd\\ ADJ. commonplace; trite. The English teacher criticized his story because of his *hackneyed* plot.

hag-gard \\'hag -ərd\\ ADJ. wasted away; gaunt. After his long illness, he was pale and *haggard*.

hag-gle\\'hag -əl\\ V. argue about prices. I prefer to shop in a store that has a one-price policy because, whenever I *haggle* with a shopkeeper, I am never certain that I paid a fair price for the articles I purchased. also N.

hal-cy-on\\'hal -sē-ən\\ ADJ. calm; peaceful. In those *halcyon* days, people were not worried about sneak attacks and bombings.

hale\\'hā(ə)l\\ ADJ. healthy. After a brief illness, he was *hale* again.

hal-lowed \\'hal -(ι)ōd\\ ADJ. blessed; consecrated. He was laid to rest in *hallowed* ground.

hal-lu-ci-na-tion\\hə‚lüs -ᵊn-ā -shən\\ N. delusion. I think you were frightened by an *hallucination* which you created in your own mind.

ham-per\\'ham -pər\\ V. obstruct. The minority party agreed not to *hamper* the efforts of the leaders to secure a lasting peace.

hap\\'hap \\ N. chance; luck. In his poem *Hap*, Thomas Hardy objects to the part chance plays in our lives.

hap-haz-ard\\ ⁽'⁾hap-'haz -ərd\\ ADJ. random; by chance. His *haphazard* reading left him unacquainted with authors of the books.

hap-less\\'hap -ləs\\ ADJ. unfortunate. This *hapless* creature had never known a moment's pleasure.

ha-rangue \\hə-'raŋ \\ N. noisy speech. In his lengthy *harangue*, the principal berated the offenders. also V.

ha-rass\\hə-'ras\\ V. to annoy by repeated attacks. When he could not pay his bills as quickly as he had promised, he was *harassed* by his creditors.

har-bin-ger\\'här -bən-jər\\ N. forerunner. The crocus is an early *harbinger* of spring. also V.

\\ŋ\\ sing   \\ō\\ go   \\ȯ\\ law   \\ȯi\\ boy   \\th\\ thin   \\t͟h\\ the   \\ü\\ loot   \\u̇\\ foot
\\y\\ yet   \\zh\\ vision   \\ä, k̲, ⁿ, œ, ō͞e, ue, ū͞e, ʸ\\ *see* Pronunciation Symbols

har-bor\'här-bər\ v. provide a refuge for; hide. The church *harbored* illegal aliens who were political refugees.

harp-ing\'härp-iŋ\ N. tiresome dwelling on a subject. After he had reminded me several times about what he had done for me, I told him to stop *harping* on my indebtedness to him. **harp**\'härp\ v.

har-ri-dan \'har -əd-ᵊn\ N. shrewish hag. Most people avoided the *harridan* because they feared her abusive and vicious language.

har-row\'har -ₒō\ v. break up ground after plowing; torture. I don't want to *harrow* you at this time by asking you to recall the details of your unpleasant experience. also N.

har-ry\'har -ē\ v. raid. The guerrilla band *harried* the enemy nightly.

haugh-ti-ness\'hȯt-ē-nəs\ N. pride; arrogance. I resent his *haughtiness* because he is no better than we are.

hau-teur\hȯ-ᵗtər \ N. haughtiness. His snobbishness is obvious to all who witness his *hauteur* when he talks to those whom he considers his social inferiors.

haw-ser\'hȯ -zər\ N. large rope. The ship was tied to the pier by a *hawser*.

haz-ard-ous \'haz -ərd-əs\ ADJ. dangerous. Your occupation is too *hazardous* for insurance companies to consider your application.

haz-y \'hā -zē\ ADJ. slightly obscure. In *hazy* weather, you cannot see the top of this mountain.

heck-ler\ 'hek-(ə)lər \ N. person who verbally harasses others. The *heckler* kept interrupting the speaker with rude remarks. **heck-le**\ 'hek-əl\ v.

he-do-nism\'hēd -ᵊn-ˌiz -əm\ N. belief that pleasure is the sole aim in life. *Hedonism* and asceticism are opposing philosophies of human behavior.

heed-less \'hēd -ləs\ ADJ. not noticing; disregarding. He drove on, *heedless* of the warnings placed at the side of the road that it was dangerous.

he-gi-ra \hi-ᵗjī -rə\ N. flight, especially Mohammed's flight from Mecca to Medina. Mohammed began his *hegira* when he was 53 years old.

\ə\ abut	\ᵊ\ kitten, F table	\ər\ further	\a\ ash	\ā\ ace	\ä\ cot, cart
\aů\ out	\ch\ chin	\e\ bet	\ē\ easy	\g\ go	\i\ hit \ī\ ice \j\ job

hei-nous \\'hā -nəs\ ADJ. atrocious; hatefully bad. Hitler's *heinous* crimes will never be forgotten.

her-biv-o-rous \\,(h)ər-'biv-ə-rəs\ ADJ. grain-eating. Some *herbivorous* animals have two stomachs for digesting their food. **her-bi-vore** \\'(h)ər-bə-,vō(ə)r\ N.

her-e-sy \\'her -ə-sē\ N. opinion contrary to popular belief; opinion contrary to accepted religion. He was threatened with excommunication because his remarks were considered to be pure *heresy*.

her-e-tic \\'her -ə-tik\ N. person who maintains opinions contrary to the doctrines of the church. She was punished by the Spanish Inquisition because she was a *heretic*.

her-met-i-cal-ly \\,(,)hər-'met -i-k(ə-)lē\ ADV. sealed by fusion so as to be airtight. After these bandages are sterilized, they are placed in *hermetically* sealed containers.

her-mit-age \\'hər -mət-ij\ N. home of a hermit. Even in his remote *hermitage* he could not escape completely from the world.

het-er-o-ge-ne-ous \\,het -ə-rə-'jē -nē-əs\ ADJ. dissimilar. In *heterogeneous* groupings, we have an unassorted grouping, while in homogeneous groupings we have people or things which have common traits.

hew \\'hyü \ V. cut to pieces with ax or sword. The cavalry rushed into the melee and *hewed* the enemy with their swords.

hi-a-tus \hī-'āt -əs\ N. gap; pause. There was a *hiatus* of twenty years in the life of Rip van Winkle. also ADJ.

hi-ber-nal \hī-'bərn -ᵊl\ ADJ. wintry. Bears prepare for their long *hibernal* sleep by overeating.

hi-ber-nate \\'hī -bər-,nāt \ V. sleep throughout the winter. Bears are one of the many species of animals that *hibernate*.

hi-er-ar-chy \\'hī-(ə-),rär -kē\ N. body divided into ranks. It was difficult to step out of one's place in this *hierarchy*.

hi-ero-glyph-ic \,hī -(ə-)rə-'glif -ik\ N. picture writing. The discovery of the Rosetta Stone enabled scholars to read the ancient Egyptian *hieroglyphics*.

hi-lar-i-ty \hil-'ar -ət-ē\ N. boisterous mirth. This *hilarity* is improper on this solemn day of mourning.

\ŋ\ **sing**	\ō\ **go**	\ò\ **law**	\ói\ **boy**	\th\ **thin**	\<u>th</u>\ **the**	\ü\ **loot**	\ú\ **foot**
\y\ **yet**	\zh\ **vision**	\à, <u>k</u>, ⁿ, œ, ōē, ue, ūē, ʸ\ *see* Pronunciation Symbols

hind-most\\'hīn(d) ˌmōst\ ADJ. furthest behind. The coward could always be found in the *hindmost* lines whenever
a battle was being waged.

hire-ling\\'hī(ə)r -liŋ\ N. one who serves for hire [usually
contemptuously]. In a matter of such importance, I do
not wish to deal with *hirelings;* I must meet with the chief.

hir-sute\\'hər ˌsüt\ ADJ. hairy. He was a *hirsute* individual
with a heavy black beard.

his-tri-on-ic\ˌhis -trē-'än -ik\ADJ. theatrical. He was proud
of his *histrionic* ability and wanted to play the role of
Hamlet. **his-tri-on-ics**\ˌhis -trē-'än -iks\N.

hoar-y\\'hō(ə)r -ē\ADJ. white with age. The man was *hoary*
and wrinkled.

hoax\\'hōks\ N. trick; practical joke. Embarrassed by the
hoax, he reddened and left the room. also V.

ho-lo-caust\\'häl -ə-ˌkȯst \ N. destruction by fire. Citizens of
San Francisco remember that the destruction of the city
was caused not by the earthquake but by the *holocaust*
that followed.

hol-ster\\'hōl(t) -stər\N. pistol case. Even when he was not
in uniform, he carried a *holster* and pistol under his arm.

hom-age\\'(h)äm-ij \N. honor; tribute. In her speech she
tried to pay *homage* to a great man.

home-spun\\'hōm ˌspən\ ADJ. domestic; made at home.
Homespun wit like *homespun* cloth was often coarse and
plain. also N.

hom-i-ly\\'häm -ə-lē\ N. sermon; serious warning. His
speeches were always *homilies,* advising his listeners to re-
pent and reform.

ho-mo-ge-ne-ous\ˌhō -mə-'jē -nē-əs\ADJ. of the same kind.
Educators try to put pupils of similar abilities into classes
because they believe that this *homogeneous* grouping is advisable. **ho-mo-ge-ne-i-ty**\ˌhō -mə-jə-'nē -ət-ē\N.

hone\\'hōn \v. sharpen. To make shaving easier, he *honed*
his razor with great care.

hood-wink\\'hȯd -ˌwiŋk \ V. deceive; delude. Having been
hoodwinked once by the fast-talking salesman, he was extremely cautious when he went to purchase a used car.

hor-ta-to-ry \'hȯrt -ə-ˌtȯr -ē\ ADJ. encouraging; exhortive. The crowd listened to his *hortatory* statements with ever growing excitement; finally they rushed from the hall to carry out his suggestions.

hor-ti-cul-tur-al \ˌhȯrt -ə-ˈkəlch(-ə) -rəl\ ADJ. pertaining to cultivation of gardens. When he bought his house, he began to look for flowers and decorative shrubs, and began to read books dealing with *horticultural* matters.

hos-tel-ry \'häs -tᵊl-rē\ N. inn. Travelers interested in economy should stay at *hostelries* and pensions rather than fashionable hotels.

hov-el \'həv-əl\ N. shack; small, wretched house. He wondered how poor people could stand living in such a *hovel*.

hov-er \'həv-ər\ V. hang about; wait nearby. The police helicopter *hovered* above the accident.

hub-bub \'həb -ˌəb\ N. confused uproar. The marketplace was a scene of *hubbub* and excitement; in all the noise, we could not distinguish particular voices.

hu-bris \'hyü-brəs\ N. arrogance; excessive self-conceit. Filled with *hubris*, Lear refused to heed his friends' warnings.

hue \'hyü\ N. color; aspect. The aviary contained birds of every possible *hue*.

hu-mane \hyü-ˈmān\ ADJ. kind. His *humane* and considerate treatment of the unfortunate endeared him to all.

hum-drum \'həm -ˌdrəm\ ADJ. dull; monotonous. After his years of adventure, he could not settle down to a *humdrum* existence.

hu-mid \'hyü -məd\ ADJ. damp. He could not stand the *humid* climate and moved to a drier area.

hu-mil-i-ty \hyü-ˈmil -ət-ē\ N. humbleness of spirit. He spoke with a *humility* and lack of pride which impressed his listeners.

hum-mock \'həm -ək\ N. small hill. The ascent of the *hummock* is not difficult and the view from the hilltop is ample reward for the effort.

hu-mus \'hyü -məs\ N. substance formed by decaying vegetable matter. In order to improve his garden, he spread *humus* over his lawn and flower beds.

\ŋ\ **sing** \ō\ **go** \ȯ\ **law** \ȯi\ **boy** \th\ **thin** \t͟h\ **the** \ü\ **loot** \u̇\ **foot**
\y\ **yet** \zh\ **vision** \à, k̲, ⁿ, œ, œ̄, ue, ū̠e, ʳ\ *see* Pronunciation Symbols

hur-tle\\'hərt-əl\\v. rush headlong. The runaway train *hurtled* towards disaster.

hus-band-ry \\'həz -bən-drē\\ N. frugality; thrift; agriculture. He accumulated his small fortune by diligence and *husbandry*.

hy-brid\\'hī -brəd\\N. mongrel; mixed breed. Mendel's formula explains the appearance of *hybrids* and pure species in breeding. also ADJ.

hy-dro-pho-bia\\ˌhī-drə-'fō-bē-ə\\N. rabies; fear of water. A dog that bites a human being must be observed for symptoms of *hydrophobia*.

hy-per-bo-le \\hī-'pər -bə-⁽'⁾lē\\ N. exaggeration; overstatement. This salesman is guilty of *hyperbole* in describing his product; it is wise to discount his claims.

hy-per-bo-re-an \\ˌhī -pər-'bōr -ē-ən\\ ADJ. situated in extreme north; arctic; cold. The *hyperborean* blasts brought snow and ice to the countryside.

hy-per-crit-i-cal \\ˌhī -pər-'krit -i-kəl\\ ADJ. excessively exacting. You are *hypercritical* in your demands for perfection; we all make mistakes.

hy-po-chon-dri-ac\\ˌhī -pə-'kän -drēˌak \\ N. person unduly worried about his health; worrier without cause about illness. The doctor prescribed chocolate pills for his patient who was a *hypochondriac*.

hyp-o-crit-i-cal \\ˌhip -ə-'krit -i-kəl\\ ADJ. pretending to be virtuous; deceiving. I resent his *hypocritical* posing as a friend for I know he is interested only in his own advancement.

hy-po-thet-i-cal\\ˌhī -pə-'thet -i-kəl\\ADJ. based on assumptions or hypotheses. Why do we have to consider *hypothetical* cases when we have actual case histories which we may examine? **hy-poth-e-sis**\\hī-'päth -ə-səs\\N.

–i–

ich-thy-ol-ogy\ ,ik-thē-'äl-ə-jē \ N. study of fish. Jacques Cousteau's programs about sea life have advanced the cause of *ichthyology.*

icon\ 'ī-,kän \ N. religious image; idol. The *icons* on the walls of the church were painted in the thirteenth century.

i-con-o-clas-tic \(ı)ī-,kän -ə-'klas-tik\ ADJ. attacking cherished traditions. George Bernard Shaw's *iconoclastic* plays often startled people.

i-de-ol-o-gy\ ,īd -ē-'äl -ə-jē\ N. ideas of a group of people. That *ideology* is dangerous to this country because it embraces undemocratic philosophies.

id-i-om\ 'id -ē-əm\ N. special usage in language. I could not understand their *idiom* because literal translation made no sense.

id-i-o-syn-cra-sy\ ,id -ē-ə-'siŋ -krə-sē\ N. peculiarity; eccentricity. One of his personal *idiosyncrasies* was his habit of rinsing all cutlery given him in a restaurant.

id-i-o-syn-crat-ic \ ,id -ē-ō-,(ı)sin-'krat -ik\ ADJ. private; peculiar to an individual. Such behavior is *idiosyncratic;* it is as easily identifiable as a signature.

i-dol-a-try\ ī-'däl -ə-trē\ N. worship of idols; excessive admiration. Such *idolatry* of singers of popular ballads is typical of the excessive enthusiasm of youth.

idyl-lic\ ī-'dil-ik\ ADJ. charmingly carefree; simple. Far from the city, she led an *idyllic* existence in her rural retreat.

ig-ne-ous\ 'ig -nē-əs\ ADJ. produced by fire; volcanic. Lava, pumice, and other *igneous* rocks are found in great abundance around Mount Vesuvius near Naples.

ig-no-ble\ ig-'nō-bəl\ ADJ. of lowly origin; unworthy. This plan is inspired by *ignoble* motives and I must, therefore, óppose it.

ig-no-min-i-ous \ ,ig -nə-'min -ē-əs\ ADJ. disgraceful. The country smarted under the *ignominious* defeat and dreamed of the day when it would be victorious. **ig-no-mi-ny**\ 'ig -nə-,min -ē\ N.

\ŋ\ sing   \ō\ go   \ȯ\ law   \ȯi\ boy   \th\ thin   \th\ the   \ü\ loot   \u̇\ foot
\y\ yet   \zh\ vision   \à, ḵ, ⁿ, œ, œ̄, ue, ūe, ʸ\ *see* Pronunciation Symbols

il-lim-it-able \\(ᐟ⁾il-ᐟ(l)im -ət-ə-bəl\\ ADJ. infinite. Man, having explored the far corners of the earth, is now reaching out into *illimitable* space.

il-lu-sion\\il-ü -zhən\\ N. misleading vision. It is easy to create an optical *illusion* in which lines of equal length appear different. **il-lu-so-ry**\\il-üs -(ə-)rē\\ ADJ.

il-lu-sive \\il-ü -siv\\ ADJ. deceiving. This mirage is an illusion; let us not be fooled by its *illusive* effect.

im-be-cil-i-ty \\im -bə-ᶦsil -ət-ē\\ N. weakness of mind. I am amazed at the *imbecility* of the readers of these trashy magazines.

im-bibe\\im-ᶦbīb \\ V. drink in. The dry soil *imbibed* the rain quickly.

im-bro-glio\\im-ᶦbrōl -(ᵢ)yō\\ N. a complicated situation; perplexity; entanglement. He was called in to settle the *imbroglio* but failed to bring harmony into the situation.

im-brue \\im-ᶦbrü \\ V. drench, stain, especially with blood. As the instigator of this heinous murder, he is as much *imbrued* in blood as the actual assassin.

im-bue \\im-ᶦbyü \\ V. saturate, fill. His visits to the famous Gothic cathedrals *imbued* him with feelings of awe and reverence.

im-mac-u-late\\im-ᶦak -yə-lət\\ADJ. pure; spotless. The West Point cadets were *immaculate* as they lined up for inspection.

im-mi-nent \\im -ə-nənt\\ ADJ. impending; near at hand. The *imminent* battle will determine our success or failure in this conflict.

im-mo-bil-i-ty \\im -(ᵢ)ō-ᶦbil -ət-ē\\ N. state of being immovable. Modern armies cannot afford the luxury of *immobility,* as they are vulnerable to attack while standing still.

im-mo-late\\ᶦim -ə˞lāt\\ V. offer as a sacrifice. The tribal king offered to *immolate* his daughter to quiet the angry gods.

im-mune \\im-ᶦyün \\ ADJ. exempt. He was fortunately *immune* from the disease and could take care of the sick.

im-mure\\im-ᶦyú(ə)r\\ V. imprison; shut up in confinement. For the two weeks before the examination, the student *immured* himself in his room and concentrated upon his studies.

\ə\ abut	\ᵊ\ kitten, F table	\ər\ **further**	\a\ **ash**	\ā\ **ace**	\ä\ **cot, cart**
\aú\ **out**	\ch\ **chin**	\e\ **bet**	\ē\ **easy**	\g\ **go**	\i\ **hit**	\ī\ **ice**	\j\ **job**

im-mu-ta-ble\⁽¹⁾im-ʹ(m)yüt -ə-bəl\ADJ. unchangeable. Scientists are constantly seeking to discover the *immutable* laws of nature.

im-pair\im-ʹpa(ə)r\ V. worsen; diminish in value. This arrest will *impair* his reputation in the community.

im-pale\im-ʹpā(ə)l\ V. pierce. He was *impaled* by the spear hurled by his adversary.

im-pal-pa-ble\⁽¹⁾im-ʹpal -pə-bəl\ADJ. imperceptible; intangible. The ash is so fine that it is *impalpable* to the touch but it can be seen as a fine layer covering the window ledge.

im-par-tial\(ʹ)im-ʹpär-shəl\ADJ. not biased; fair. As members of the jury, you must be *impartial*, showing no favoritism to either party but judging the case on its merits.

im-passe\im -ʹpas\ N. predicament from which there is no escape. In this *impasse*, all turned to prayer as their last hope.

im-pas-sive \⁽¹⁾im-ʹpas -iv\ ADJ. without feeling; not affected by pain. The American Indian has been incorrectly depicted as an *impassive* individual, undemonstrative and stoical.

im-peach\im-ʹpēch \ V. charge with crime in office; indict. The angry congressman wanted to *impeach* the President.

im-pec-ca-ble\⁽¹⁾im-ʹpek -ə-bəl\ADJ. faultless. He was proud of his *impeccable* manners.

im-pe-cu-nious\im -pi-ʹkyü -nyəs\ADJ. without money. Now that he was wealthy, he gladly contributed to funds to assist the *impecunious* and the disabled.

im-pede\im-ʹpēd\V. hinder; block; delay. A series of accidents *impeded* the launching of the space shuttle.

im-ped-i-ment\im-ʹped-ə-mənt\N. hindrance; stumbling-block. She had a speech *impediment* that prevented her speaking clearly.

im-pend-ing\im-ʹpen -diŋ\ADJ. nearing; approaching. The entire country was saddened by the news of his *impending* death.

im-pen-i-tent \⁽¹⁾im-ʹpen -ə-tənt\ ADJ. not repentant. We could see by his brazen attitude that he was *impenitent*.

\ŋ\ sing   \ō\ go   \ȯ\ law   \ȯi\ boy   \th\ thin   \t͟h\ the   \ü\ loot   \u̇\ foot
\y\ yet   \zh\ vision   \à, k̲, ⁿ, œ, œ̄, ue, ūe, ʸ\ *see* Pronunciation Symbols

im·pe·ri·ous \im-'pir -ē-əs\ ADJ. domineering. His *imperious* manner indicated that he had long been accustomed to assuming command.

im·per·me·able \⁽¹⁾im-'pər -mē-ə-bəl\ ADJ. impervious; not permitting passage through its substance. This new material is *impermeable* to liquids.

im·per·ti·nent \⁽¹⁾im-'pərt -ᵊn-ənt\ ADJ. insolent. I regard your remarks as *impertinent* and resent them.

im·per·turb·a·bil·i·ty \im -pər₋tər -bə-'bil -ət-ē\ N. calmness. We are impressed by his *imperturbability* in this critical moment and are calmed by it.

im·per·turb·a·ble \im -pər-'tər -bə-bəl\ ADJ. calm; placid. He remained *imperturbable* and in full command of the situation in spite of the hysteria and panic all around him.

im·per·vi·ous \⁽¹⁾im-'pər -vē-əs\ ADJ. not penetrable; not permitting passage through. You cannot change their habits for their minds are *impervious* to reasoning.

im·pet·u·ous \im-'pech -(ə-)wəs\ ADJ. violent; hasty; rash. We tried to curb his *impetuous* behavior because we felt that in his haste he might offend some people.

im·pe·tus \'im -pət-əs\ N. moving force. It is a miracle that there were any survivors since the two automobiles that collided were traveling with great *impetus*.

im·pi·e·ty \⁽¹⁾im-'pī -ət-ē\ N. irreverence; wickedness. We must regard your blasphemy as an act of *impiety*.

im·pinge \im-'pinj\ v. infringe; touch; collide with. How could they be married without *impinging* on one another's freedom?

im·pi·ous \'im -pē-əs\ ADJ. irreverent. The congregation was offended by his *impious* remarks.

im·pla·ca·ble \⁽¹⁾im-'plak -ə-bəl\ ADJ. incapable of being pacified. Madame Defarge was the *implacable* enemy of the Evremonde family.

im·plau·si·ble \(')im-'plò-zə-bəl\ ADJ. unlikely; unbelievable. Though her alibi seemed *implausible*, it in fact turned out to be true.

im·ple·ment \im -plə₋mənt\ v. supply what is needed; furnish with tools. I am unwilling to *implement* this plan until I have assurances that it has the full approval of your officials. **im·ple·ment** \im -plə-mənt\ N.

\ə\ abut \ᵊ\ kitten, F table \ər\ **further** \a\ **ash** \ā\ **ace** \ä\ cot, cart
\aů\ **out** \ch\ **chin** \e\ bet \ē\ **easy** \g\ **go** \i\ hit \ī\ ice \j\ job

im·pli·ca·tion \ˌim -plə-ˈkā -shən\ N. that which is hinted at or suggested. If I understand the *implications* of your remark, you do not trust our captain.

im·plic·it \im-ˈplis -ət\ ADJ. understood but not stated. It is *implicit* that you will come to our aid if we are attacked.

im·ply \im-ˈplī\ V. suggest a meaning not expressed; signify. Even though your statement does not declare that you are at war with that country, your actions *imply* that that is the actual situation.

im·pol·i·tic \(ˈ)im-ˈpäl -ə-ˌtik\ ADJ. not wise. I think it is *impolitic* to raise this issue at the present time because the public is too angry.

im·pon·der·a·ble \(ˈ)im-ˈpän -d(ə-)rə-bəl\ ADJ. weightless. I can evaluate the data gathered in this study; the *imponderable* items are not so easily analyzed.

im·port \ˈim -ˌpō(ə)rt\ N. significance. I feel that you have not grasped the full *import* of the message sent to us by the enemy. **im·port** \im-ˈpō(ə)rt\ V.

im·por·tu·nate \im-ˈpȯrch -(ə-)nət\ ADJ. urging; demanding. He tried to hide from his *importunate* creditors until his allowance arrived.

im·por·tune \ˌim-pər-ˈt(y)ün\ V. beg earnestly. I must *importune* you to work for peace at this time.

im·pos·ture \im-ˈpäs-chər\ N. assuming a false identity; masquerade. She was imprisoned for her *imposture* of a doctor.

im·po·tent \ˈim -pət-ənt\ ADJ. weak; ineffective. Although he wished to break the nicotine habit, he found himself *impotent* in resisting the craving for a cigarette.

im·pov·er·ished \im-ˈpäv-(ə-)rishd\ ADJ. poor. The loss of their farm left the family *impoverished* and hopeless.

im·pre·cate \ˈim -pri-ˌkāt\ V. curse; pray that evil will befall. To *imprecate* Hitler's atrocities is not enough; we must insure against any future practice of genocide.

im·preg·na·ble \im-ˈpreg -nə-bəl\ ADJ. invulnerable. Until the development of the airplane as a military weapon, the fort was considered *impregnable*.

\ŋ\ **sing**   \ō\ **go**   \ȯ\ **law**   \ȯi\ **boy**   \th\ **thin**   \t͟h\ **the**   \ü\ **loot**   \u̇\ **foot**
\y\ **yet**   \zh\ **vision**   \à, k̲, ⁿ, œ, œ̄, ue, ue̅, ᵛ\ *see* Pronunciation Symbols

im-promp-tu\im-'präm(p) -ₒt(y)ü\ADJ. without previous preparation. His listeners were amazed that such a thorough presentation could be made in an *impromptu* speech.

im-pro-pri-e-ty\im -p(r)ǝ-'prī -ǝt-ē\N. state of being inappropriate. Because of the *impropriety* of his costume, he was denied entrance into the dining room.

im-prov-i-dent\⁽¹⁾im-'präv -ǝd-ǝnt\ADJ. thriftless. He was constantly being warned to mend his *improvident* ways and begin to "save for a rainy day."

im-pro-vise\im -prǝ-'vīz\ V. compose on the spur of the moment. He would sit at the piano and *improvise* for hours on themes from Bach and Handel.

im-pru-dent\(')im-'prüd-ǝnt\ADJ. lacking caution; injudicious. It is *imprudent* to exercise vigorously and become overheated when you are unwell.

im-pugn\im-'pyün\ V. doubt; challenge; gainsay. I cannot *impugn* your honesty without evidence.

im-pu-ni-ty\im-'pyü -nǝt-ē\N. freedom from punishment. The bully mistreated everyone in the class with *impunity* for he felt that no one would dare retaliate.

im-pu-ta-tion\im -pyǝ-'tā -shǝn\N. charge; reproach. You cannot ignore the *imputations* in his speech that you are the guilty party.

im-pute\im-'pyüt\ V. attribute; ascribe. If I wished to *impute* blame to the officers in charge of this program, I would come out and state it definitely and without hesitation.

in-ad-ver-tence\in -ǝd-'vǝrt -ǝn(t)s\N. oversight; carelessness. By *inadvertence*, he omitted two questions on the examination.

in-al-ien-a-ble\⁽¹⁾in-'āl -yǝ-nǝ-bǝl\ADJ. not to be taken away; nontransferable. The Declaration of Independence mentions the *inalienable* rights that all of us possess.

in-ane\in-'ān\ ADJ. silly; senseless. Such comments are *inane* because they do not help us solve our problem. **in-an-i-ty**\in-'an -ǝt-ē\N.

in-an-i-mate\⁽¹⁾in-'an -ǝ-mǝt\ ADJ. lifeless. She was asked to identify the still and *inanimate* body.

\ǝ\ abut \ᵊ\ kitten, F table \ǝr\ **further** \a\ ash \ā\ ace \ä\ cot, cart
\aů\ **out** \ch\ chin \e\ bet \ē\ **easy** \g\ go \i\ hit \ī\ ice \j\ job

in-ar-tic-u-late \,in -(,)är -'tik -yə-lət\ ADJ. speechless; producing indistinct speech. He became *inarticulate* with rage and uttered sounds without meaning.

in-can-des-cent \,in-kən-'des-ᵊnt\ ADJ. strikingly bright; shining with intense heat. If you leave on an *incandescent* light bulb, it quickly grows too hot to touch.

in-can-ta-tion \in ,kan -'tā -shən\ N. singing or chanting of magic spells; magical formula. Uttering *incantations* to make the brew more potent, the witch doctor stirred the liquid in the caldron.

in-ca-pac-i-tate \,in -kə-'pas -ə-,tāt\ V. disable. During the winter, many people were *incapacitated* by respiratory ailments.

in-car-cer-ate \in-'kär -sə-,rāt\ V. imprison. The warden will *incarcerate* the felon.

in-car-nate \in-'kär -nət\ ADJ. endowed with flesh; personified. Your attitude is so fiendish that you must be a devil *incarnate*. also V.

in-car-na-tion \in ,kär -'nā -shən\ N. act of assuming a human body and human nature. The *incarnation* of Jesus Christ is a basic tenet of Christian theology.

in-cen-di-ar-y \in-'sen -dē,er -ē\ N. arsonist. The fire spread in such an unusual manner that the fire department chiefs were certain that it had been set by an *incendiary*. also ADJ.

in-cen-tive \in-'sent -iv\ N. spur; motive. Students who dislike school must be given an *incentive* to learn.

in-ces-sant \(')in-'ses -ᵊnt\ ADJ. uninterrupted. The crickets kept up an *incessant* chirping which disturbed our attempts to fall asleep.

in-cho-ate \in-'kō -ət\ ADJ. recently begun; rudimentary; elementary. Before the Creation, the world was an *inchoate* mass.

in-ci-dence \'in(t) -səd-ən(t)s\ N. falling on a body; a casual occurrence. We must determine the angle of *incidence* of the rays of light.

in-ci-den-tal \,in(t)-sə-'dent-ᵊl\ ADJ. not essential; minor. The scholarship covered his major expenses at college and some of his *incidental* expenses as well.

\ŋ\ sing   \ō\ go   \ò\ law   \òi\ boy   \th\ thin   \th̲\ the   \ü\ loot   \u̇\ foot
\y\ yet   \zh\ vision   \à, k̲, ⁿ, œ, œ̄, ue, ūe, ʸ\ *see* Pronunciation Symbols

in-cip-i-ent\in-'sip -ē-ənt\ADJ. beginning; in an early stage. I will go to sleep early for I want to break an *incipient* cold.

in-ci-sive \in-'sī -siv\ ADJ. cutting; sharp. His *incisive* remarks made us see the fallacy in our plans.

in-cite\in-'sīt\ V. arouse to action. The demagogue *incited* the mob to take action into its own hands.

in-clem-ent\⁽¹⁾in-'klem -ənt\ADJ. stormy; unkind. I like to read a good book in *inclement* weather.

in-clu-sive \in-'klü-siv\ ADJ. tending to include all. This meeting will run from January 10 to February 15 *inclusive*.

in-cog-ni-to\in -ˌkäg -hēt ˑ₍ˌ₎ō\ADV, ADJ. with identity concealed; using an assumed name. The monarch enjoyed traveling through the town *incognito* and mingling with the populace. also N.

in-co-her-ence\ˌin-kō-'hir-ən(t)s\N. lack of relevance; lack of intelligibility. The bereaved father sobbed and stammered, caught up in the *incoherence* of his grief. **in-co-her-ent**\in-kō-'hir-ənt\ADJ.

in-com-mo-di-ous \in -kə-'möd -ē-əs\ ADJ. not spacious. In their *incommodious* quarters, they had to improvise for closet space.

in-com-pat-i-ble \ˌin -kəm-'pat -ə-bəl\ ADJ. inharmonious. The married couple argued incessantly and finally decided to separate because they were *incompatible*.

in-con-gru-i-ty\ˌin -kən-'grü -ət-ē\N. lack of harmony; absurdity. The *incongruity* of his wearing sneakers with formal attire amused the observers.

in-con-gru-ous \⁽¹⁾in -'kän -grə-wəs\ ADJ. not fitting; absurd. These remarks do not have any relationship to the problem at hand; they are *incongruous* and should be stricken from the record.

in-con-se-quen-tial\₍ˌ₎in ˌkän(t)-sə-'kwən -chəl\ADJ. of trifling significance. Your objections are *inconsequential* and may be disregarded.

\ə\ **abut**	\ᵊ\ **kitten, F table**	\ər\ **further**	\a\ **ash**	\ā\ **ace**	\ä\ **cot, cart**	
\aů\ **out**	\ch\ **chin**	\e\ **bet**	\ē\ **easy**	\g\ **go**	\i\ **hit**	\ī\ **ice**	\j\ **job**

in-con-ti-nent \⁽ᵗ⁾in·känt -ᵊn-ənt\ ADJ. lacking self-restraint; licentious. His *incontinent* behavior off stage shocked many people and they refused to attend the plays and movies in which he appeared.

in-con-tro-vert-i-ble \₍₍₎in·kän -trə·vərt -ə-bəl\ ADJ. indisputable. We must yield to the *incontrovertible* evidence which you have presented and free your client.

in-cor-po-re-al \in -kȯr⁽ᵗ⁾·pōr -ē-əl\ ADJ. immaterial; without a material body. We must devote time to the needs of our *incorporeal* mind as well as our corporeal body.

in-cor-ri-gi-ble \in⁽ᵗ⁾·kȯr-ə-jə-bəl\ ADJ. uncorrectable. Because he was an *incorrigible* criminal, he was sentenced to life imprisonment.

in-cre-du-li-ty \in -kri·d(y)ü -lət-ē\ N. a tendency to disbelief. Your *incredulity* in the face of all the evidence is hard to understand.

in-cred-u-lous \in⁽ᵗ⁾·krej -ə-ləs\ ADJ. withholding belief; skeptical. The *incredulous* judge refused to accept the statement of the defendant.

in-cre-ment \iŋ-krə-mənt\ N. increase. The new contract calls for a 10 percent *increment* in salary for each employee for the next two years.

in-crim-i-nate \in·krim -ə·nāt\ V. accuse. The evidence gathered against the racketeers *incriminates* some high public officials as well.

in-cu-bate \iŋ -kyə·bāt\ V. hatch; scheme. Inasmuch as our supply of electricity is cut off, we shall have to rely on the hens to *incubate* these eggs.

in-cu-bus \iŋ -kyə-bəs\ N. burden; mental care; nightmare. The *incubus* of financial worry helped bring on his nervous breakdown.

in-cul-cate \in·kəl ̱·kāt\ V. teach. In an effort to *inculcate* religious devotion, the officials ordered that the school day begin with the singing of a hymn.

in-cum-bent \in·kəm -bənt\ N. officeholder. The newly elected public official received valuable advice from the present *incumbent*. also ADJ.

\ŋ\ **sing**   \ō\ **go**   \ȯ\ **law**   \ȯi\ **boy**   \th\ **thin**   \t̲h̲\ **the**   \ü\ **loot**   \u̇\ **foot**
\y\ **yet**   \zh\ **vision**   \à, k̲, ⁿ, œ, ō̄e, ue, ūe, ʸ\ *see* Pronunciation Symbols

incur

in-cur\in-'kər\v. bring upon oneself. His parents refused to pay any future debes he might *incur*.

in-cur-sion \in-'kər -zhən\ N. temporary invasion. The nightly *incursions* and hit-and-run raids of our neighbors across the border tried the patience of the country to the point where we decided to retaliate in force.

in-de-fat-i-ga-ble\in -di-'fat -i-gə-bəl\ADJ. tireless. He was *indefatigable* in his constant efforts to raise funds for the Red Cross.

in-dem-ni-fy\in-'dem -nə-ˌfī\ v. make secure against loss; compensate for loss. The city will *indemnify* all home owners whose property is spoiled by this project.

in-den-ture\in-'den -chər\v. bind as servant or apprentice to master. Many immigrants could come to America only after they had *indentured* themselves for several years. also N.

in-dict\in-'dīt\ v. charge. If the grand jury *indicts* the suspect, he will go to trial.

in-dig-e-nous\in-'dij -ə-nəs\ADJ. native. Tobacco is one of the *indigenous* plants which the early explorers found in this country.

in-di-gent\'in -di-jənt\ADJ. poor. Because he was *indigent*, he was sent to the welfare office.

in-dig-ni-ty\in-'dig -nət-ē\N. offensive or insulting treatment. Although he seemed to accept cheerfully the *indignities* heaped upon him, he was inwardly very angry. **in-dig-nant**\in-'dig -nənt\ADJ.

in-dis-put-a-ble\ˌin -dis-'pyüt -ə-bəl\ADJ. too certain to be disputed. In the face of these *indisputable* statements, I withdraw my complaint.

in-dis-sol-u-ble\ˌin-dis-'äl-yə-bəl\ADJ. permanent. The *indissoluble* bonds of marriage are all too often being dissolved.

in-dite\in-'dīt\ v. write; compose. Cyrano *indited* many letters for Christian.

in-do-lence\'in -də-lən(t)s\N. laziness. The sultry weather in the tropics encourages a life of *indolence*.

in-dom-i-ta-ble\in-'däm -ət-ə-bəl\ ADJ. unconquerable. The founders of our country had *indomitable* willpower.

\ə\ abut   \ᵊ\ kitten, F table   \ər\ further   \a\ ash   \ā\ ace   \ä\ cot, cart
\au̇\ out   \ch\ chin   \e\ bet   \ē\ easy   \g\ go   \i\ hit   \ī\ ice   \j\ job

in-du-bi-ta-bly\⁽'⁾in-d̶(y)ü -bət-ə-blē\ ADV. beyond a doubt. Because his argument was *indubitably* valid, the judge accepted it.

in-duc-tive \in-d̶ək -tiv\ ADJ. pertaining to induction or proceeding from the specific to the general. The discovery of the planet Pluto is an excellent example of the results that can be obtained from *inductive* reasoning.

in-dul-gent\in-d̶əl -jənt\ ADJ. humoring; yielding; lenient. An *indulgent* parent may spoil a child by creating an artificial atmosphere of leniency.

in-e-bri-et-y \in -i-'brī -ət-ē\ N. habitual intoxication. Because of his *inebriety*, he was discharged from his position as family chauffeur.

in-ef-fa-ble\⁽'⁾in-'ef -ə-bəl\ ADJ. unutterable; cannot be expressed in speech. Such *ineffable* joy must be experienced; it cannot be described.

in-ef-fec-tu-al \,in-ə-'fek-chə(-wə)l\ ADJ. not effective; weak. Because the candidate failed to get across his message to the public, his campaign was *ineffectual*.

in-e-luc-ta-ble\in -i-'lək -tə-bəl\ ADJ. irresistible; not to be escaped. He felt that his fate was *ineluctable* and refused to make any attempt to improve his lot.

in-ept\in-'ept \ ADJ. unsuited; absurd; incompetent. The constant turmoil in the office proved that he was an *inept* administrator.

in-eq-ui-ty \(')in-'ek-wət-ē\ N. unfairness. In demanding equal pay for equal work, women protest the basic *inequity* of a system that gives greater financial rewards to men.

in-er-tia\in-'ər -shə\ N. state of being inert or indisposed to move. Our *inertia* in this matter may prove disastrous; we must move to aid our allies immediately.

in-ex-o-ra-ble \⁽'⁾in-'eks -(ə-)rə-bəl\ ADJ. relentless; unyielding; implacable. After listening to the pleas for clemency, the judge was *inexorable* and gave the convicted man the maximum punishment allowed by law.

in-fal-li-ble \⁽'⁾in-'fal -ə-bəl\ ADJ. unerring. We must remember that none of us is *infallible*.

in-fa-mous\'in -fə-məs\ ADJ. notoriously bad. Jesse James was an *infamous* outlaw.

---

in·fan·tile \ˈin-fən-ˌtīl\ ADJ. childish; extremely immature. When will he outgrow such *infantile* behavior?

in·fer \in-ˈfər\ v. deduce; conclude. We must be particularly cautious when we *infer* that a person is guilty on the basis of circumstantial evidence.

in·fer·ence \ˈin-f(ə-)rən(t)s\ N. conclusion drawn from data. I want you to check this *inference* because it may have been based on insufficient information.

in·fer·nal \in-ˈfərn-əl\ ADJ. pertaining to hell; devilish. They could think of no way to hinder his *infernal* scheme.

in·fi·del \ˈin-fəd-əl\ N. unbeliever. The Saracens made war against the *infidels*.

in·fin·i·tes·i·mal \(ı)in-ˌfin-ə-ˈtes -ə-məl\ ADJ. very small. In the twentieth century, physicists have made their greatest discoveries about the characteristics of *infinitesimal* objects like the atom and its parts.

in·fir·mi·ty \in-ˈfər -mət-ē\ N. weakness. His greatest *infirmity* was lack of willpower.

in·flat·ed \in-ˈflāt -əd\ ADJ. enlarged (with air or gas). After the balloons were *inflated*, they were distributed among the children.

in·flux \ˈin-ˌfləks\ N. flowing into. The *influx* of refugees into the country has taxed the relief agencies severely.

in·frac·tion \in-ˈfrak -shən\ N. violation. Because of his many *infractions* of school regulations, he was suspended by the dean.

in·fringe \in-ˈfrinj\ v. violate; encroach. I think your machine *infringes* on my patent.

in·ge·nue \ˈan -jə-nü\ N. an artless girl; an actress who plays such parts. Although she was forty, she still insisted that she be cast as an *ingenue* and refused to play more mature roles.

in·gen·u·ous \in-ˈjen -yə-wəs\ ADJ. naive; young; unsophisticated. These remarks indicate that you are *ingenuous* and unaware of life's harsher realities.

in·grate \ˈin -ˌgrāt\ N. ungrateful person. You are an *ingrate* since you have treated my gifts with scorn.

in·gra·ti·ate \in-ˈgrā -shē-ˌāt\ v. become popular with. He tried to *ingratiate* himself into her parents' good graces.

\ə\ abut	\ᵊ\ kitten, F table	\ər\ further	\a\ ash	\ā\ ace	\ä\ cot, cart
\au̇\ out	\ch\ chin	\e\ bet	\ē\ easy	\g\ go	\i\ hit	\ī\ ice	\j\ job

in-her-ent \in-'hir -ənt\ ADJ. firmly established by nature or habit. His *inherent* love of justice compelled him to come to their aid.

in-hib-it \in-'hib -ət\ V. prohibit; restrain. The child was not *inhibited* in his responses. **in-hi-bi-tion** \,in -(h)ə-'bish -ən\ N.

in-im-i-cal \in-'im -i-kəl\ ADJ. unfriendly; hostile. She felt that they were *inimical* and were hoping for her downfall.

in-im-i-ta-ble \(')in-'im-ət-ə-bəl\ ADJ. matchless; not able to be imitated. We admire Auden for his *inimitable* use of language; he is one of a kind.

in-iq-ui-tous \in-'ik -wət-əs\ ADJ. unjust; wicked. I cannot approve of the *iniquitous* methods you used to gain your present position. **in-iq-ui-ty** \in-'ik -wət-ē\ N.

in-kling \'iŋ -kliŋ\ N. hint. This came as a complete surprise to me as I did not have the slightest *inkling* of your plans.

in-nate \in-'āt \ ADJ. inborn. His *innate* talent for music was soon recognized by his parents.

in-noc-u-ous \in-'äk -yə-wəs\ ADJ. harmless. Let him drink it; it is *innocuous*.

in-no-va-tion \,in -ə-'vā -shən\ N. change; introduction of something new. He loved *innovations* just because they were new.

in-nu-en-do \,in -yə-'wen -,dō\ N. hint; insinuation. I resent the *innuendos* in your statement more than the statement itself.

in-op-por-tune \(,)in-,äp-ər-'t(y)ün\ ADJ. untimely; poorly chosen. A rock concert is an *inopportune* setting for a quiet conversation.

in-or-di-nate \in-'ȯrd -ᵊn-ət\ ADJ. unrestrained; excessive. She had an *inordinate* fondness for candy.

in-sa-tia-ble \(')in-'sā -shə-bəl\ ADJ. not easily satisfied; greedy. His thirst for knowledge was *insatiable;* he was always in the library.

in-scru-ta-ble \in-'skrüt -ə-bəl\ ADJ. incomprehensible; not to be discovered. I fail to understand the reasons for your outlandish behavior; your motives are *inscrutable*.

in-sen-sate \(')in-'sen -,sāt\ ADJ. without feeling. He lay there as *insensate* as a log.

\ŋ\ **sing** \ō\ **go** \ȯ\ **law** \ȯi\ **boy** \th\ **thin** \th\ **the** \ü\ **loot** \u̇\ **foot**
\y\ **yet** \zh\ **vision** \á, k̲, ⁿ, œ, œ̄, ue, ūe, ʸ\ *see* Pronunciation Symbols

in-sid-i-ous\in-'sid -ē-əs\ ADJ. treacherous; stealthy; sly. The fifth column is *insidious* because it works secretly within our territory for our defeat.

in-sin-u-ate\in-'sin -yə-ˌwāt\ V. hint; imply. What are you trying to *insinuate* by that remark?

in-sip-id \in-'sip -əd\ ADJ. tasteless; dull. I am bored by your *insipid* talk.

in-so-lent \'in(t) -s(ə-)lənt\ ADJ. haughty and contemptuous. I resent your *insolent* manner.

in-sol-ven-cy\⁽¹⁾in-'säl -vən-sē\ N. bankruptcy; lack of ability to repay debts. When rumors of his *insolvency* reached his creditors, they began to press him for payment of the money due them.

in-som-ni-a\in-'säm -nē-ə\ N. wakefulness; inability to sleep. He refused to join us in a midnight cup of coffee because he claimed it gave him *insomnia*.

in-sou-ci-ant\in-'sü -sē-ənt\ ADJ. indifferent; without concern or care. Your *insouciant* attitude at such a critical moment indicates that you do not understand the gravity of the situation.

in-sti-gate\'in(t) -stə-ˌgāt\ V. urge; start; provoke. I am afraid that this statement will *instigate* a revolt.

in-su-lar\'in(t)s -(y)ə-lər\ ADJ. like an island; narrow-minded. In an age of such rapid means of communication, we cannot afford to be hemmed in by such *insular* ideas.

in-su-per-a-ble\⁽¹⁾in-'sü -p(ə-)rə-bəl\ ADJ. insurmountable; invincible. In the face of *insuperable* difficulties they maintained their courage and will to resist.

in-sur-gent\in-'sər -jənt\ ADJ. rebellious. We will not discuss reforms until the *insurgent* troops have returned to their homes. also N.

in-te-grate \'int -ə-ˌgrāt \ V. make whole; combine; make into one unit. He tried to *integrate* all their activities into one program.

in-teg-ri-ty \in-'teg -rət-ē\ N. wholeness; purity; uprightness. He was a man of great *integrity*.

in-tel-lect\'int -ᵊl-ˌekt\ N. higher mental powers. He thought college would develop his *intellect*.

\ə\ abut   \ᵊ\ kitten, F table   \ər\ further   \a\ ash   \ā\ ace   \ä\ cot, cart
\aú\ out   \ch\ chin   \e\ bet   \ē\ easy   \g\ go   \i\ hit   \ī\ ice   \j\ job

in-tel-li-gen-tsia\in-tel -ə-'jen(t) -sē-ə\ N. the intelligent and educated classes [often used derogatorily]. He preferred discussions about sports and politics to the literary conversations of the *intelligentsia*.

in-ter\in-'tər\ v. bury. They are going to *inter* the body tomorrow.

in-ter-dict\int -ər-'dikt\ v. prohibit; forbid. Civilized nations must *interdict* the use of nuclear weapons if we expect our society to live. **in-ter-dict**\'int -ər-ˌdikt\ N.

in-ter-im\'int -ə-rəm\ N. meantime. The company will not consider our proposal until next week; in the *interim*, let us proceed as we have in the past. also ADJ.

in-ter-loc-u-to-ry \ˌint -ər-'läk -yə-ˌtōr -ē\ ADJ. conversational; intermediate, not final. This *interlocutory* decree is only a temporary setback; the case has not been settled.

in-ter-ment\in-'tər -mənt\ N. burial. *Interment* will take place in the church cemetery at 2 P.M. Wednesday.

in-ter-mi-na-ble \⁽'⁾in-'tərm -(ə-)nə-bəl\ ADJ. endless. Although his speech lasted for only twenty minutes, it seemed *interminable* to his bored audience.

in-ter-mit-tent\ˌint -ər-'mit -ᵊnt\ADJ. periodic; on and off. Our picnic was marred by *intermittent* rains.

in-ter-ne-cine\ˌint -ər-'nes -ˌēn \ ADJ. mutually destructive. The rising death toll on both sides indicates the *internecine* nature of this conflict.

in-ter-stic-es \in-'tər -stə-ˌsēz \ N. chinks; crevices. The mountain climber sought to obtain a foothold in the *interstices* of the cliff.

in-ti-mate\'int -ə-ˌmāt\ v. hint. She *intimated* rather than stated her preferences. **in-ti-mate**\'int -ə-mət\ADJ, N.

in-tim-i-da-tion\in-ˌtim -ə-ˌdā -shən\N. fear. A ruler who maintains his power by *intimidation* is bound to develop clandestine resistance.

in-trac-ta-ble\⁽'⁾in-'trak -tə-bəl\ADJ. unruly; refractory. The horse was *intractable* and refused to enter the starting gate.

in-tran-si-gence\in-'tran(t)s -ə-jən(t)s\N. state of stubborn unwillingness to compromise. The *intransigence* of both parties in the dispute makes an early settlement almost impossible to obtain.

\ŋ\ **sing**   \ō\ **go**   \o\ **law**   \oi\ **boy**   \th\ **thin**   \th\ **the**   \ü\ **loot**   \u\ **foot**
\y\ **yet**   \zh\ **vision**   \à, ḵ, ⁿ, œ, œ̄, ue, ūe, ᵊ\ *see* Pronunciation Symbols

in·tran·si·gent\in-'tran(t)s -ə-jənt\ADJ. refusing any compromise. The strike settlement has collapsed because both sides are *intransigent*.

in·trep·id\in-'trep -əd\ADJ. fearless. For his *intrepid* conduct in battle, he was promoted.

in·trin·sic\in-'trin -zik\ADJ. belonging to a thing in itself; inherent. Although the *intrinsic* value of this award is small, I shall always cherish it.

in·tro·vert\'in -trə-ɣərt\N. one who is introspective; inclined to think more about oneself. In his poetry, he reveals that he is an *introvert* by his intense interest in his own problems. also v.

in·trude\in-'trüd\V. trespass; enter as an uninvited person. He hesitated to *intrude* on their conversation.

in·tu·i·tion\in -t(y)ú-'ish -ən\N. power of knowing without reasoning. She claimed to know the truth by *intuition*. **in·tu·i·tive**\in-'t(y)ü-ət-iv\ADJ.

in·un·date\'in -ₜₒn-ₜdāt\V. overflow; flood. The tremendous waves *inundated* the town.

in·ure\in-'(y)ú(ə)r\V. accustom; harden. He was *inured* to the Alaskan cold.

in·val·i·date\ⁱⁱin-'val -ə-ₜdāt\V. weaken; destroy. The relatives who received little or nothing sought to *invalidate* the will by claiming that the deceased had not been in his right mind when he had signed the document.

in·vec·tive\in-'vek -tiv\N. abuse. He had expected criticism but not the *invective* which greeted his proposal.

in·veigh\in-'vā\V. denounce; utter censure or invective. He *inveighed* against the demagoguery of the previous speaker and urged that the audience reject his philosophy as dangerous.

in·vei·gle\in-'vā -gəl\V. lead astray; wheedle. He was *inveigled* into joining the club.

in·verse\ⁱⁱin-'vərs\ADJ. opposite. There is an *inverse* ratio between the strength of light and its distance. **in·verse** \'in -ɣərs\N.

in·vet·er·ate\in-'vet -ə-rət\ADJ. deep-rooted; habitual. He is an *inveterate* smoker.

\ə\ abut   \ᵊ\ kitten, F table   \ər\ **further**   \a\ **ash**   \ā\ **ace**   \ä\ cot, cart
\aú\ **out**   \ch\ **chin**   \e\ **bet**   \ē\ **easy**   \g\ **go**   \i\ **hit**   \ī\ **ice**   \j\ **job**

in-vid-i-ous\in-'vid -ē-əs\ADJ. designed to create ill will or envy. We disregarded her *invidious* remarks because we realized how jealous she was.

in-vin-ci-ble\(')in-'vin(t)-sə-bəl\ADJ. unconquerable. Superman is *invincible.*

in-vi-o-la-bil-i-ty \(')in-ˌvī -ə-lə-'bil -ət-ē\ N. security from being destroyed, corrupted or profaned. They respected the *inviolability* of her faith and did not try to change her manner of living.

in-voke\in-'vōk\v. call upon; ask for. She *invoked* her advisor's aid in filling out her financial aid forms.

in-vul-ner-a-ble \(')in-'vəln -(ə-)rə-bəl\ ADJ. incapable of injury. Achilles was *invulnerable* except in his heel.

i-o-ta\ī-'ōt -ə\ N. very small quantity. He hadn't an *iota* of common sense.

ir-as-ci-ble\ir-'as -ə-bəl\ADJ. irritable; easily angered. His *irascible* temper frightened me.

irate\ī-'rāt\ADJ. angry. When John's mother found out he had overdrawn his checking account for the third month in a row, she was so *irate* she could scarcely speak to him.

ir-i-des-cent \ˌir -ə-'des -ᵊnt\ ADJ. exhibiting rainbowlike colors. He admired the *iridescent* hues of the oil that floated on the surface of the water.

irk-some \'ərk -səm\ ADJ. repetitious; tedious. He found working on the assembly line *irksome* because of the monotony of the operation he had to perform.

i-ron-i-cal \ī-'rän -i-kəl\ ADJ. resulting in an unexpected and contrary manner. It is *ironical* that his success came when he least wanted it.

i-ro-ny\'ī -rə-nē\N. hidden sarcasm or satire; use of words that convey a meaning opposite to the literal meaning. Gradually his listeners began to realize that the excessive praise he was lavishing was merely *irony;* he was actually denouncing his opponent.

ir-rec-on-cil-able\ˌ(ˌ)ir-ˌ(r)ek -ənˈsī -lə-bəl\ADJ. incompatible; not able to be resolved. Because the separated couple were *irreconcilable,* the marriage counselor recommended a divorce.

\ŋ\ sing   \ō\ go   \ȯ\ law   \ȯi\ boy   \th\ thin   \th̲\ the   \ü\ loot   \u̇\ foot
\y\ yet   \zh\ vision   \à, k̲, ⁿ, œ, œ̅, ue, ue̅, ʸ\ *see* Pronunciation Symbols

ir-rel-e-vant\⁽ʼ⁾ir-ʹ(r)el -ə-vənt\ ADJ. not applicable; unrelated. This statement is *irrelevant* and should be disregarded by the jury.

ir-re-me-di-a-ble\ir -i-ʹmēd -ē-ə-bəl\ ADJ. incurable; uncorrectable. The error he made was *irremediable*.

ir-rep-a-ra-ble\⁽ʼ⁾ir-ʹ(r)ep -(ə-)rə-bəl\ ADJ. not able to be corrected or repaired. Your apology cannot atone for the *irreparable* damage you have done to his reputation.

ir-rev-er-ent\⁽ʼ⁾ir-ʹ(r)ev -(ə-)rənt\ ADJ. lacking proper respect. The worshippers resented his *irreverent* remarks about their faith.

ir-rev-o-ca-ble\⁽ʼ⁾ir-ʹ(r)ev -ə-kə-bəl\ ADJ. unalterable. Let us not brood over past mistakes since they are *irrevocable*.

i-so-tope\ʹī -sə-ˌtōp\ N. varying form of an element. The study of the *isotopes* of uranium led to the development of the nuclear bomb.

it-er-ate\ʹit -ə-ˌrāt\ V. utter a second time; repeat. I will *iterate* the warning I have previously given to you.

i-tin-er-ant\ī-ʹtin -ə-rənt\ ADJ. wandering; traveling. He was an *itinerant* peddler and traveled through Pennsylvania and Virginia selling his wares. also N.

i-tin-er-ar-y\ī-ʹtin -ə-ˌrer -ē\ N. plan of a trip. Before leaving for his first visit to France and England, he discussed his *itinerary* with people who had been there and with his travel agent.

\ə\ **abut**	\ᵊ\ **kitten, F table**	\ər\ **further**	\a\ **ash**	\ā\ **ace**	\ä\ **cot, cart**
\au̇\ **out**	\ch\ **chin**	\e\ **bet**	\ē\ **easy**	\g\ **go**	\i\ **hit**	\ī\ **ice**	\j\ **job**

–j–

jad-ed\\jād -əd\\ADJ. fatigued; surfeited. He looked for exotic foods to stimulate his *jaded* appetite.

jar-gon\\jär -gən\\N. language used by special group; gibberish. We tried to understand the *jargon* of the peddlers in the market-place but could not find any basis for comprehension.

jaun-diced\\jȯn -dəst\\ADJ. yellowed; prejudiced; envious. He gazed at the painting with *jaundiced* eyes.

jaunt\\'jȯnt\\N. trip; short journey. He took a quick *jaunt* to Atlantic City.

jaun-ty\\'jȯnt-ē\\ADJ. stylish; perky; carefree. She wore her beret at a *jaunty* angle.

je-june\\ji⸳jün\\ADJ. lacking interest; barren; meager. The plot of the play is *jejune* and fails to capture the interest of the audience.

jeop-ar-dy\\'jep -ərd-ē\\N. exposure to death or danger. He cannot be placed in double *jeopardy*.

jet-ti-son\\'jet -ə-sən\\V. throw overboard. In order to enable the ship to ride safely through the storm, the captain had to *jettison* much of his cargo. also N.

jin-go-ism\\'jiŋ -(ˌ)gō-ˌiz -əm\\N. extremely aggressive and militant patriotism. We must be careful to prevent a spirit of *jingoism* from spreading at this time; the danger of a disastrous war is too great.

jo-cose\\jō⸳kōs\\ADJ. giving to joking. The salesman was so *jocose* that many of his customers suggested that he become a "stand-up" comic.

joc-u-lar\\'jäk -yə-lər\\ADJ. said or done in jest. Do not take my *jocular* remarks seriously.

jo-cund\\'jäk -ənd\\ADJ. merry. Santa Claus is always vivacious and *jocund*.

ju-bi-la-tion\\ˌjü -bə⸳lā-shən\\N. rejoicing. There was great *jubilation* when the armistice was announced.

ju-di-cious\\jü⸳dish -əs\\ADJ. wise; determined by sound judgment. I believe that this plan is not *judicious;* it is too risky.

jug-ger-naut\\'jəg-ər-ˌnȯt\\N. irresistible crushing force. Nothing could survive in the path of the *juggernaut*.

---

jun-cture\\'jəŋ(k) -chər\\ N. crisis; joining point. At this critical *juncture*, let us think carefully before determining the course we shall follow.

jun-ket\\'jəŋ -kət\\ N. a merry feast or picnic. The opposition claimed that his trip to Europe was merely a political *junket*. also V.

jun-ta \\'hùn -tə\\ N. group of men joined in political intrigue; cabal. As soon as he learned of its existence, the dictator ordered the execution of all of the members of the *junta*.

ju-ris-pru-dence \\ ˌjùr -ə-'sprüd -ᵊn(t)s\\ N. science of law. He was more a student of *jurisprudence* than a practitioner of the law.

jux-ta-pose\\'jək -stə-ˌpōz \\ V. place side by side. Comparison will be easier if you *juxtapose* the two objects.

–k–

ka·lei·do·scope \kə'līd -ə͵skōp\ N. tube in which patterns made by the reflection in mirrors of colored pieces of glass, etc., produce interesting symmetrical effects. People found a new source of entertainment while peering through Sir David Brewster's invention, the *kaleidoscope;* they found the everchanging patterns fascinating.

ken \'ken\ N. range of knowledge. I cannot answer your question since this matter is beyond my *ken.*

kin·dred \'kin-drəd\ ADJ. related; similar in nature or character. Tom Sawyer and Huck Finn were two *kindred* spirits. also N.

ki·net·ic \kə'net -ik\ ADJ. producing motion. Designers of the electric automobile find that their greatest obstacle lies in the development of light and efficient storage batteries, the source of the *kinetic* energy needed to propel the vehicle.

ki·osk \kē ͵äsk\ N. summerhouse; open pavilion. She waited at the subway *kiosk.*

kis·met \'kiz ͵met\ N. fate. *Kismet* is the Arabic word for "fate."

kith \'kith\ N. familiar friends. He always helped both his *kith* and kin.

klep·to·ma·ni·ac \klep -tə-'mā -nē-͵ak\ N. person who has a compulsive desire to steal. They discovered that the wealthy customer was a *kleptomaniac* when they caught her stealing some cheap trinkets.

knav·ery \'nāv -(ə-)rē\ N. rascality. We cannot condone such *knavery* in public officials.

knead \'nēd\ V. mix; work dough. Her hands grew strong from *kneading* bread.

knell \'nel\ N. tolling of a bell at a funeral; sound of the funeral bell. "The curfew tolls the *knell* of parting day." also V.

knoll \'nōl\ N. little round hill. Robert Louis Stevenson's grave is on a *knoll* in Samoa.

---

lab-y-rinth\\lab -ə₁rin(t)th\ N. maze. Tom and Betty were lost in the *labyrinth* of secret caves.

lac-er-ate\\las -ə₁rāt\ V. mangle; tear. Her body was *lacerated* in the automobile crash. **lac-er-ate**\las -ə-rət\ADJ.

lach-ry-mose\\lak -rə₁mōs\ ADJ. producing tears. His voice has a *lachrymose* quality which is more appropriate at a funeral than a class reunion.

lack-a-dai-si-cal\\lak -ə-'dā -zi-kəl\ADJ. affectedly languid. He was *lackadaisical* and indifferent about his part in the affair.

lack-ey\\lak -ē\N. footman; toady. The duke was followed by his *lackeys*. also V.

lack-lus-ter\\'lak-₁ləs-tər\ADJ. dull. We were disappointed by the *lackluster* performance.

la-con-ic\lə'kän -ik\ADJ. brief and to the point. Will Rogers' *laconic* comments on the news made him world famous.

lag-gard\\lag -ərd\ADJ. slow; sluggish. The sailor had been taught not to be *laggard* in carrying out orders. also N.

la-gniappe\\lan ₁yap\ N. trifling present given to a customer. The butcher threw in some bones for the dog as a *lagniappe*.

la-goon\lə'gün\N. shallow body of water near a sea; lake. They enjoyed their swim in the calm *lagoon*.

la-i-ty\\'lā -ət-ē\N. laymen; persons not connected with the clergy. The *laity* does not always understand the clergy's problems.

lam-bent\\lam -bənt\ADJ. flickering; softly radiant. They sat quietly before the *lambent* glow of the fireplace.

lam-i-nat-ed\\'lam -ə₁nāt -əd\ADJ. made of thin plates or scales. Banded gneiss is a *laminated* rock.

lam-poon\lam'pün\ V. ridicule. This article *lampoons* the pretensions of some movie moguls. also N.

lan-guid\\'laŋ -gwəd\ADJ. weary; sluggish; listless. Her siege of illness left her *languid* and pallid.

lan-guish\\laŋ -gwish\V. lose animation; lose strength. In stories, lovelorn damsels used to *languish* and pine away.

---

lan-guor\\'laŋ -(g)ər\ N. lassitude; depression. His friends tried to overcome the *languor* into which he had fallen by taking him to parties and to the theater.

lank\\'laŋk\ ADJ. long and thin. *Lank*, gaunt, Abraham Lincoln was a striking figure.

lap-i-dar-y\\'lap -ə͵der -ē\ N. worker in precious stones. He employed a *lapidary* to cut the large diamond. also ADJ.

lar-ce-ny\\'lärs -nē\ N. theft. Because of the prisoner's record, the district attorney refused to reduce the charge from grand *larceny* to petit larceny.

lar-gess\lär-'zhes\ N. generous gift. Lady Bountiful distributed *largess* to the poor.

las-civ-i-ous\lə-'siv -ē-əs\ ADJ. lustful. The *lascivious* books were confiscated and destroyed.

las-si-tude\\'las -ə͵t(y)üd\ N. languor; weariness. The hot, tropical weather created a feeling of *lassitude* and encouraged drowsiness.

la-tent\\'lāt -ᵊnt\ ADJ. dormant; hidden. His *latent* talent was discovered by accident.

lat-er-al\\'lat -ə-rəl\ ADJ. coming from the side. In order to get good plant growth, the gardener must pinch off all *lateral* shoots. also N, V.

lat-i-tude\\'lat -ə͵t(y)üd\ N. freedom from narrow limitations. I think you have permitted your son too much *latitude* in this matter.

laud-a-ble\\'lȯd -ə-bəl\ ADJ. praiseworthy; commendable. His *laudable* deeds will be remembered by all whom he aided.

lau-da-to-ry\\'lȯd -ə͵tȯr -ē\ ADJ. expressing praise. The critics' *laudatory* comments helped to make her a star.

lave\\'lāv\ V. wash. The running water will *lave* away all stains.

lav-ish\\'lav -ish\ ADJ. liberal; wasteful. The actor's *lavish* gifts pleased her. also V.

lech-er-ous\\'lech -(ə-)rəs\ ADJ. impure in thought and act; lustful; unchaste. He is a *lecherous* and wicked old man.

\ŋ\ **sing**	\ō\ **go**	\ȯ\ **law**	\ȯi\ **boy**	\th\ **thin**	\th̲\ **the**	\ü\ **loot**	\u̇\ **foot**
\y\ **yet**	\zh\ **vision**	\à, k̲, ⁿ, œ, ō̄e, ue, ū̄e, ʸ\ *see* Pronunciation Symbols

lech-er-y \\'lech -(ə-)rē\ N. gross lewdness; lustfulness. In his youth he led a life of *lechery* and debauchery; he did not mend his ways until middle age.

lec-tern \\'lek -tərn\ N. reading desk. The chaplain delivered his sermon from a hastily improvised *lectern*.

lee-way \\'lē-‚wā\ N. room to move; margin. When you set a deadline, allow a little *leeway*.

leg-a-cy \\'leg-ə-sē\ N. a gift made by a will; anything handed down from the past. Part of my *legacy* from my parents is an album of family photographs.

leg-end \\'lej-ənd\ N. explanatory list of symbols on a map. The *legend* at the bottom of the map made it clear which symbols stood for rest areas along the highway and which stood for public camp sites. (secondary meaning)

leg-er-de-main \‚lej-ərd-ə-'mān\ N. sleight of hand. The magician demonstrated his renowned *legerdemain*.

le-nien-cy \\'lē-nē-ən-sē\ N. mildness; permissiveness. Considering the gravity of the offense, we were surprised by the *leniency* of the sentence.

le-o-nine \\'lē-ə-‚nīn\ N. like a lion. He was *leonine* in his rage.

le-sion \\'lē -zhən\ N. unhealthy change in structure; injury. Many *lesions* are the result of disease.

le-thal \\'lē -thəl\ ADJ. deadly. It is unwise to leave *lethal* weapons where children may find them.

le-thar-gic \lə-'thär -jik\ ADJ. drowsy; dull. The stuffy room made him *lethargic*.

lev-i-ty \\'lev -ət-ē\ N. lightness. Such *levity* is improper on this serious occasion.

lewd \\'lüd\ ADJ. lustful. They found his *lewd* stories objectionable.

lex-i-cog-ra-pher \‚lek -sə-'käg -rə-fər\ N. compiler of a dictionary. The new dictionary is the work of many *lexicographers* who spent years compiling and editing the work.

lex-i-con \\'lek -sə-‚kän\ N. dictionary. I cannot find this word in any *lexicon* in the library.

\ə\ **abut**	\ᵊ\ **kitten, F table**	\ər\ **further**	\a\ **ash**	\ā\ **ace**	\ä\ **cot, cart**
\aú\ **out**	\ch\ **chin**	\e\ **bet**	\ē\ **easy**	\g\ **go**	\i\ **hit**	\ī\ **ice**	\j\ **job**

li-ai-son\\'lē -ə‚zän\\ N. officer who acts as go-between for two armies. As the *liaison*, he had to avoid offending the leaders of the two armies.

li-ba-tion\\lī -'bā-shən\\ N. drink. He offered a *libation* to the thirsty prisoner.

li-bel-ous\\'lī -b(ə-)ləs\\ ADJ. defamatory; injurious to the good name of a person. He sued the newspaper because of its *libelous* story.

lib-er-tine\\'lib -ər‚tēn\\ N. debauched person, roué. Although she was aware of his reputation as a *libertine*, she felt she could reform him and help him break his dissolute way of life. also ADJ.

li-bid-i-nous\\lə-'bid -°n-əs\\ ADJ. lustful. They objected to his *libidinous* behavior.

li-bi-do\\lə-'bēd -₍₎ō\\ N emotional urges behind human activity. The psychiatrist maintained that suppression of the *libido* often resulted in maladjustment and neuroses.

li-bret-to\\lə-'bret -₍₎ō\\ N. text of an opera. The composer of an opera's music is remembered more frequently than the author of its *libretto*.

li-cen-tious\\lī-'sen -chəs\\ ADJ. wanton; lewd; dissolute. The *licentious* monarch helped bring about his country's downfall.

lieu\\'lü\\ N. instead of. They accepted his check in *lieu* of cash.

lil-li-pu-tian\\‚lil-ə-'pyü-shən\\ ADJ. extremely small. The model was built on a *lilliputian* scale. also N.

lim-ber\\'lim-bər\\ ADJ. flexible. Hours of ballet classes kept him *limber*.

lim-bo\\'lim -₍₎bō\\ N. region near heaven or hell where certain souls are kept; a prison (slang). Among the divisions of Hell are Purgatory and *Limbo*.

lim-pid\\'lim -pəd\\ ADJ. clear. A *limpid* stream ran through his property.

lin-ea-ments\\'lin-ē-ə-mənts\\ N. features of the face. She quickly sketched the *lineaments* of his face.

| \\ŋ\\ **sing** | \\ō\\ **go** | \\ȯ\\ **law** | \\ȯi\\ **boy** | \\th\\ **thin** | \\t͟h\\ **the** | \\ü\\ **loot** | \\u̇\\ **foot** |
| \\y\\ **yet** | \\zh\\ **vision** | \\à, k̲, ⁿ, œ, œ̅, ue, ūe, ᵛ\\ *see* Pronunciation Symbols |

lin·guis·tic\liŋ-'gwis -tik\ADJ. pertaining to language. The modern tourist will encounter very little *linguistic* difficulty as English has become an almost universal language.

li·on·ize\ 'lī-ə-,nīz\ v. treat as a celebrity. She enjoyed being *lionized* and adored by the public.

liq·ui·date\'lik -wə,dāt\ v. settle accounts; clear up. He was able to *liquidate* all his debts in a short period of time.

list·less\'list-ləs\ADJ. lacking in spirit or energy. We had expected him to be full of enthusiasm and were surprised by his *listless* attitude.

lit·a·ny\'lit -ᵊn-ē\ N. supplicatory prayer. On this solemn day, the congregation responded to the prayers of the priest during the *litany* with fervor and intensity.

lithe\'līth\ ADJ. flexible; supple. Her figure was *lithe* and willowy.

lit·i·ga·tion\,lit -ə-'gā -shən\ N. lawsuit. Try to settle this amicably; I do not want to start *litigation*.

li·to·tes\'līt -ə-,tēz\ N. understatement for emphasis. To say, "He little realizes," when we mean that he does not realize at all, is an example of the kind of understatement we call *litotes*.

liv·id\'liv -əd\ADJ. lead-colored; black and blue; enraged. His face was so *livid* with rage that we were afraid he might have an attack of apoplexy.

loath\'lōth\ ADJ. averse; reluctant. They were both *loath* for him to go.

loathe\'lōth\ v. detest. We *loathed* the wicked villain.

lode\'lōd\ N. metal-bearing vein. If this *lode* which we have discovered extends for any distance, we have found a fortune.

lofty\'lòf-tē\ADJ. very high. They used to tease him about his *lofty* ambitions.

loi·ter\ 'lòit-ər\v. hang around; linger. The policeman told him not to *loiter* in the alley.

loll\ 'läl\v. lounge about. They *lolled* around in their chairs watching television.

---

lon·gev·i·ty \län·ˈjev -ət-ē\ N. long life. The old man was proud of his *longevity*.

lope \ˈlōp\ V. gallop slowly. As the horses *loped* along, we had an opportunity to admire the ever-changing scenery. also N.

lo·qua·cious \lō-ˈkwā -shəs\ ADJ. talkative. She is very *loquacious* and can speak on the telephone for hours.

lout \ˈlaut\ N. clumsy person. The delivery boy is an awkward *lout*.

lu·bric·i·ty \lü-ˈbris -ət-ē\ N. slipperiness; evasiveness. He exasperated the reporters by his *lubricity*; they could not pin him down to a definite answer.

lu·cent \ˈlüs -ᵊnt\ ADJ. shining. The moon's *lucent* rays silvered the river.

lu·cid \ˈlü -səd\ ADJ. bright; easily understood. His explanation was *lucid* and to the point.

lu·cra·tive \ˈlü -krət-iv\ ADJ. profitable. He turned his hobby into a *lucrative* profession.

lu·cre \ˈlü -kər\ N. money. Preferring *lucre* to fame, he wrote stories of popular appeal.

lu·di·crous \ˈlüd -ə-krəs\ ADJ. laughable; trifling. Let us be serious; this is not a *ludicrous* issue.

lu·gu·bri·ous \lù-ˈgü -brē-əs\ ADJ. mournful. The *lugubrious* howling of the dogs added to our sadness.

lu·mi·nous \ˈlü -mə-nəs\ ADJ. shining; issuing light. The sun is a *luminous* body.

lu·nar \ˈlü -nər\ ADJ. pertaining to the moon. *Lunar* craters can be plainly seen with the aid of a small telescope.

lu·rid \ˈlùr -əd\ ADJ. wild; sensational. The *lurid* stories he told shocked his listeners.

lus·cious \ˈləsh -əs\ ADJ. pleasing to taste or smell. The ripe peach was *luscious*.

lus·ter \ˈləs -tər\ N. shine; gloss. The soft *luster* of the silk in the dim light was pleasing. also N.

lus·trous \ˈləs -trəs\ ADJ. shining. Her large and *lustrous* eyes gave a touch of beauty to an otherwise drab face.

lux·u·ri·ant \(ˌ)ləg-ˈzhùr -ē-ənt\ ADJ. fertile; abundant; ornate. Farming was easy in this *luxuriant* soil.

−m−

ma·ca·bre \mə-'käb(-rə)\ ADJ. gruesome; grisly. The city morgue is a *macabre* spot for the uninitiated.

mac·er·ate \'mas -ə-ˌrāt\ V. to soften by soaking or steeping. The leaves were *macerated* by the damp, boggy soil.

Ma·chi·a·vel·lian \ˌmak -ē-ə-'vel -ē-ən\ ADJ. crafty; double-dealing. I do not think he will be a good ambassador because he is not accustomed to the *Machiavellian* maneuverings of foreign diplomats.

mach·i·na·tion \ˌmak -ə-'nā -shən\ N. scheme. I can see through your wily *machinations*.

mad·ri·gal \'mad -ri-gəl\ N. pastoral song. His program of folk songs included several *madrigals* which he sang to the accompaniment of a lute.

mael·strom \'mā(ə)l -strəm\ N. whirlpool. The canoe was tossed about in the *maelstrom*.

mag·nan·i·mous \mag-'nan -ə-məs\ ADJ. generous. The philanthropist was most *magnanimous*.

mag·nate \'mag -ˌnāt\ N. person of prominence or influence. The steel *magnate* decided to devote more time to city politics.

mag·nil·o·quent \mag-'nil -ə-kwənt\ ADJ. boastful, pompous. In their stories of the trial, the reporters ridiculed the *magniloquent* speeches of the defense attorney.

mag·ni·tude \'mag -nə-ˌt(y)üd\ N. greatness; extent. It is difficult to comprehend the *magnitude* of his crime.

maim \'mām\ V. mutilate; injure. The hospital could not take care of all who had been wounded or *maimed* in the railroad accident.

mal·a·droit \ˌmal -ə-'dröit\ ADJ. clumsy; bungling. In his usual *maladroit* way, he managed to upset the cart and spill the food.

mal·aise \mə-'lāz\ N. uneasiness; distress. She felt a sudden vague *malaise* when she heard sounds at the door.

mal·a·prop·ism \'mal-ə-ˌpräp-ˌiz-əm\ N. comic misuse of a word. When Mrs. Malaprop criticizes Lydia for being "as headstrong as an allegory on the banks of the Nile," she confuses "allegory" and "alligator" in a typical *malapropism*.

---

mal-con-tent \ˌmal -kən-ˈtent\ N. person dissatisfied with existing state of affairs. He was one of the few *malcontents* in Congress; he constantly voiced his objections to the Presidential program, also ADJ.

mal-e-dic-tion \ˌmal -ə-ˈdik -shən\ N. curse. The witch uttered *maledictions* against her captors.

mal-e-fac-tor \ˈmal -əˌfak -tər\ N. criminal. We must try to bring these *malefactors* to justice.

ma-lev-o-lent \mə-ˈlev -ə-lənt\ ADJ. wishing evil. We must thwart his *malevolent* schemes.

ma-li-cious \mə-ˈlish -əs\ ADJ. dictated by hatred or spite. The *malicious* neighbor spread the gossip.

ma-lign \mə-ˈlīn\ V. speak evil of; defame. Because of her hatred of the family, she *maligns* all who are friendly to them. also ADJ.

ma-lig-nant \mə-ˈlig -nənt\ ADJ. having an evil influence; virulent. This is a *malignant* disease; we may have to use drastic measures to stop its spread.

ma-lin-ger-er \mə-ˈliŋ -gər-ər\ N. one who feigns illness to escape duty. The captain ordered the sergeant to punish all *malingerers*.

mall \ˈmȯl\ N. public walk. The *Mall* in Central Park has always been a favorite spot for Sunday strollers.

mal-le-a-ble \ˈmal -ē-ə-bəl\ ADJ. capable of being shaped by pounding. Gold is a *malleable* metal.

mam-mal \ˈmam -əl\ N. a vertebrate animal whose female suckles its young. Many people regard the whale as a fish and do not realize that it is a *mammal*.

mam-moth \ˈmam -əth\ ADJ. gigantic. The *mammoth* corporations of the twentieth century are a mixed blessing. also N.

man-date \ˈman ˌdāt\ N. order; charge. In his inaugural address, the President stated that he had a *mandate* from the people to seek an end to social evils such as poverty, poor housing, etc. also V.

man-da-tory \ˈman -dəˌtōr -ē\ ADJ. obligatory. These instructions are *mandatory;* any violation will be severely punished.

\ŋ\ sing   \ō\ go   \ȯ\ law   \ȯi\ boy   \th\ thin   \t͟h\ the   \ü\ loot   \u̇\ foot
\y\ yet   \zh\ vision   \à, k̲, ⁿ, œ, œ̄, ue, ūe, ʳ\ *see* Pronunciation Symbols

mangy\'mān-jē\ ADJ. shabby; wretched. We finally threw out the *mangy* rug that the dog had destroyed.

ma-ni-a-cal\mə-'nī -ə-kəl\ ADJ. raving mad. His *maniacal* laughter frightened us.

man-i-fest\'man -ə͵fest\ ADJ. understandable; clear. His evil intentions were *manifest* and yet we could not stop him. also V, N.

man-i-fes-to\͵man -ə-'fes -(͵)tō\ N. declaration; statement of policy. This statement may be regarded as the *manifesto* of the party's policy.

man-i-fold\'man -ə͵fōld\ ADJ. numerous; varied. I cannot begin to tell you how much I appreciate your *manifold* kindnesses. also ADV, N.

ma-nip-u-late\mə-'nip -yə-͵lāt \ V. operate with the hands. How do you *manipulate* these puppets?

man-u-mit\͵man -yə-'mit\ V. emancipate; free from bondage. Enlightened slave owners were willing to *manumit* their slaves and thus put an end to the evil of slavery in the country.

ma-raud-er\mə-'ròd -ər\ N. raider; intruder. The sounding of the alarm frightened the *marauders*. **ma-raud**\mə-'ròd\ V.

mar-i-tal\'mar -ət-°l\ ADJ. pertaining to marriage. After the publication of his book on *marital* affairs, he was often consulted by married people on the verge of divorce.

mar-i-time\'mar -ə͵tīm\ ADJ. bordering on the sea; nautical. The *Maritime* Provinces depend on the sea for their wealth.

marred\'märd\ ADJ. damaged; disfigured. She had to refinish the *marred* surface of the table. **mar**\'mär\ V.

mar-row\'mar -(͵)ō\ N. soft tissue filling the bones. The frigid cold chilled the traveler to the *marrow*.

mar-su-pi-al\mär-'sü -pē-əl\ N. one of a family of mammals that nurse their offspring in a pouch. The most common *marsupial* in North America is the opossum. also ADJ.

mar-tial\'mär -shəl\ ADJ. warlike. The sound of *martial* music is always inspiring.

\ə\ abut   \ᵊ\ kitten, F table   \ər\ further   \a\ ash   \ā\ ace   \ä\ cot, cart
\aù\ out   \ch\ chin   \e\ bet   \ē\ easy   \g\ go   \i\ hit   \ī\ ice   \j\ job

mar-ti-net\ˌmärt -ᵊn-ˈet \ N. strict disciplinarian. The commanding officer was a *martinet* who observed each regulation to the letter.

mas-ti-cate\ˈmas -təˌkāt\ V. chew. We must *masticate* our food carefully and slowly in order to avoid stomach disorders.

ma-ter-nal\mə-ˈtərn -ᵊl\ADJ. motherly. Many animals display *maternal* instincts only while their offspring are young and helpless.

ma-tri-arch\ˈmā-trē-ˌärk \ N. woman who rules a family or larger social group. The *matriarch* ruled her gypsy tribe with a firm hand.

ma-tri-cide\ˈma -trəˌsīd \ N. murder of a mother by a child. A crime such as *matricide* is inconceivable.

ma-trix\ˈmā -triks\ N. mold or die. The cast around the *matrix* was cracked.

maud-lin\ˈmȯd -lən\ADJ. effusively sentimental. I do not like such *maudlin* pictures. I call them tearjerkers.

maul\ˈmȯl \ V. handle roughly. The rock star was *mauled* by his overexcited fans.

maun-der\ˈmȯn -dər\ V. talk incoherently; utter drivel. You do not make sense; you *maunder* and garble your words.

mau-so-le-um\ˌmȯ -sə-ˈlē -əm\ N. monumental tomb. His body was placed in the family *mausoleum*.

mauve\ˈmōv \ ADJ. pale purple. The *mauve* tint in the lilac bush was another indication that spring had finally arrived.

mav-er-ick\ˈmav-(ə)-rik \N. rebel; nonconformist. To the masculine literary establishment, George Sand with her insistence on wearing trousers and smoking cigars was clearly a *maverick* who fought her proper womanly role.

mawk-ish\ˈmȯ -kish\ADJ. sickening; insipid. Your *mawkish* sighs fill me with disgust.

max-im\ˈmak -səm\N. proverb; a truth pithily stated. Aesop's fables illustrate moral *maxims*.

| \ŋ\ sing | \ō\ go | \ȯ\ law | \ȯi\ boy | \th\ thin | \th\ the | \ü\ loot | \u̇\ foot |
| \y\ yet | \zh\ vision | \ä, k, ⁿ, œ, ōͤ, ue, ūͤ, ᵞ\ *see* Pronunciation Symbols |

may-hem\\'mā ˌhem\ N. injury to body. The riot was marked not only by *mayhem* with its attendant loss of life and limb but also by arson and pillage.

mea-ger\'mē-gər\ADJ. scanty; inadequate. His salary was far too *meager* for him to afford to buy a new car.

me-an-der\mē-'an -dər\v. to wind or turn in its course. It is difficult to sail up this stream because of the way it *meanders* through the countryside. also N.

med-dle-some\'med -ᵊl-səm\ADJ. interfering. He felt his marriage was suffering because of his *meddlesome* mother-in-law.

me-di-ate\'mēd -ē-ˌāt\ v. settle a dispute through the services of an outsider. Let us *mediate* our differences rather than engage in a costly strike. **me-di-ate**\'mēd-ē-ət\ADJ.

me-di-o-cre\ˌmēd -ē-'ō -kər\ADJ. ordinary; commonplace. We were disappointed because he gave a rather *mediocre* performance in this role.

med-i-ta-tion\ˌmed -ə-'tā -shən\N. reflection; thought. She reached her decision only after much *meditation*.

med-ley\'med -lē\N. mixture. The band played a *medley* of Gershwin tunes.

meg-a-lo-ma-nia\ˌmeg-ə-lō-'mā-nē-ə\N. mania for doing grandiose things. Developers who spend millions trying to build the world's tallest skyscraper suffer from *megalomania*.

mé-lange\mā-'län zh\ N. medley; miscellany. This anthology provides a *mélange* of the author's output in the fields of satire, criticism and political analysis.

me-lee\'mā ˌlā\ N. fight. The captain tried to ascertain the cause of the *melee* which had broken out among the crew members.

mel-lif-lu-ous\me-'lif -lə-wəs\ ADJ. flowing smoothly; smooth. Italian is a *mellifluous* language.

me-men-to\mi-'ment -ˌ(ˌ)ō\ N. token; reminder. Take this book as a *memento* of your visit.

me-mo-ri-al-ize\mə-'mōr -ē-ə-ˌlīz\ .v. commemorate. Let us *memorialize* his great contribution by dedicating this library in his honor.

\ə\ abut	\ᵊ\ kitten, F table	\ər\ further	\a\ ash	\ā\ ace	\ä\ cot, cart
\aü\ out	\ch\ chin	\e\ bet	\ē\ easy	\g\ go	\i\ hit	\ī\ ice	\j\ job

men·da·cious\men-dā -shəs\ ADJ. lying; false. He was a pathological liar, and his friends learned to discount his *mendacious* stories.

men·di·cant\'men -di-kənt\ N. beggar. From the moment we left the ship, we were surrounded by *mendicants* and peddlers. also ADJ.

me·ni·al\'mē-nē-əl\ADJ. suitable for servants; low. I cannot understand why a person of your ability and talent should engage in such *menial* activities. also N.

men·tor\'men -ˌtȯ(ə)r\ N. teacher, guide. During this very trying period, he could not have had a better *mentor,* for the teacher was sympathetic and understanding.

mer·can·tile\'mər -kən-ˌtēl\ ADJ. concerning trade. I am more interested in the opportunities available in the *mercantile* field than I am in those in the legal profession.

mer·ce·nar·y\'mərs -ᵊn-ˌer -ē\ADJ. interested in money or gain. I am certain that your action was prompted by *mercenary* motives. also N.

mer·cu·ri·al\₍ᵢ₎mər-ᴊkyùr -ē-əl\ ADJ. fickle; changing. He was of a *mercurial* temperament and therefore unpredictable.

mer·e·tri·cious\ˌmer -ə-ᴊtrish -əs\ADJ. flashy; tawdry. Her jewels were inexpensive but not *meretricious.*

me·sa\'mā -sə\ N. high, flat-topped hill. The *mesa,* rising above the surrounding desert, was the most conspicuous feature of the area.

mes·mer·ize\'mez -mə-ˌrīz\ V. hypnotize. The incessant drone seemed to *mesmerize* him and place him in a hypnotic trance.

met·al·lur·gi·cal\ˌmet -ᵊl-ᵊr -ji-kəl\ADJ. pertaining to the art of removing metals from ores. During the course of his *metallurgical* research, the scientist developed a steel alloy of tremendous strength.

met·a·mor·pho·sis\ˌmet -ə-ᴊmȯr -fə-səs\ N. change of form. The *metamorphosis* of caterpillar to butterfly is typical of many such changes in animal life.

met·a·phor \'met -ə-ˌfȯ(ə)r\ N. implied comparison. "He soared like an eagle" is an example of a simile; "He is an eagle in flight," a *metaphor.*

\ŋ\ sing   \ō\ go   \ȯ\ law   \ȯi\ boy   \th\ thin   \th\ the   \ü\ loot   \ù\ foot
\y\ yet   \zh\ vision   \à, k̲, ⁿ, œ, œ̄, ue, ūe, ᴿ\ *see* Pronunciation Symbols

met·a·phys·i·cal \\,met -ə-ˈfiz -i-kəl\\ ADJ. pertaining to speculative philosophy. The modern poets have gone back to the fanciful poems of the *metaphysical* poets of the seventeenth century for many of their images. **met·a·phys·ics**\\,met -ə-ˈfiz -ik\\ N.

mete\\ˈmēt \\ V. measure; distribute. He tried to be impartial in his efforts to *mete* out justice.

me·thod·i·cal\\mə-ˈthäd-i-kəl\\ADJ. systematic. An accountant must be *methodical* and maintain order among his financial records.

me·tic·u·lous\\mə-ˈtik -yə-ləs\\ADJ. excessively careful. He was *meticulous* in checking his accounts.

me·trop·o·lis \\mə-ˈträp -(ə-)ləs\\ N. large city. Every evening this terminal is filled with the thousands of commuters who are going from this *metropolis* to their homes in the suburbs.

met·tle\\ˈmet -ᵊl\\ N. courage; spirit. When challenged by the other horses in the race, the thoroughbred proved its *mettle* by its determination to hold the lead.

mi·as·ma\\mī-ˈaz -mə\\N. swamp gas; odor of decaying matter. I suspect that this area is infested with malaria as I can readily smell the *miasma*.

mi·cro·cosm\\ˈmī -krə-ˌkäz -əm\\N. small world. In the *microcosm* of our small village, we find illustrations of all the evils that beset the universe.

mien\\ˈmēn \\ N. demeanor; bearing. She had the gracious *mien* of a queen.

mi·grant\\ˈmī -grənt\\ADJ. changing its habitat; wandering. These *migrant* birds return every spring. also N.

mi·gra·to·ry\\ˈmī -grə-ˌtōr -ē\\ADJ. wandering. The return of the *migratory* birds to the northern sections of this country is a harbinger of spring.

mi·lieu\\mēl-ˈyə(r) \\ N. environment; means of expression. His *milieu* is watercolor although he has produced excellent oil paintings and lithographs.

mil·i·tant\\ˈmil -ə-tənt\\ADJ. combative; bellicose. Although at this time he was advocating a policy of neutrality, one could usually find him adopting a more *militant* attitude. also N.

mil·i·tate\\'mil -ə-ˌtāt \ v. work against. Your record of lateness and absence will *militate* against your chances of promotion.

mil·len·ni·um \mə-ˈlen -ē-əm\ N. thousand-year period; period of happiness and prosperity. I do not expect the *millennium* to come during my lifetime.

mim·ic·ry\\'mim-i-krē\N. imitation. Her gift for *mimicry* was so great that her friends said that she should be in the theater.

min·a·ret\ˌmin -ə-ˈret\ N. slender tower attached to a mosque. From the balcony of the *minaret* we obtained an excellent view of the town and the neighboring countryside.

mi·na·to·ry \'min -ə-ˌtōr -ē\ ADJ. threatening. All abusive and *minatory* letters received by the mayor and other public officials were examined by the police.

minc·ing \'min(t) -siŋ\ ADJ. affectedly dainty. Yum-Yum walked across the stage with *mincing* steps.

min·ion\'min -yən\N. a servile dependent. He was always accompanied by several of his *minions* because he enjoyed their subservience and flattery.

mi·nu·ti·ae \mə-ˈn(y)ü-shē-ˌē\N. petty details. She would have liked to ignore the *minutiae* of daily living.

mi·rage \mə-ˈräzh\ N. unreal reflection; optical illusion. The lost prospector was fooled by a *mirage* in the desert.

mire\\'mī(ə)r\v. entangle; stick in swampy ground. Their rear wheels became *mired* in mud. also N.

mirth\'mərth\N. merriment; laughter. Sober Malvolio found Sir Toby's *mirth* improper.

mis·ad·ven·ture\ˌmis -əd-ˈven -chər\ N. mischance; ill luck. The young explorer met death by *misadventure*.

mis·an·thrope \'mis -ᵊn̩ˌthrōp \ N. one who hates mankind. We thought the hermit was a *misanthrope* because he shunned our society.

mis·ap·pre·hen·sion \ˌ(ˌ)mis͵ap -riˈhen -chən\ N. error; misunderstanding. To avoid *misapprehension*, I am going to ask all of you to repeat the instructions I have given.

mis·ce·ge·na·tion\ˌ(ˌ)mis͵ej -ə-ˈnā -shən\N. intermarriage between races. Some states passed laws against *miscegenation*.

\ŋ\ **sing**   \ō\ **go**   \o\̇ **law**   \o\̇i **boy**   \th\ **thin**   \t̲h̲\ **the**   \ü\ **loot**   \u\̇ **foot**
\y\ **yet**   \zh\ **vision**   \à, ḵ, ⁿ, œ, œ̄, ue, ūe, ᵞ\ *see* Pronunciation Symbols

mis-cel-la-ny\\'mis -ə-ͺlā -nē\\ N. mixture of writings on various subjects. This is an interesting *miscellany* of nineteenth-century prose.

mis-chance\\⁽¹⁾mis(h)-ͺ'chan(t)s \\ N. ill luck. By *mischance*, he lost his week's salary.

mis-con-strue\\ͺmis-kən-'strü\\ V. interpret incorrectly; misjudge. She took the passage seriously rather than humorously because she *misconstrued* the author's ironic tone.

mis-cre-ant\\'mis -krē-ənt\\ N. wretch; villain. His kindness to the *miscreant* amazed all of us who had expected to hear severe punishment pronounced. also ADJ.

mis-de-mean-or\\ͺmis -di-'mē -nər\\ N. minor crime. The culprit pleaded guilty to a *misdemeanor* rather than face trial for a felony.

mis-giv-ing\\⁽¹⁾mis-ͺ'giv -iŋ\\ N. doubt about a future event. Hamlet described his *misgivings* to Horatio but decided to fence with Laertes despite his foreboding of evil.

mis-hap\\'mis ͺ-hap\\ N. accident. With a little care you could have avoided this *mishap*.

mis-no-mer\\⁽¹⁾mis-'nō -mər\\ N. wrong name; incorrect designation. His tyrannical conduct proved to all that his nickname, King Eric the Just, was a *misnomer*.

mi-sog-a-my\\'mə-'sä-ga-mē\\ N. hatred of marriage. He remained a bachelor not because of *misogamy* but because of ill fate; his fiancee died before the wedding.

mi-sog-y-nist\\mə-'säj -ə-nəst\\ N. hater of women. She accused him of being a *misogynist* because he had been a bachelor all his life.

mis-sile\\'mis -əl\\ N. object to be thrown or projected. Scientists are experimenting with guided *missiles*. also ADJ.

mis-sive\\'mis-iv\\ N. letter. The ambassador received a *missive* from the Secretary of State.

mite\\'mīt \\ N. very small object or creature; small coin. The criminal was so heartless that he even stole the widow's *mite*.

mit-i-gate\\'mit -ə-ͺgāt \\ V. appease. Nothing he did could *mitigate* her wrath; she was unforgiving.

---

mne-mon-ic \ni-'män-ik\ ADJ. pertaining to memory. He used *mnemonic* tricks to master new words. also N.

mo-bile \'mō -bəl\ ADJ. movable; not fixed. The *mobile* blood bank operated by the Red Cross visited our neighborhood today. **mo-bil-i-ty** \mō-'bil -ət-ē\ N.

mode \'mōd\ N. prevailing style. She was not used to their lavish *mode* of living.

mod-i-cum \'mäd -i-kəm\ N. limited quantity. Although his story is based on a *modicum* of truth, most of the events he describes are fictitious.

mod-ish \'mōd -ish\ ADJ. fashionable. She always discarded all garments which were no longer *modish*.

mod-u-la-tion \,mäj -ə-'lā -shən\ N. toning down; changing from one key to another. When she spoke, it was with quiet *modulation* of voice.

mo-gul \'mō-(,)gəl\ N. powerful person. The oil *moguls* made great profits when the price of gasoline rose.

moi-e-ty \'mȯi -ət-ē\ N. half; part. There is a *moiety* of the savage in her personality which is not easily perceived by those who do not know her well.

mol-e-cule \'mäl -i-₁kyü(ə)l\ N. the smallest part of a homogeneous substance. In chemistry, we study how atoms and *molecules* react to form new substances.

mol-li-fy \'mäl -ə-₁fī\ V. soothe. We tried to *mollify* the hysterical child by promising her many gifts.

molt \'mōlt\ V. shed or cast off hair or feathers. The male robin *molted* in the spring. also N.

mol-ten \'mōlt -ᵊn\ ADJ. melted. The city of Pompeii was destroyed by volcanic ash rather than by *molten* lava flowing from Mount Vesuvius.

mo-men-tous \mō-'ment -əs\ ADJ. very important. On this *momentous* occasion, we must be very solemn.

mo-men-tum \mō-'ment -əm\ N. quantity of motion of a moving body; impetus. The car lost *momentum* as it tried to ascend the steep hill.

mon-ar-chy \'män-ər-kē\ N. government under a single ruler. England today remains a *monarchy*.

\ŋ\ sing   \ō\ go   \ȯ\ law   \ȯi\ boy   \th\ thin   \t̲h̲\ the   \ü\ loot   \u̇\ foot
\y\ yet   \zh\ vision   \à, k̲, ⁿ, œ, œ̄, ue, ūe, ʸ\ *see* Pronunciation Symbols

mo-nas-tic \mə-'nas-tik\ ADJ. related to monks. Wanting to live a religious life, he took his *monastic* vows.

mon-e-tar-y \'män -ə,ter -ē\ ADJ. pertaining to money. She was in complete charge of all *monetary* matters affecting the household.

mono-lith-ic \,män-əl-'ith-ik\ ADJ. solidly uniform; unyielding. The patriots sought to present a *monolithic* front.

mon-o-the-ism \'män -ə-(,)thē-,iz -əm\ N. belief in one God. Abraham was the first to proclaim his belief in *monotheism*.

mo-not-o-ny \mə-'nät-ᵊn-ē\ N. sameness leading to boredom. He took a clerical job, but soon grew to hate the *monotony* of his daily routine.

mon-u-men-tal \,män-yə-'ment-ᵊl\ ADJ. massive. Writing a dictionary is a *monumental* task.

mood-i-ness \'müd -ē-nəs\ N. fits of depression or gloom. We could not discover the cause of his recurrent *moodiness*.

moor \'mu̇(ə)r\ N. marshy wasteland. These *moors* can only be used for hunting; they are too barren for agriculture. also V.

moot \'müt\ ADJ. debatable. Our tariff policy is a *moot* subject.

mor-a-to-ri-um \,mȯr -ə-ᵗōr -ē-əm\ N. legal delay of payment. If we declare a *moratorium* and delay collection of debts for six months, I am sure the farmers will be able to meet their bills.

mor-bid \'mȯr -bəd\ ADJ. given to unwholesome thought; gloomy. These *morbid* speculations are dangerous; we must lighten our thinking by emphasis on more pleasant matters.

mor-dant \'mȯrd -ᵊnt\ ADJ. biting; sarcastic; stinging. Actors feared the critic's *mordant* pen.

mo-res \'mȯ(ə)r ,āz\ N. customs. The *mores* of Mexico are those of Spain with some modifications.

mor-i-bund \'mȯr -ə-(,)bənd\ ADJ. at the point of death. The doctors called the family to the bedside of the *moribund* patient.

---

mo·rose\mə-'rōs\ ADJ. ill-humored; sullen. When we first meet Hamlet, we find him *morose* and depressed.

mor·ti·cian \mȯr-'tish-ən\ N. undertaker. The *mortician* prepared the corpse for burial.

mor·ti·fy\'mȯrt-ə-ˌfī\ V. humiliate; punish the flesh. She was so *mortified* by her blunder that she ran to her room in tears.

mote\'mōt\ N. small speck. The tiniest *mote* in the eye is very painful.

mo·tif\mō-'tēf\ N. theme. This simple *motif* runs throughout the entire score.

mot·ley \'mät-lē\ ADJ. parti-colored; mixed. The captain had gathered a *motley* crew to sail the vessel.

mot·tled\'mät-əld\ADJ. spotted. When he blushed, his face took on a *mottled* hue.

moun·te·bank\'maùnt-i-ˌbaŋk\ N. charlatan; boastful pretender. The patent medicine man was a *mountebank*.

mud·dle\'məd-əl\V. confuse; mix up. His thoughts were *muddled* and chaotic. also N.

mug·gy \'məg-ē\ ADJ. warm and damp. August in New York City is often *muggy*.

mug·wump\'məg-ˌwəmp\ N. defector from a party. When he refused to support his party's nominees, he was called a *mugwump* and deprived of his seniority privileges in Congress.

mulct\'məlkt\ V. defraud a person of something. The lawyer was accused of trying to *mulct* the boy of his legacy. also N.

mul·ti·far·i·ous\ˌməl-tə-'far-ē-əs\ADJ. varied; greatly diversified. A career woman and mother, she was constantly busy with the *multifarious* activities of her daily life.

mul·ti·form \'məl-ti-ˌfȯrm\ ADJ. having many forms. Snowflakes are *multiform* but always hexagonal.

mul·ti·lin·gual \ˌməl-ti-'liŋ-g(yə-)wəl\ ADJ. having many languages. Because they are bordered by so many countries, the Swiss people are *multilingual*.

\ŋ\ **sing**	\ō\ **go**	\ȯ\ **law**	\ȯi\ **boy**	\th\ **thin**	\th̲\ **the**	\ü\ **loot**	\ù\ **foot**
\y\ **yet**	\zh\ **vision**		\à, k̲, ⁿ, œ, œ̄, ue, ūe,ʸ\ *see* Pronunciation Symbols				

mul·ti·plic·i·ty \ˌməl -tə-ˈplis -ət-ē\ N. state of being numerous. He was appalled by the *multiplicity* of details he had to complete before setting out on his mission.

mun·dane \ˌmən -ˈdān\ ADJ. worldly as opposed to spiritual. He was concerned only with *mundane* matters, especially the daily stock market quotations.

mu·nif·i·cent \myù-ˈnif -ə-sənt\ ADJ. very generous. The *munificent* gift was presented to the bride.

murk·i·ness \ˈmər -kē-nəs\ N. darkness; gloom. The *murkiness* and fog of the waterfront that evening depressed me.

muse \ˈmyüz\ V. ponder. For a moment he *mused* about the beauty of the scene, but his thoughts soon changed as he recalled his own personal problems. also N.

musk·y \ˈməs -kē\ ADJ. having the odor of musk. She left a trace of *musky* perfume behind her.

must·y \ˈməs -tē\ ADJ. stale; spoiled by age. The attic was dark and *musty*.

mu·ta·ble \ˈmyüt -ə-bəl\ ADJ. changing in form; fickle. His opinions were *mutable* and easily influenced by anyone who had any powers of persuasion.

mu·ti·late \ˈmyüt -ᵊl-ˌāt\ V. maim. The torturer threatened to *mutilate* his victim.

mu·ti·nous \ˈmyüt -ᵊn-əs\ ADJ. unruly; rebellious. The captain had to use force to quiet his *mutinous* crew.

my·o·pic \mīˈō -pik\ ADJ. nearsighted. In thinking only of your present needs and ignoring the future, you are being rather *myopic*. **my·o·pia** \mīˈō -pē-ə\ N.

myr·i·ad \ˈmir -ē-əd\ N. very large number. *Myriads* of mosquitoes from the swamps invaded our village every twilight. also ADJ.

-n-

na-dir \\'nā ˌdi(ə)r\\ N. lowest point. Although few people realized it, the Dow-Jones average had reached its *nadir* and would soon begin an upward surge.

na-ive-té \\ˌ(ˌ)nä ˌēv(-ə)ˌ'tā\\ N. quality of being unsophisticated. I cannot believe that such *naiveté* is unassumed in a person of her age and experience.

nar-cis-sist \\'när-sə-səst\\ N. conceited, self-centered person. A *narcissist* is his own best friend. **nar-cis-sism** \\'när-sə-siz-əm\\ N; **nar-cis-sis-tic** \\'när-sə-'sis-tik\\ ADJ.

na-scent \\'nas -ᵊnt\\ ADJ. incipient; coming into being. If we could identify these revolutionary movements in their *nascent* state, we would be able to eliminate serious trouble in later years.

na-tal \\'nāt -ᵊl\\ ADJ. pertaining to birth. He refused to celebrate his *natal* day because it reminded him of the few years he could look forward to.

nau-se-ate \\'nò -z(h)ēˌāt\\ V. cause to become sick; fill with disgust. The foul smells began to *nauseate* him.

nau-ti-cal \\'nòt -i-kəl\\ ADJ. pertaining to ships or navigation. The Maritime Museum contains many models of clipper ships, logbooks, anchors and many other items of a *nautical* nature.

nave \\'nāv\\ N. main body of a church. The *nave* of the cathedral was empty at this hour.

neb-u-lous \\'neb -yə-ləs\\ ADJ. cloudy; hazy. Your theories are too *nebulous;* please clarify them.

ne-crol-o-gy \\nə-'kräl -ə-jē\\ N. obituary notice; list of the dead. The *necrology* of those buried in this cemetery is available in the office.

nec-ro-man-cy \\'nek -rəˌman(t) -sē\\ N. black magic; dealings with the dead. Because he was able to perform feats of *necromancy,* the natives thought he was in league with the devil.

ne-far-i-ous \\ni-'far -ē-əs\\ ADJ. very wicked. He was universally feared because of his many *nefarious* deeds.

ne-ga-tion \\ni-'gā -shən\\ N. denial. I must accept his argument since you have been unable to present any *negation* of his evidence.

\\ŋ\\ sing　\\ō\\ go　\\ò\\ law　\\òi\\ boy　\\th\\ thin　\\t͟h\\ the　\\ü\\ loot　\\u̇\\ foot
\\y\\ yet　\\zh\\ vision　\\à, k̲, ⁿ, œ, ō̄e, ue, ūe, ʸ\\ see Pronunciation Symbols

neg-li-gence\ˈneg-li-jən(t)s\ N. carelessness. *Negligence* can prove costly near complicated machinery.

nem-e-sis\ˈhem -ə-səs\ N. revenging agent. Captain Bligh vowed to be Christian's *nemesis*.

ne-o-phyte\ˈnē -ə͵fīt \ N. recent convert; beginner. This mountain slope contains slides that will challenge experts as well as *neophytes*.

nep-o-tism\ˈnep -ə͵tiz -əm\ N. favoritism (to a relative). John left his position with the company because he felt that advancement was based on *nepotism* rather than ability.

net-tle \ˈnet -ᵊl\ V. annoy; vex. Do not let him *nettle* you with his sarcastic remarks.

nex-us\ˈnek -səs\ N. connection. I fail to see the *nexus* which binds these two widely separated events.

nib\ˈnib\ N. beak; pen point. The *nibs* of fountain pens often became clotted and corroded.

ni-ce-ty\ˈnī -sət-ē\ N. precision; minute distinction. I cannot distinguish between such *niceties* of reasoning.

nig-gard-ly\ˈnig -ərd-lē\ ADJ. meanly stingy; parsimonious. The *niggardly* pittance the widow receives from the government cannot keep her from poverty.

nig-gle\ˈnig-əl\ V. spend too much time on minor points; carp. Let's not *niggle* over details. **nig-gling** \ˈnig-(ə-)liŋ\ ADJ.

ni-hil-ism\ˈnī-(h)ə-͵liz-əm\ N. denial of traditional values; total skepticism. *Nihilism* holds that existence has no meaning.

nir-va-na\ni(ə)r-ˈvän -ə\ N. in Buddhist teachings, the ideal state in which the individual loses himself in the attainment of an impersonal beatitude. He tried to explain the concept of *nirvana* to his skeptical students.

noc-tur-nal \näk-ˈtərn -ᵊl\ ADJ. done at night. Mr. Jones obtained a watchdog to prevent the *nocturnal* raids on his chicken coops.

noi-some \ˈnȯi -səm\ ADJ. foul smelling; unwholesome. I never could stand the *noisome* atmosphere surrounding the slaughter houses.

---

no-mad-ic \nō-'mad -ik\ ADJ. wandering. Several *nomadic* tribes of Indians would hunt in this area each year.

no-men-cla-ture\ 'nō-mən-,klā-chər\ N. terminology; system of names. She struggled to master scientific *nomenclature.*

non-age\ 'nän-ij\ N. immaturity. She was embarrassed by the *nonage* of her contemporaries who never seemed to grow up.

non-cha-lance\,nän -shə-'län(t)s\ N. indifference; lack of interest. Few people could understand how he could listen to the news of the tragedy with such *nonchalance;* the majority regarded him as callous and unsympathetic.

non-com-mit-tal \,nän -kə-'mit -ᵊl\ ADJ. neutral; unpledged; undecided. We were annoyed by his *noncommittal* reply for we had been led to expect definite assurances of his approval.

non-en-ti-ty \nä-'hen(t) -ət-ē\ N. nonexistence; person of no importance. Of course you are a *nonentity;* you will continue to be one until you prove your value to the community.

non-plus \'nän -'pləs\ V. bring to a halt by confusion. In my efforts to correct this situation I was *nonplussed* by the stupidity of my assistants. also N.

non se-qui-tur\⁽¹⁾nän -'sek -wət-ər\ N. a conclusion that does not follow from the facts stated. Your term paper is full of *non sequiturs;* I cannot see how you reached the conclusions you state.

nose-gay \'nōz ;gā\ N. fragrant bouquet. These spring flowers will make an attractive *nosegay.*

nos-tal-gia \nä-'stal -jə\ N. homesickness; longing for the past. The first settlers found so much work to do that they had little time for *nostalgia.*

no-to-ri-ous \nō-'tōr -ē-əs\ ADJ. outstandingly bad; unfavorably known. Captain Kidd was a *notorious* pirate.

nov-el-ty\ 'näv-əl-tē\ N. something new; newness. The computer is no longer a *novelty* around the office. **nov-el**\ 'näv-əl\ ADJ.

nov-ice\ 'näv -əs\ N. beginner. Even a *novice* can do good work if he follows these simple directions.

---

nox·ious\\'näk -shəs\\ADJ. harmful. We must trace the source of these *noxious* gases before they asphyxiate us.

nu·ance\\'n(y)ü ˌän(t)s \\ N. shade of difference in meaning or color. The unskilled eye of the layman has difficulty in discerning the *nuances* of color in the paintings.

nu·bile\\'n(y)ü -bəl\\ADJ. marriageable. Mrs. Bennet, in *Pride and Prejudice* by Jane Austen, was worried about finding suitable husbands for her five *nubile* daughters.

nu·ga·to·ry \\'n(y)ü -gə-ˌtōr -ē\\ ADJ. futile; worthless. This agreement is *nugatory* for no court will enforce it.

nu·mis·ma·tist\\n(y)ü-ˈmiz -mət-əst\\N. person who collects coins. The *numismatist* had a splendid collection of antique coins.

nup·tial\\ 'nəp-shəl \\ADJ. related to marriage. Their *nuptial* ceremony was performed in Golden Gate Park.

nur·ture\\'nər-chər\\V. bring up; feed; educate. We must *nurture* the young so that they will develop into good citizens. also N.

nu·tri·ent \\'n(y)ü -trē-ənt\\ ADJ. providing nourishment. During the convalescent period, the patient must be provided with *nutrient* foods. also N.

—O—

oaf\ˈōf \ N. stupid, awkward person. He called the unfortunate waiter a clumsy *oaf.*

ob-du-rate\ˈäb -d(y)ə-rət\ ADJ. stubborn. He was *obdurate* in his refusal to listen to our complaints.

obei-sance\ō-ˈbās -ᵊn(t)s\ N. bow. She made an *obeisance* as the king and queen entered the room.

ob-e-lisk\ˈäb -ə-ˌlisk \ N. tall column tapering and ending in a pyramid. Cleopatra's Needle is an *obelisk* in Central Park, New York City.

o-bese\ō-ˈbēs \ ADJ. fat. It is advisable that *obese* people try to lose weight.

ob-fus-cate\ˈäb -fə-ˌskāt \ V. confuse; muddle. Do not *obfuscate* the issues by dragging in irrelevant arguments.

o-bit-u-ary\ə-ˈbich -ə-ˌwer -ē\ N. death notice. I first learned of his death when I read the *obituary* in the newspaper.

ob-jec-tive\əb-ˈjek-tiv\ ADJ. not influenced by emotions; fair. Even though he was her son, she tried to be *objective* about his behavior.

ob-jec-tive\əb-ˈjek-tiv\ N. goal; aim. A degree in medicine was her ultimate *objective.*

ob-jur-gate\ˈäb -jər-ˌgāt \ V. scold; rebuke severely. I am afraid he will *objurgate* us publicly for this offense.

ob-jur-ga-tion\ˌäb -jər-ˈgā -shən\ N. severe rebuke; scolding. *Objurgations* and even threats of punishment did not deter the young hoodlums.

ob-la-tion\ə-ˈblā -shən\ N. the Eucharist; pious donation. The wealthy man offered *oblations* so that the church might be able to provide for the needy.

o-blig-a-to-ry\ə-ˈblig -ə-ˌtōr -ē\ ADJ. binding; required. It is *obligatory* that books borrowed from the library be returned within two weeks.

o-blique\ō-ˈblēk \ ADJ. slanting; deviating from the perpendicular or from a straight line. The sergeant ordered the men to march "*Oblique* Right." also N.

o-bliq-ui-ty\ō-ˈblik -wət-ē\ N. departure from right principles; perversity. His moral decadence was marked by his *obliquity* from the ways of integrity and honesty.

\ŋ\ **sing**   \ō\ **go**   \o\ **law**   \oi\ **boy**   \th\ **thin**   \th\ **the**   \ü\ **loot**   \u̇\ **foot**
\y\ **yet**   \zh\ **vision**   \à, k̠, ⁿ, œ, œ̄, ue, ūe, ʸ\ *see* Pronunciation Symbols

o·blit·er·ate\ə-ˈblit -ə-ˌrāt \ V. destroy completely. The tidal wave *obliterated* several island villages.

o·bliv·i·on\ə-ˈbliv -ē-ən\ N. forgetfulness. His works had fallen into a state of *oblivion;* no one bothered to read them.

ob·lo·quy \ˈäb -lə-kwē\ N. slander; disgrace; infamy. I resent the *obloquy* that you are casting upon my reputation.

ob·nox·ious\äb-ˈnäk -shəs\ ADJ. offensive. I find your behavior *obnoxious;* please amend your ways.

ob·se·qui·ous\əb-ˈsē -kwē-əs\ ADJ. slavishly attentive; servile; sycophantic. Nothing is more disgusting to me than the *obsequious* demeanor of the people who wait upon you.

ob·ses·sion\äb-ˈsesh -ən\ N. fixed idea; continued brooding. This *obsession* with the supernatural has made him unpopular with his neighbors.

ob·so·lete\äb -sə-ˈlēt\ ADJ. outmoded. That word is *obsolete;* do not use it.

ob·ste·tri·cian\äb -stə-ˈtrish -ən\ N. physician specializing in delivery of babies. In modern times, the delivery of children has passed from the midwife to the more scientifically trained *obstetrician.*

ob·strep·er·ous \əb-ˈstrep -(ə-)rəs\ ADJ. boisterous; noisy. The crowd became *obstreperous* and shouted their disapproval of the proposals made by the speaker.

ob·trude\əb-ˈtrüd\ V. push into prominence. The other members of the group object to the manner in which you *obtrude* your opinions into matters of no concern to you.

ob·tru·sive\əb-ˈtrü -siv\ ADJ. pushing forward. I found him a very *obtrusive* person, constantly seeking the center of the stage.

ob·tuse\äb-ˈt(y)üs\ ADJ. blunt; stupid. Because he was so *obtuse,* he could not follow the teacher's reasoning and asked foolish questions.

ob·vi·ate \ˈäb -vē-ˌāt\ V. make unnecessary; get rid of. I hope this contribution will *obviate* any need for further collections of funds.

Oc·ci·dent\äk -səd-ənt\N. the West. It will take time for the *Occident* to understand the ways and customs of the Orient. **oc·ci·den·tal**\äk-sə‚dent -ᵊl\ADJ.

oc·cult\ə-ˈkəlt\ ADJ. mysterious; secret; supernatural. The *occult* rites of the organization were revealed only to members. also N.

oc·u·list\äk -yə-ləst\N. physician who specializes in treatment of the eyes. In many states, an *oculist* is the only one who may apply medicinal drops to the eyes for the purpose of examining them.

o·di·ous\ōd -ē-əs\ADJ. hateful. I find the task of punishing you most *odious*.

o·di·um\ōd -ē-əm\ N. repugnance; dislike. I cannot express the *odium* I feel at your heinous actions.

o·dor·if·er·ous\ōd -ə-ˈrif -(ə-)rəs\ADJ. giving off an odor. The *odoriferous* spices stimulated his jaded appetite.

o·dor·ous\ōd -ə-rəs\ADJ. having an odor. This variety of hybrid tea rose is more *odorous* than the one you have in your garden.

of·fal\ȯ -fəl\N. waste; garbage. In America, we discard as *offal* that which could feed families in less fortunate parts of the world.

of·fi·cious\ə-ˈfish -əs\ADJ. meddlesome; excessively trying to please. Browning informs us that the Duke resented the bough of cherries some *officious* fool brought to the Duchess.

o·gle\ōg -əl\V. glance coquettishly at; make eyes at. Sitting for hours at the sidewalk cafe, the old gentleman would *ogle* the young girls and recall his youthful romances. also N.

ol·fac·to·ry \äl¹fak -t(ə-)rē\ ADJ. concerning the sense of smell. The *olfactory* organ is the nose.

ol·i·gar·chy \äl -ə‚gär -kē\ N. government by a few. The feudal *oligarchy* was supplanted by an autocracy.

om·i·nous\äm -ə-nəs\ADJ. threatening. These clouds are *ominous;* they portend a severe storm.

om·nip·o·tent \äm-ˈnip -ət-ənt\ ADJ. all-powerful. The monarch regarded himself as *omnipotent* and responsible to no one for his acts. also N.

\ŋ\ sing   \ō\ go   \ȯ\ law   \ȯi\ boy   \th\ thin   \th\ the   \ü\ loot   \u̇\ foot
\y\ yet   \zh\ vision   \à, k̲, ⁿ, œ, œ̄, ue, ūe, ʳ\ *see* Pronunciation Symbols

om·ni·pres·ent \äm -ni-ˈprez -ᵊnt\ ADJ. universally present; ubiquitous. On Christmas Eve, Santa Claus is *omnipresent*.

om·ni·scient \äm-ˈnish -ənt\ ADJ. all-knowing. I do not pretend to be *omniscient*, but I am positive about this item.

om·niv·o·rous\äm-ˈniv -(ə-)rəs\ADJ. eating both plant and animal food; devouring everything. Some animals, including man, are *omnivorous* and eat both meat and vegetables; others are either carnivorous or herbivorous.

on·er·ous \ˈän -ə -rəs\ ADJ. burdensome. He asked for an assistant because his work load was too *onerous*. **o·nus**\ˈō -nəs\N.

on·o·mat·o·poe·ia \än -ə-ˌmat -ə-ˈpē -(y)ə\ N. words formed in imitation of natural sounds. Words like "rustle" and "gargle" are illustrations of *onomatopoeia*.

on·slaught\ˈän -ˌslȯt\ N. vicious assault. We suffered many casualties during the unexpected *onslaught* of the enemy troops.

o·nus\ˈō -nəs\N. burden; responsibility. The emperor was spared the *onus* of signing the surrender papers; instead, he relegated the assignment to his generals.

o·pal·es·cent \ˌō -pə-ˈles -ᵊnt\ADJ. iridescent. The Ancient Mariner admired the *opalescent* sheen on the water.

o·paque\ō-ˈpāk\ ADJ. dark; not transparent. I want something *opaque* placed in this window so that no one will be able to watch me. also N.

o·pi·ate\ō -pē-ət\N. sleep producer; deadener of pain. By such *opiates*, he made the people forget their difficulties and accept their unpleasant circumstances. also ADJ.

op·por·tune\ˌäp -ər-ˈt(y)ün\ ADJ. timely; well chosen. You have come at an *opportune* moment for I need a new secretary.

op·por·tun·ist \ˌäp -ər-ˈt(y)ü -nəst\ N. individual who sacrifices principles for expediency by taking advantage of circumstances. I do not know how he will vote on this question as he is an *opportunist*.

op·pro·bri·ous\ə-ˈprō -brē -əs\ADJ. disgraceful. I find your conduct so *opprobrious* that I must exclude you from classes.

---

op-pro-bri-um\ə-ˈprō-brē-əm\ N. infamy; vilification. He refused to defend himself against the slander and *opprobrium* hurled against him by the newspapers; he preferred to rely on his record.

op-ti-cian\äp-ˈtish-ən\ N. maker and seller of eyeglasses. The patient took the prescription given him by his oculist to the *optician*.

op-ti-mal\ˈäp-tə-məl\ ADJ. most favorable. If you wait for the *optimal* moment to act, you may never begin your project. **op-ti-mum**\äp-tə-məm\ N.

op-ti-mist\ˈäp-tə-məst\ N. person who looks on the bright side. The pessimist says the glass is half-empty; the *optimist* says it is half-full.

op-tom-e-trist\äp-ˈtäm-ə-trəst\ N. one who fits glasses to remedy visual defects. Although an *optometrist* is qualified to treat many eye disorders, he may not use medicines or surgery in his examinations.

op-u-lence\ˈäp-yə-lən(t)s\ N. wealth. Visitors from Europe are amazed at the *opulence* of this country.

o-pus\ˈō-pəs\ N. work. Although many critics hailed his Fifth Symphony as his major work, he did not regard it as his major *opus*.

or-a-to-ri-o\ȯr-ə-ˈtōr-ē-ˌō\ N. dramatic poem set to music. The Glee Club decided to present an *oratorio* during their recital.

or-di-nance\ˈȯrd-nən(t)s\ N. decree. Passing a red light is a violation of a city *ordinance*.

o-ri-en-ta-tion\ˌōr-ē-ən-ˈtā-shən\ N. act of finding oneself in society. Freshman *orientation* provides the incoming students with an opportunity to learn about their new environment and their place in it.

or-i-fice\ˈȯr-ə-fəs\ N. mouthlike opening; small opening. The Howe Caverns were discovered when someone observed that a cold wind was issuing from an *orifice* in the hillside.

or-nate\ȯr-ˈnāt\ ADJ. excessively decorated; highly decorated. Furniture of the Baroque period can be recognized by its *ornate* carvings.

\ŋ\ sing   \ō\ go   \ȯ\ law   \ȯi\ boy   \th\ thin   \th\ the   \ü\ loot   \u̇\ foot
\y\ yet   \zh\ vision   \ä, k̲, ⁿ, œ, œ̄, ue, ūe, ʸ\ *see* Pronunciation Symbols

or·ni·thol·o·gist \ˌȯr -nə-ˈthäl -ə-jəst\ N. scientific student of birds. Audubon's drawings of American bird life have been of interest not only to the *ornithologists* but also to the general public.

or·ni·thol·o·gy \ˌȯr -nə-ˈthäl -ə-jē\ N. study of birds. Audubon's studies of American birds greatly influenced the course of *ornithology* in this country.

o ro·tund \ȯr -ə-ˌtənd\ ADJ. having a round, resonant quality; inflated speech. The politician found that his *orotund* voice was an asset when he spoke to his constituents.

or·thog·ra·phy \ȯr-ˈthäg -rə-fē\ N. correct spelling. Many of us find English *orthography* difficult to master because so many of our words are not written phonetically.

os·cil·late \ˈäs -ə-ˌlāt\ V. vibrate pendulumlike; waver. It is interesting to note how public opinion *oscillates* between the extremes of optimism and pessimism.

os·si·fy \ˈäs -ə-ˌfī\ V. change or harden into bone. When he called his opponent a "bonehead," he implied that his adversary's brain had *ossified* and that he was not capable of clear thinking.

os·ten·si·ble \ä-ˈsten(t) -sə-bəl\ ADJ. apparent; professed; pretended. Although the *ostensible* purpose of this expedition is to discover new lands, we are really interested in finding new markets for our products.

os·ten·ta·tious \ˌäs -tən-ˈtā -shəs\ ADJ. showy; pretentious. The real hero is never *ostentatious*.

os·tra·cize \ˈäs -trə-ˌsīz\ V. exclude from public favor; ban. As soon as the newspapers carried the story of his connection with the criminals, his friends began to *ostracize* him. **os·tra·cism** \ˈäs -trə-ˌsiz -əm\ N.

oust \ˈaust\ V. expel; drive out. The world wondered if the United States could *oust* Noriega from power.

o·vert \ō-ˈvərt\ ADJ. open to view. According to the United States Constitution, a person must commit an *overt* act before he may be tried for treason.

\ə\ **abut**	\ᵊ\ **kitten, F table**	\ər\ **further**	\a\ **ash**	\ā\ **ace**	\ä\ **cot, cart**
\aù\ **out**	\ch\ **chin**	\e\ **bet**	\ē\ **easy**	\g\ **go**	\i\ **hit**	\ī\ **ice**	\j\ **job**

o-ver-ween-ing \ō -vər-ˈwē -niŋ\ ADJ. presumptuous; arrogant. His *overweening* pride in his accomplishments was not justified.

ovine\ˈō-ˌvīn\ADJ. like a sheep. How *ovine* these true-believers were, following their shepherds thoughtlessly.

ovoid\ˈō-ˌvȯid\ADJ. egg-shaped. At Easter she had to cut out hundreds of brightly colored *ovoid* shapes.

–p–

pach-y-derm\ 'pak-i-ˌdərm\ N. thick-skinned animal. The elephant is probably the best-known *pachyderm*.

pac-i-fist\ 'pas-ə-fəst\ N. one opposed to force; antimilitarist. The *pacifists* urged that we reduce our military budget and recall our troops stationed overseas.

pad-dock\ 'pad-ək\ N. saddling enclosure at race track; lot for exercising horses. The *paddock* is located directly in front of the grandstand so that all may see the horses being saddled and the jockeys mounted.

pae-an\ 'pē-ən\ N. song of praise or joy. They sang *paeans* for their safe arrival.

pains-tak-ing\ 'pān-ˌstā-kiŋ\ ADJ. showing hard work; taking great care. The new high-frequency word list is the result of *painstaking* efforts on the part of our research staff.

pal-at-able\ 'pal-ət-ə-bəl\ ADJ. agreeable; pleasing to the taste. Paying taxes can never be made *palatable*.

pa-la-tial\ pə-ˈlā-shəl\ ADJ. magnificent. He proudly showed us through his *palatial* home.

pa-la-ver\ pə-ˈlav-ər\ N. discussion; misleading speech; chatter. In spite of all the *palaver* before the meeting, the delegates were able to conduct serious negotiations when they sat down at the conference table. also V.

pal-ette\ 'pal-ət\ N. board on which painter mixes pigments. At the present time, art supply stores are selling a paper *palette* which may be discarded after use.

pal-let\ 'pal-ət\ N. small, poor bed. The weary traveler went to sleep on his straw *pallet*.

pal-li-ate\ 'pal-ē-ˌāt\ V. ease pain; make less guilty or offensive. Doctors must *palliate* that which they cannot cure.

pal-li-a-tion\ pal-ē-ˈā-shən\ N. act of making less severe or violent. If we cannot find a cure for this disease at the present time, we can, at least, endeavor to seek its *palliation*.

pal-lid\ 'pal-əd\ ADJ. pale; wan. Because his occupation required that he work at night and sleep during the day, he had an exceptionally *pallid* complexion.

\ə\ abut	\ᵊ\ kitten, F table	\ər\ further	\a\ ash	\ā\ ace
\ä\ cot, cart				
\aù\ out	\ch\ chin	\e\ bet	\ē\ easy	\g\ go
\i\ hit	\ī\ ice	\j\ job		

pal-pa-ble\\'pal -pə-bəl\\ ADJ. tangible; easily perceptible. I cannot understand how you could overlook such a *palpable* blunder. **pal-pa-bly**\\'pal -pə-blē\\ ADV.

pal-pi-tate \\'pal -pə͵tāt\\ v. throb; flutter. As he became excited, his heart began to *palpitate* more and more erratically.

pal-try \\'pol -trē\\ ADJ. insignificant; petty. This is a *paltry* sum to pay for such a masterpiece.

pan-a-cea \\pan-ə͵'sē -ə\\ N. cure-all; remedy for all diseases. There is no easy *panacea* that will solve our complicated international situation.

Pan-de-mo-ni-um \\pan -də͵'mō -nē -əm\\ N. wild tumult. When the ships collided in the harbor, *pandemonium* broke out among the passengers.

pan-der\\'pan -dər\\ v. cater to the low desires of others. Books which *pander* to man's lowest instincts should be banned.

pan-e-gy-ric\\pan -ə͵'jir -ik\\ N. formal praise. The modest hero blushed as he listened to the *panegyrics* uttered by the speakers about his valorous act.

pan-o-ply\\'pan -ə-plē\\ N. full set of armor. The medieval knight in full *panoply* found his movements limited by the weight of his armor.

pan-ora-ma\\pan -ə͵'ram -ə\\ N. comprehensive view; unobstructed view in all directions. Tourists never forget the impact of their first *panorama* of the Grand Canyon.

pan-to-mime \\pant -ə͵mīm\\ N. acting without dialogue. Because he worked in *pantomime,* the clown could be understood wherever he appeared. also v.

pa-py-rus \\pə͵'pī -rəs\\ N. ancient paper made from stem of papyrus plant. The ancient Egyptians were among the first to write on *papyrus.*

par-a-ble\\'par -ə-bəl\\ N. short, simple story teaching a moral. Let us apply to our own conduct the lesson that this *parable* teaches.

par-a-digm\\'par-ə-͵dīm\\ N. model; example; pattern. Pavlov's experiment in which he trains a dog to salivate on hearing a bell is a *paradigm* of the conditioned-response experiment in behavioral psychology.

par-a-dox \ˈpar -ə͵däks\ N. statement that looks false but is actually correct; a contradictory statement. Wordsworth's "The child is father to the man" is an example of *paradox*. **par-a-dox-i-cal** \par-ə-däk -si-kəl\ ADJ. **par-a-dox-i-cal-ly** \par -ə-däk -si-k(ə)lē\ ADV.

par-a-gon \ˈpar -ə͵gän \ N. model of perfection. The class disliked him because the teacher was always pointing to him as a *paragon* of virtue.

par-al-lel-ism \ˈpar -ə͵lel͵iz -əm\N. state of being parallel; similarity. There is a striking *parallelism* between the two ages.

pa-ram-e-ter \pə-ˈram-ət-ər\ N. limit; independent variable. We need to define the *parameters* of the problem.

par-amour \ˈpar-ə͵mú(ə)r\ N. illicit lover. She sought a divorce on the grounds that her husband had a *paramour* in another town.

par-a-noi-a \͵par -ə-ˈnói -ə\ N. chronic form of insanity marked by delusions of grandeur or persecution. The psychiatrists analyzed his ailment as *paranoia*. **para-noid** \ˈpar -ə͵nóid\ ADJ. or N.

par-a-pet \ˈpar -ə-pət\ N. low wall at edge of roof or balcony. The best way to attack the soldiers fighting behind the *parapets* on the roof is by bombardment from the air.

par-a-pher-na-lia \͵par -ə-fə(r)ˈnäl -yə\ N. equipment; odds and ends. His desk was cluttered with paper, pen, ink, dictionary and other *paraphernalia* of the writing craft.

par a-phrase \ˈpar -ə͵frāz\ V. restate a passage in one's own words while retaining thought of author. In 250 words or less, *paraphrase* this article. also N.

par-a-site \ˈpar -ə͵sīt\ N. animal or plant living on another; toady; sycophant. The tapeworm is an example of the kind of *parasite* that may infest the human body. **par-a-sit-ic** \͵par-ə ˈsit -ik\ ADJ.—**par-a-sit-ism** \ˈpar -ə-sə͵tiz -əm\ N.—**par-a-sit-ize** \ˈpar -ə-sə-͵tīz\ V.

pa-ri-ah \pə-ˈrī -ə\ N. social outcast. I am not a *pariah* to be shunned and ostracized.

\ə\ abut \ᵊ\ kitten, F table \ər\ further \a\ ash \ā\ ace \ä\ cot, cart
\aú\ out \ch\ chin \e\ bet \ē\ easy \g\ go \i\ hit \ī\ ice \j\ job

par-i-ty \'par -ət-ē\ N. equality; close resemblance. I find your analogy inaccurate because I do not see the *parity* between the two illustrations.

par-lance\'pär -lən(t)s\ N. language; idiom. All this legal *parlance* confuses me; I need an interpreter.

par-ley \'pär -lē\ N. conference. The peace *parley* has not produced the anticipated truce. also V.

par-o-dy\'par -əd-ē\ N. humorous imitation; travesty. We enjoyed the clever *parodies* of popular songs which the chorus sang. also V.

par-ox-ysm \'par -ək͵siz -əm\ N. fit or attack of pain, laughter, rage. When he heard of his sons' misdeeds, he was seized by a *paroxysm* of rage. **par-ox-ys-mal**\͵par -ək-'siz -məl\ADJ.

par-ri-cide\'par -ə͵sīd \ N. person who murders his own father; murder of a father. The jury was shocked by the details of this vicious *parricide* and found the man who had killed his father guilty of murder in the first degree.

par-ry\'par -ē\V. ward off a blow. He was content to wage a defensive battle and tried to *parry* his opponent's thrusts.

par-si-mo-ni-ous \pär -sə-'mō -nē-əs\ ADJ. stingy; excessively frugal. His *parsimonious* nature did not permit him to enjoy any luxuries. **par-si-mo-ny**\'pär -sə͵mō -nē\N.— **par-si-mo-ni-ous-ly**\͵par -sə-'mō -nē-əs-lē\ADV.

par-tial-i-ty\͵pär-shē -'al -ət-ē\ N. inclination; bias. As a judge, not only must I be unbiased, but I must also avoid any evidence of *partiality* when I award the prize. **par-tial** \'pär -shəl\ADJ.—**par-tial-ly**\'pärsh -(ə-)lē\ADV.

par-ti-san \'pärt-ə-zən\ADJ. one-sided; prejudiced; committed to a party. On certain issues of conscience, she refused to take a *partisan* stand. also N.

par-tu-ri-tion\͵pärt -ə-'rish -ən\N. delivery; childbirth. The difficulties anticipated by the obstetricians at *parturition* did not materialize; it was a normal delivery.

par-ve-nu \'pär -və͵n(y)ü\ N. upstart; newly rich person. Although extremely wealthy, he was regarded as a *parvenu* by the aristocratic members of society.

pas-sé\pa-'sā \ADJ. old-fashioned; past the prime. His style is *passé* and reminiscent of the Victorian era.

---

passive

pas-sive \\'pas -iv\\ ADJ. not active; acted upon. Mahatma Gandhi urged his followers to pursue a program of *passive* resistance as he felt that it was more effective than violence and acts of terrorism. also N. **pas-sive-ly** \\'pas -iv-lē\\ ADV.—**pas-siv-i-ty** \\paˌsiv -ət-ē\\ N.

pas-tiche \\pasˈtēsh\\ N. imitation of another's style in musical composition or in writing. We cannot even say that his music is a *pastiche* of this composer or that; it is, rather, reminiscent of many musicians.

pas-to-ral \\'pas -t(ə)rəl\\ ADJ. rural. In these stories of *pastoral* life, we find an understanding of the daily tasks of country folk.

pa-tent \\'pat -ᵊnt\\ ADJ. open for the public to read; obvious. It was *patent* to everyone that the witness spoke the truth. also N.

pa-thet-ic \\pəˈthet -ik\\ ADJ. causing sadness, compassion, pity; touching. Everyone in the auditorium was weeping by the time he finished his *pathetic* tale about the orphaned boy. **pa-thet-i-cal-ly** \\pəˈthet -i-k(ə-)lē\\ ADV.

patho-log-i-cal \\ˌpath -ə-ˈläj -i-kəl\\ ADJ. pertaining to disease. As we study the *pathological* aspects of this disease, we must not overlook the psychological elements. **pa-thol-o-gy** \\pəˈthäl -ə-jē\\ N.—**pa-thol-o-gist** \\pəˈthäl -ə-jəst\\ N.

pa-thos \\'pā ˌthäs\\ N. tender sorrow; pity; quality in art or literature that produces these feelings. The quiet tone of *pathos* that ran through the novel never degenerated into the maudlin or the overly sentimental.

pa-ti-na \\pə-ˈtē-nə\\ N. green crust on old bronze works; tone slowly taken by varnished painting. Judging by the *patina* on this bronze statue, we can conclude that this is the work of a medieval artist.

pa-tois \\'pa ˌtwä\\ N. local or provincial dialect. His years of study of the language at the university did not enable him to understand the *patois* of the natives.

pa-tri-arch \\'pā -trēˌärk\\ N. father and ruler of a family or tribe. In many primitive tribes, the leader and lawmaker was the *patriarch*. **pa-tri-ar-chal** \\'pā -trēˌär -kəl\\ ADJ.—**pa-tri-arch-ate** \\'pā -trēˌär -kət\\ N.—**pa-tri-ar-chy** \\'pā -trēˌär -kē\\ N.

pa·tri·cide\pā -trə⸱ˈsīd \ N. person who murders his father; murder of a father. The words parricide and *patricide* have exactly the same meaning.

pa·tri·mo·ny\ˌpa -trə⸱mō -nē\ N. inheritance from father. As predicted by his critics, he spent his *patrimony* within two years of his father's death. **pat·ri·mo·ni·al**\ˌpa -trə-ˈmo -nē-əl\ ADJ.

pa·tron·ize\ˈpā-trə-ˌnīz\ V. support; act superior toward. Experts in a field sometimes appear to *patronize* people who are less knowledgeable of the subject.

pau·ci·ty\ˈpȯ -sət-ē\ N. scarcity. The poor test papers indicate that the members of this class have a *paucity* of intelligence.

pec·ca·dil·lo\ˌpek-ə-ˈdil-ˌ(ˌ)ō\ N. slight offense. If we examine these escapades carefully, we will realize that they are mere *peccadilloes* rather than major crimes.

pe·cu·ni·ar·y\pi⸱ˈkyü -nē⸱er -ē\ ADJ. pertaining to money. I never expected a *pecuniary* reward for my work in this activity.

ped·a·gogue \ˈped -ə⸱ˌgäg\ N. teacher; dull and formal teacher. He could never be a stuffy *pedagogue;* his classes were always lively and filled with humor.

ped·ant \ˈped -ᵊnt\ N. scholar who overemphasizes book learning or technicalities. His insistence that the book be memorized marked the teacher as a *pedant* rather than a scholar. **ped·ant·ry**\ˈped -ᵊn-trē\ N.

pe·dan·tic \pi⸱ˈdant -ik\ ADJ. showing off learning; bookish. What you say is *pedantic* and reveals an unfamiliarity with the realities of life. **ped·ant**\ˈped -ᵊnt\ N.

pe·des·tri·an\pə-ˈdes-trē-ən\ ADJ. ordinary; unimaginative. Unintentionally boring, he wrote page after page of *pedestrian* prose.

pe·di·a·tri·cian\ˌpēd -ē-ə⸱ˈtrish -ən\ N. expert in children's diseases. The family doctor advised the parents to consult a *pediatrician* about their child's ailment. **pe·di·at·rics**\ˌpēd ‑ē⸱ˈa -triks\ N.—**pe·di·at·ric**\ˌpēd -ē-ˈa -trik\ N.

---

ped-i-ment \\'ped -ə-mənt\\ N. triangular part above columns in Greek buildings. The *pediment* of the building was filled with sculptures and adorned with elaborate scrollwork.

pe-jo-ra-tive \\pi-'jȯr -ət-iv\\ ADJ. having a deteriorating or depreciating effect on the meaning of a word. His use of *pejorative* language indicated his contempt for his audience.

pell-mell \\'pel 'mel\\ ADV. in confusion; disorderly. The excited students dashed *pell-mell* into the stadium to celebrate the victory.

pel-lu-cid \\pe-'lü -səd\\ ADJ. transparent; limpid; easy to understand. After reading these stodgy philosophers, I find his *pellucid* style very enjoyable.

pen-ance \\'pen-ən(t)s\\ N. self-imposed punishment for sin. The Ancient Mariner said, "I have *penance* done and *penance* more will do," to atone for the sin of killing the albatross.

pen-chant \\'pen -chənt\\ N. strong inclination; liking. He had a *penchant* for sculpture.

pen-dant \\'pen -dənt\\ ADJ. hanging down from something. Her *pendant* earrings glistened in the light.

pen-dent \\'pen -dənt\\ ADJ. suspended; jutting; pending. The *pendent* rock hid the entrance to the cave.

pen-du-lous \\'pen -jə-ləs\\ ADJ. hanging; suspended. The *pendulous* chandeliers swayed in the breeze and gave the impression that they were about to fall from the ceiling.

pen-i-tent \\'pen -ə-tənt\\ ADJ. repentant. When he realized the enormity of his crime, he became remorseful and *penitent*. also N. **pen-i-tence** \\'pen -ə-ten(t)s\\ N.—**pen-i-ten-tial** \\pen -ə-'ten -chəl\\ ADJ.

pen-sive \\'pen(t)-siv\\ ADJ. dreamily thoughtful; thoughtful with a hint of sadness. The *pensive* youth gazed at the painting for a long time and then sighed. **pen-sive-ly** \\'pen(t)-siv-lē\\ ADV.

pen-um-bra \\pə-'nəm -brə\\ N. partial shadow (in an eclipse). During an eclipse, we can see an area of total darkness and a lighter area which is the *penumbra*.

\\ə\\ abut   \\'ə\\ kitten, F table   \\ər\\ **further**   \\a\\ ash   \\ā\\ ace   \\ä\\ cot, cart
\\au̇\\ **out**   \\ch\\ chin   \\e\\ bet   \\ē\\ **easy**   \\g\\ go   \\i\\ hit   \\ī\\ ice   \\j\\ job

pe·nu·ri·ous \pə-ˈn(y)ur̓ -ē-əs\ ADJ. stingy; parsimonious. He was a *penurious* man, averse to spending money even for the necessities of life.

pen·u·ry \ˈpen -yə-rē\ N. extreme poverty. We find much *penury* and suffering in this slum area.

pe·on \ˈpē-,än\ N. unskilled laborer; drudge. He was doomed to be a *peon*, to live a lowly life of drudgery and toil.

per·cus·sion \pər-ˈkəsh -ən\ ADJ. striking one object against another sharply. The drum is a *percussion* instrument.

per·di·tion \pər-ˈdish-ən\ N. damnation; complete ruin. He was damned to eternal *perdition*.

per·e·gri·na·tion \ˌper-ə-grə-ˈnā -shən\ N. journey. His *peregrinations* in foreign lands did not bring understanding; he mingled only with fellow tourists and did not attempt to communicate with the native population.

pe·remp·to·ry \pə-ˈrem(p) -t(ə)rē\ ADJ. demanding and leaving no choice. I resent your *peremptory* attitude. **pe·remp·to·ri·ly** \pə-ˈrem(p)-t(ə)rə-ly\ ADV.

pe·ren·ni·al \pə-ˈren -ē-əl\ N. something long-lasting. These plants are hardy *perennials* and will bloom for many years. also ADJ. **pe·ren·ni·al·ly** \pə-ˈren -ē-ə-lē\ ADV.

per·fid·i·ous \(ˌ)pər-ˈfid-ē-əs\ ADJ. basely false. Your *perfidious* gossip is malicious and dangerous. **per·fid·i·ous·ly** \pər-ˈfid -ē-əs-lē\ ADV.

per·fi·dy \ˈpər -fəd-ē\ N. violation of a trust. When we learned of his *perfidy*, we were shocked and dismayed.

per·force \pər-ˈfō(ə)rs\ ADV. of necessity. I must *perforce* leave, as my train is about to start.

per·func·to·ry \pər-ˈfəŋ(k)-t(ə-)rē\ ADJ. superficial; listless; not thorough. He overlooked many weaknesses when he inspected the factory in his *perfunctory* manner. **per·func·to·ri·ly** \pər-ˈfəŋ(k)-t(ə-) rə-lē\ ADV.

peri·gee \ˈper-ə-(ˌ)jē\ N. point of moon's orbit when it is nearest the earth. The rocket which was designed to take photographs of the moon was launched as the moon approached its *perigee*.

pe·rim·e·ter \pə-ˈrim -ət-ər\ N. outer boundary. To find the *perimeter* of any quadrilateral, we add the four sides.

\ŋ\ sing   \ō\ go   \ȯ\ law   \ȯi\ boy   \th\ thin   \th\ the   \ü\ loot   \u̇\ foot
\y\ yet   \zh\ vision   \à, ḵ, ⁿ, œ, œ̄, ue, ūe, ʼ\ see Pronunciation Symbols

per-i-pa-tet-ic\per -ə-pə-'tet -ik\ADJ. walking about; moving. The *peripatetic* school of philosophy derives its name from the fact that Aristotle walked with his pupils while discussing philosophy with them.

pe-riph-ery\pə-'rif -(ə-)rē\N. edge, especially of a round surface. He sensed that there was something just beyond the *periphery* of his vision. **pe-riph-er-al**\pə-'rif -(ə-)rəl\ADJ.

per-ju-ry\'pərj-(ə-)rē\N. false testimony while under oath. When several witnesses appeared to challenge his story, he was indicted for *perjury*. **per-jure**\'pər -jər\V.—**per-jur-er**\'pər -jər-ər\N.

per-me-able\'pər -mē-ə-bəl\ADJ. porous; allowing passage through. Glass is *permeable* to light. **per-me-a-bil-i-ty**\pər -mē-ə-'bil -ət-ē\N.

per-me-ate\'pər -mē-,āt\V. pass through; spread. The odor of frying onions *permeated* the air. **per-me-ation**\,pər -mē-'ā -shən\N.

per-ni-cious\pər-'nish -əs\ADJ. very destructive. He argued that these books had a *pernicious* effect on young and susceptible minds. **per-ni-cious-ly**\pər-'nish -əs-lē\ADV.

per-ora-tion\'per -ər-,ā -shən\N. conclusion of an oration. The *peroration* was largely hortatory and brought the audience to its feet clamoring for action at its close.

per-pe-trate\'pər -pə-,trāt\V. commit an offense. Only an insane person could *perpetrate* such a horrible crime. **per-pe-tra-tion**\,pər -pə-'trā -shən\N.—**per-pe-tra-tor**\'pər -pə-,trāt -ər\N.

per-pet-u-al\pər-'pech -(ə-)wəl\ADJ. everlasting. Ponce de Leon hoped to find *perpetual* youth. **per-pet-u-al-ly**\pər-'pech-(ə-)wəl-lē\ADV.

per-qui-site\'pər -kwə-zət\N. any gain above stipulated salary. The *perquisites* attached to this job make it even more attractive than the salary indicates.

per-si-flage\'pər -si-,fläzh\N. flippant conversation; banter. This *persiflage* is not appropriate when we have such serious problems to discuss.

\ə\ abut   \ʰ\ kitten, F table   \ər\ further   \a\ ash   \ā\ ace   \ä\ cot, cart
\aú\ out   \ch\ chin   \e\ bet   \ē\ easy   \g\ go   \i\ hit   \ī\ ice   \j\ job

per-son-able \pərs -nə-bəl\ ADJ. attractive. The man I am seeking to fill this position must be *personable* since he will be representing us before the public.

per-spi-ca-cious \pər -spə-'kā -shəs\ ADJ. having insight; penetrating; astute. We admired his *perspicacious* wisdom and sagacity. **per-spi-cac-i-ty**\pər -spə-'kas -ət-ē\ N.

per-spi-cu-i-ty\pər -spə-'kyü -ət-ē\ N. clearness of expression; freedom from ambiguity. One of the outstanding features of this book is the *perspicuity* of its author; his meaning is always clear.

per-spic-u-ous\pər-'spik -yə-wəs\ ADJ. plainly expressed. His *perspicuous* comments eliminated all possibility of misinterpretation.

pert \'pərt\ ADJ. impertinent; forward. I think your *pert* and impudent remarks call for an apology.

per-ti-na-cious \pərt -ᵊn-'ā -shəs\ ADJ. stubborn; persistent. He is bound to succeed because his *pertinacious* nature will not permit him to quit. **per-ti-nac-i-ty**\pərt -ᵊn-'as -ət-ē\ N.

per-ti-nent \'pərt-ᵊn-ənt\ ADJ. suitable; to the point. The lawyer wanted to know all the *pertinent* details. **per-ti-nence**\'pərt -ᵊn-ən(t)s\ N.

per-turb \pər 'tərb\ V. disturb greatly. I am afraid this news will *perturb* him. **per-tur-ba-tion** \pərt -ər-'bā -shən\ N.

pe-rus-al\pə-'rü-zəl\ N. reading. I am certain that you have missed important details in your rapid *perusal* of this document. **peruse**\pə-'rüz\ V.

per-va-sive\pər-'vā-siv\ ADJ. spread throughout; permeating. The *pervasive* odor of mothballs clung to the clothes and did not fade away until they had been thoroughly aired. **per-vade**\pər-'vād\ ADJ.

per-verse \(ͺ)pər-'vərs\ ADJ. stubborn; intractable. Because of your *perverse* attitude, I must rate you as deficient in cooperation. **per-verse-ly**\pər-'vərs -lē\ ADV.—**per-verse-ness**\pər-'vərs -nəs\ N.

per-ver-sion\pər-'vər -zhən\ N. corruption; turning from right to wrong. Inasmuch as he had no motive for his crimes, we could not understand his *perversion*.

\ŋ\ **sing**   \ō\ **go**   \ȯ\ **law**   \ȯi\ **boy**   \th\ **thin**   \th̲\ **the**   \ü\ **loot**   \u̇\ **foot**
\y\ **yet**   \zh\ **vision**   \á, k̲, ⁿ, œ, œ̄, ue, ūe, ᴼ\ *see* Pronunciation Symbols

per-ver-si-ty \pər-ˈvər -sət-ē\ N. stubborn maintenance of a wrong cause. I cannot forgive your *perversity* in repeating such an impossible story.

pes-si-mism \ˈpəs -ə-ˌmiz -əm\ N. belief that life is basically bad or evil; gloominess. The good news we have been receiving lately indicates that there is little reason for your *pessimism*. **pes-si-mist** \ˈpəs -ə-məst\ N.—**pes-si-mis-tic** \ˌpes -ə-ˈmis -tik\ ADJ.

pes-ti-len-tial \ˌpes -tə-ˈlen -chəl\ ADJ. causing plague; baneful. People were afraid to explore the *pestilential* swamp. **pes-ti-lence** \ˈpes -tə-lən (t)s\ N.–**pes-ti-len-tial-ly** \ˌpes -tə-ˈlench -(ə-)lē\ ADV.

pet-ri-fy \ˈpe -trə-ˌfī\ V. turn to stone. His sudden and un-expected appearance seemed to *petrify* her. **pet-ri-fac-tion** \ˌpe -trə-ˈfak -shən\ N.

pet-u-lant \ˈpech -ə-lənt\ ADJ. touchy; peevish. The feverish patient was *petulant* and restless. **pet-u-lance** \ˈpech -ə-lən(t)s\ N.–**pet-u-lant-ly** \ˈpech -ə-lənt-lē\ ADV.

phar-i-sa-i cal \ˌfar -ə-ˈsā -ə-kəl\ ADJ. pertaining to the Pharisees, who paid scrupulous attention to tradition; self-righteous; hypocritical. Walter Lippman has pointed out that moralists who do not attempt to explain the moral code they advocate are often regarded as *pharisaical* and ignored. **phar-i-sa-i-cal-ly** \ˌfar -ə-ˈsā -ə-k(ə-)lē\ ADV.

phi-al \ˈfī (-ə)l\ N. small bottle. Even though it is small, this *phial* of perfume is expensive.

phi-lan-der \fə-ˈlan -dər\ V. make love lightly; flirt. Do not *philander* or trifle with my affections because love is too serious. **phi-lan-der-er** \fə-ˈlan -dər-ər\ N.

phi-lan-thro-pist \fə-ˈlan(t)-thrə-pəst\ N. lover of mankind; doer of good. As he grew older, he became famous as a *philanthropist* and benefactor of the needy. **phi-lan-thro-py** \fə-ˈlan(t)-thrə-pē\ N.—**phil-an-throp-ic** \ˌfil -ən-ˈthräp -ik\ ADJ.

phi-lis-tine \ˈfil -ə-ˌstēn \ N. narrow-minded person, uncultured and exclusively interested in material gain. We need more men of culture and enlightenment; we have too many *philistines* among us. also ADJ.

\ə\ abut	\ˈ\ kitten, F table	\ər\ further	\a\ ash	\ā\ ace	\ä\ cot, cart
\aů\ out	\ch\ chin	\e\ bet	\ē\ easy	\g\ go	\i\ hit \ī\ ice \j\ job

phi-lol-o-gy \fə-'läl -ə-jē\ N. study of language. The professor of *philology* advocated the use of Esperanto as an international language. **phil-o-log-i-cal** \fil -ə-'läj -i-kəl\ ADJ.—**phi-lol-o-gist**\fə-'läl -ə-jəst\ N.

phleg-mat-ic\fleg-'mat -ik\ADJ. calm; not easily disturbed. The nurse was a cheerful but *phlegmatic* person.

pho-bia\'fō -bē-ə\ N. morbid fear. His fear of flying was more than mere nervousness; it was a real *phobia*.

phys-i-og-no-my \fiz -ē-'ä(g) -nə-mē\ N. face. He prided himself on his ability to analyze a person's character by studying his *physiognomy*.

phys-i-o-log-i-cal\fiz -ē-ə-'läj -i-kəl\ADJ. pertaining to the science of the function of living organisms. To understand this disease fully, we must examine not only its *physiological* aspects but also its psychological elements. **phys-i-ol-o-gist**\fiz -ē-'äl -ə-jəst\ N.—**phys-i-ol-o-gy** \fiz -ē-'äl -ə-jē\ N.

pi-ca-resque\pik -ə-'resk\ ADJ. pertaining to rogues in literature. *Tom Jones* has been hailed as one of the best *picaresque* novels in the English language.

pie-bald\'pī -ˌbȯld\ ADJ. mottled; spotted. You should be able to identify this horse easily as it is the only *piebald* horse in the race. also N.

pied\'pīd\ ADJ. variegated; multicolored. The *Pied* Piper of Hamelin got his name from the multicolored clothing he wore.

pil-lage\'pil -ij\ V. plunder. The enemy *pillaged* the quiet village and left it in ruins. also N.

pil-lo-ry\'pil-(ə-)rē\ V. punish by placing in a wooden frame and subjecting to ridicule. Even though he was mocked and *pilloried,* he maintained that he was correct in his beliefs. also N.

pin-ion\'pin -yən\ V. restrain. They *pinioned* his arms against his body but left his legs free so that he could move about. also N.

pin-na-cle\'pin -i-kəl\ N. peak. We could see the morning sunlight illuminate the *pinnacle* while the rest of the mountain lay in shadow.

\ŋ\ sing   \ō\ go   \ȯ\ law   \ȯi\ boy   \th\ thin   \t͟h\ the   \ü\ loot   \u̇\ foot
\y\ yet   \zh\ vision   \ä, k̲, ⁿ, œ, œ̄, ue, ūe, ʸ\ *see* Pronunciation Symbols

pi-ous \\'pī -əs\\ ADJ. devout. The *pious* parents gave their children a religious upbringing. **pi-ous-ly**\\'pī -əs-lē\\ADV.

pi-quant \\'pē -kənt\\ ADJ. pleasantly tart-tasting; stimulating. The *piquant* sauce added to our enjoyment of the meal. **pi-quan-cy**\\'pē -kən-sē\\ N.

pique\\'pēk\\ N. irritation; resentment. She showed her *pique* by her refusal to appear with the other contestants at the end of the contest. also V.

pithy\\'pith -ē\\ADJ. concise; meaty. I enjoy reading his essays because they are always compact and *pithy*.

pit-tance\\'pit -ᵊn(t) N. a small allowance or wage. He could not live on the *pittance* he received as a pension and had to look for an additional source of revenue.

pla-cate\\'plāk- ˌāt\\ V. pacify; conciliate. The teacher tried to *placate* the angry mother. **pla-ca-ble**\\'plak -ə-bəl\\ADJ.

plac-id\\'plas -əd\\ADJ. peaceful; calm. After his vacation in this *placid* section, he felt soothed and rested. **pla-cid-i-ty**\\plə-'sid -ət-ē\\N.—**plac-id-ly**\\'plas -əd-lē\\ADV.

pla-gia-rism\\'plā -jəˌriz -əm\\N. theft of another's ideas or writings passed on as original. The editor recognized the *plagiarism* and rebuked the culprit who had presented the manuscript as original. **pla-gia-rize**\\'plā -jəˌrīz \\ V.—**pla-gia-rist**\\'plā -jəˌrəst\\N.

plain-tive\\'plānt -iv\\ADJ. mournful. The dove has a *plaintive* and melancholy call. **plain-tive-ly**\\'plānt -iv-lē\\ADV.

plat-i-tude\\'plat -əˌt(y)üd \\ N. trite remark; commonplace statement. The *platitudes* in his speech were applauded by the vast majority in his audience; only a few people perceived how trite his remarks were. **plat-i-tu-di-nous** \\plat-ə-'t(y)üd -nəs\\ADJ.

pla-ton-ic \\plə -'tän -ik\\ ADJ. purely spiritual; theoretical; without sensual desire. Although a member of the political group, he took only a *platonic* interest in its ideals and goals.

plau-di-to-ry\\ 'plȯ-də-ˌtōr-ē\\ADJ. approving; applauding. The theatrical company reprinted the *plauditory* comments of the critics in its advertisement.

\\ə\\ abut　\\ᵊ\\ kitten, F table　\\ər\\ further　\\a\\ ash　\\ā\\ ace　\\ä\\ cot, cart
\\aú\\ out　\\ch\\ chin　\\e\\ bet　\\ē\\ easy　\\g\\ go　\\i\\ hit　\\ī\\ ice　\\j\\ job

plau-si-ble \'plȯ -zə-bəl\ ADJ. having a show of truth but open to doubt; specious. Even though your argument is *plausible*, I still would like to have more proof. **plau-si-bil-i-ty** \ˌplȯ -zə-ˈbil -ət-ē\ N.—**plau-si-bly** \'plȯ -zə-blē\ ADV.

ple-be-ian \pli-ˈbē -(y)ən\ ADJ. common; pertaining to the common people. His speeches were aimed at the *plebeian* minds and emotions; they disgusted the more refined.

pleb-i-scite \'pleb -ə-ˌsīt\ N. expression of the will of a people by direct election. I think this matter is so important that it should be decided not by a handful of legislators but by a *plebiscite* of the entire nation.

ple-na-ry \'plē -nə-rē\ ADJ. complete; full. The union leader was given *plenary* power to negotiate a new contract with the employers.

pleni-po-ten-tia-ry \ˌplen -ə-pə-ˈtench -(ə-)rē\ ADJ. fully empowered. Since he was not given *plenipotentiary* powers by his government, he could not commit his country without consulting his superiors. also N.

plen-i-tude \'plen-ə-ˌt(y)üd\ N. abundance; completeness. Looking in the pantry, we admired the *plenitude* of fruits and pickles we had preserved during the summer.

pleth-o-ra \'pleth -ə-rə\ N. excess; overabundance. She offered a *plethora* of reasons for her shortcomings.

plumb \'pləm\ ADJ. checking perpendicularity; vertical. Before hanging wallpaper it is advisable to drop a *plumb* line from the ceiling as a guide. also N. and V.

po-di-a-trist \pə-ˈdi -ə-trəst\ N. doctor who treats ailments of the feet. He consulted a *podiatrist* about his fallen arches. **po-di-a-try** \pə-ˈdī -ə-trē\ N.

po-di-um \'pōd -ē-əm\ N. pedestal; raised platform. The audience applauded as the conductor made his way to the *podium*.

poi-gnant \'poi -nyənt\ ADJ. keen; piercing; severe. Her *poignant* grief left her pale and weak. **poi-gnan-cy** \'pȯi -nyən-sē\ N.

po-lem-ic \pə-ˈlem -ik\ N. controversy; argument in support of point of view. His essays were, for the main part, *polemics* in support of the party's policy. also ADJ.—**po-lem-i-cist** \pə-ˈlem -ə-səst\ N.

---

pol·i·tic\\'päl -ə˛tik\\ ADJ. expedient; prudent; well devised. Even though he was disappointed, he did not think it *politic* to refuse this offer.

pol·i·ty\\'päl -ət-ē\\ N. form of government of nation or state. Our *polity* should be devoted to the concept that the government should strive for the good of all citizens.

po·lyg·a·mist\\pə-'lig -ə-məst\\ N. one who has more than one spouse at a time. He was arrested as a *polygamist* when his two wives filed complaints about him. **po·lyg·a·my** \\pə-'lig -ə-mē\\N.—**po·lyg·a·mous**\\pə-'lig -ə-məs\\ADJ.

poly·glot\\'päl -i˛glät\\ ADJ. speaking several languages. New York City is a *polyglot* community because of the thousands of immigrants who settle there. also N.

pon·der·ous\\'pän-d(ə-)rəs\\ADJ. weighty; unwieldy. His humor lacked the light touch; his jokes were always *ponderous*.

por·tend\\pȯr-'tend\\ V. foretell; presage. The king did not know what these omens might *portend* and asked his soothsayers to interpret them.

por·tent\\'pȯ(ə)r ˛tent\\ N. sign; omen; forewarning. He regarded the black cloud as a *portent* of evil.

por·ten·tous\\pȯr-'tent -əs\\ADJ. ominous; serious. I regard our present difficulties and dissatisfactions as *portentous* omens of future disaster.

port·ly\\'pȯrt -lē\\ADJ. stately; stout. The overweight gentleman was shown a size 44 *portly* suit.

pos·ter·i·ty\\pä-'ster -ət-ē\\ N. descendants; future generations. We hope to leave a better world to *posterity*.

post·hu·mous\\'päs -chə-məs\\ADJ. after death (as of child born after father's death or book published after author's death). The critics ignored his works during his lifetime; it was only after the *posthumous* publication of his last novel that they recognized his great talent.

post·pran·di·al\\pōs(t)-'pran-dē-əl\\ADJ. after dinner. The most objectionable feature of these formal banquets is the *postprandial* speech.

pos·tu·late\\'päs -chə-lət\\ N. self-evident truth. We must accept these statements as *postulates* before pursuing our discussions any further. also V.

po-ta-ble\'pōt -ə-bəl\ADJ. suitable for drinking. The recent drought in the Middle Atlantic states has emphasized the need for extensive research in ways of making sea water *potable*. also N.

po-tent\'pōt-ᵊnt\ADJ. powerful; persuasive; greatly influential. The jury was swayed by the highly *potent* testimony of the crime's sole eyewitness. **po-ten-cy**\'pōt-ᵊn-sē\N.

po-ten-tate\'pōt -ᵊnˌtāt\ N. monarch; sovereign. The *potentate* spent more time at Monte Carlo than he did at home with his people.

po-ten-tial \pə-'ten -chəl\ADJ. expressing possibility; latent. This juvenile delinquent is a *potential* murderer. also N. **po-ten-ti-al-i-ty**\pəˌten -chē-'al -ət-ē\N.—**po-ten-tial-ly** \pə-'tench -(ə-)lē\ADV.

po-tion\'pō -shən\N. dose (of liquid). Tristan and Isolde drink a love *potion* in the first act of the opera.

pot-pour-ri\pō-pu̇-'rē\ N. heterogeneous mixture; medley. He offered a *potpourri* of folk songs from many lands.

poul-tice\'pōl -təs\N. soothing application applied to sore and inflamed portions of the body. He was advised to apply a flaxseed *poultice* to the inflammation. also V.

prac-ti-ca-ble\'prak -ti-kə-bəl\ADJ. feasible. The board of directors decided that the plan was *practicable* and agreed to undertake the project. **prac-ti-ca-bil-i-ty**\prak -ti-kə-'bil -ət-ē\ N.

prac-ti-cal\'prak -ti-kəl\ADJ. based on experience; useful. He was a *practical* man, opposed to theory. **prac-ti-cal-i-ty** \prak -ti-'kal -ət-ē\ N.—**prac-ti-cal-ly** \'prak -ti-k(ə-)lē\ ADV.

prag-mat-ic\prag-'mat -ik\ADJ. practical; concerned with practical values. This test should provide us with a *pragmatic* analysis of the value of this course.

prag-ma-tist\'prag-mət-əst\N. practical person. No *pragmatist* enjoys becoming involved in a game he can never win.

prate\'prāt \V. speak foolishly; boost idly. Let us not *prate* about our qualities; rather, let our virtues speak for themselves.

\ŋ\ sing   \ō\ go   \o\ law   \oi\ boy   \th\ thin   \t͟h\ the   \ü\ loot   \u̇\ foot
\y\ yet   \zh\ vision   \à, k̲, ⁿ, œ, œ̄, ue, ue̅, ʳ\ *see* Pronunciation Symbols

prat-tle\\'prat -ᵊl\\ V. babble. The little girl *prattled* endlessly about her dolls. also N.

pre-am-ble \\'prē ₋am -bəl\\ N. introductory statement. In the *Preamble* to the Constitution, the purpose of the document is set forth.

pre-car-i-ous\\pri-'kar -ē-əs\\ ADJ. uncertain; risky. I think this stock is a *precarious* investment and advise against its purchase. **pre-car-i-ous-ly**\\pri-'kar -ē-əs-lē\\ADV.—**pre-car-i-ous-ness**\\pri-'kar -ē-əs-nəs\\N.

prec-e-dent\\'pres -əd-ənt\\N. something preceding in time which may be used as an authority or guide for future action. This decision sets a *precedent* for future cases of a similar nature.

pre-ce-dent\\pri-'sēd -ᵊnt\\ADJ. preceding in time, rank, etc. Our discussions, *precedent* to this event, certainly did not give you any reason to believe that we would adopt your proposal.

pre-cept\\'prē ₋sept\\ N. practical rule guiding conduct. "Love thy neighbor as thyself" is a worthwhile *precept*.

prec-i-pice\\'pres(-ə-)pəs\\N. cliff; dangerous position. Suddenly Indiana Jones found himself dangling from the edge of a *precipice*.

pre-cip-i-tate\\pri-'sip -ət-ət\\ADJ. headlong; rash. Do not be *precipitate* in this matter; investigate further. **pre-cip-i-tate-ly** \\pri-'sip -ət-ət-lē\\ ADV.—**pre-cip-i-tate-ness** \\pri-'sip -ət-ət-nəss\\N.

pre-cip-i-tate \\pri-'sip -ə-₋tāt\\ V. throw headlong; hasten. We must be patient as we cannot *precipitate* these results.

pre-cip-i-tous\\pri-'sip -ət-əs\\ADJ. steep. This hill is difficult to climb because it is so *precipitous*. **pre-cip-i-tous-ly** \\pri-'sip -ət-əs-lē\\ADV.

pre-clude\\pri-'klüd\\ V. make impossible; eliminate. This contract does not *preclude* my being employed by others at the same time that I am working for you.

pre-co-cious\\pri-'kō -shəs\\ADJ. developed ahead of time. By his rather adult manner of discussing serious topics, the child demonstrated that he was *precocious*. **pre-co-cious-ly**\\pri-'kō-shəs-lē\\ADV.—**pre-coc-i-ty**\\pri-'käs -ət-ē\\N.

pre-cur-sor\pri-'kər -sər\ N. forerunner. Gray and Burns were *precursors* of the Romantic Movement in English literature.

pred-a-to-ry\'pred -ə;tōr -ē\ ADJ. plundering. The hawk is a *predatory* bird. **pred-a-tor**\'pred -ət-ər\N.

pre-di-lec-tion \pred -ᵊl-'ek -shən\ N. partiality; preference. Although the artist used various media from time to time, he had a *predilection* for watercolor.

pre-em-i-nent \prē-'em -ə-nənt\ ADJ. outstanding; superior. The king traveled to Boston because he wanted the *preeminent* surgeon in the field to perform the operation. **pre-em-i-nence**\prē-'em-ə-nən(t)s\ N.— **pre-em-i-nent-ly** \prē-'em -ə-nənt-lē\ADV.

pre-empt\prē-'em(p)t\V.appropriate beforehand.Your attempt to *preempt* this land before it is offered to the public must be resisted. **pre-emp-tion**\prē-'em(p)-shən\N.

pref-a-to-ry\'pref -e;tōr -ē\ADJ. introductory. The chairman made a few *prefatory* remarks before he called on the first speaker.

pre-hen-sile\prē-'hen(t) -səl\ ADJ. capable of grasping or holding. Monkeys use not only their arms and legs but also their *prehensile* tails in traveling through the trees.

pre-lude\'prel-;(y)üd \ N. introduction; forerunner. I am afraid that this border raid is the *prelude* to more serious attacks.

pre-med-i-tate\pri-'med-ə-tāt\v. plan in advance. She had *premeditated* the murder for months, reading about common poisons and buying weed killer that contained arsenic.

pre-mo-ni-tion\prē -mə-'nish-ən\N. forewarning. We ignored these *premonitions* of disaster because they appeared to be based on childish fears.

pre-mon-i-to-ry\pri-'män -ə;tōr -ē\ ADJ. serving to warn. You should have visited a doctor as soon as you felt these *premonitory* chest pains.

pre-pon-der-ance \pri-'pän-d(ə-)rən(t)s\N. superiority of power, quantity, etc. The rebels sought to overcome the *preponderance* of strength of the government forces by

---

\ŋ\ sing \ō\ go \o\ law \oi\ boy \th\ thin \th\ the \ü\ loot \u\ foot
\y\ yet \zh\ vision \à, k̲, ⁿ, œ, œ̄, ue, ūē, ʳ\ *see* Pronunciation Symbols

engaging in guerrilla tactics. **pre-pon-der-ant**\pri-ʲpän -d(ə-)rənt\ ADJ.—**pre-pon-der-ant-ly** \pri-ʲpän -d(ə-)rənt-lē\ ADV.

pre-pon-der-ate\pri-ʲpän -də͵rāt\ V. be superior in power; outweigh. I feel confident that the forces of justice will *preponderate* eventually in this dispute.

pre-pos-ter-ous\pri-ʲpäs -t(ə-)rəs\ADJ. absurd; ridiculous. The excuse he gave for his lateness was so *preposterous* that everyone laughed.

pre-rog-a-tive\pri-ʲräg -ət-iv\N. privilege; unquestionable right. The President cannot levy taxes; that is the *prerogative* of the legislative branch of government.

pres-age\ʲpres -ij\V. foretell. The vultures flying overhead *presaged* the discovery of the corpse in the desert.

pre-sen-ti-ment\pri-ʲzent -ə-mənt\ N. premonition; foreboding. Hamlet felt a *presentiment* about his meeting with Laertes.

pres-tige\pre-ʲstēzh\ N. impression produced by achievements or reputation. The wealthy man sought to obtain social *prestige* by contributing to popular charities. **pres-ti-gious**\pre-ʲstij -əs\ADJ.

pre-sump-tion\pri-ʲzəm(p)-shən\N. arrogance; effrontery. She had the *presumption* to disregard our advice. **pre-sump-tive**\pri-ʲzəm(p)-tiv\ADJ.

pre-ten-tious\pri-ʲten -chəs\ADJ. ostentatious; ambitious. I do not feel that your limited resources will permit you to carry out such a *pretentious* program. **pre-ten-tious-ly** \pri-ʲten -chəs-lē\ ADV.—**pre-ten-tious-ness** \pri-ʲten -chəs-nəs\N.

pre-ter-nat-u-ral\͵prēt-ər-ʲnach(-ə)-rəl\ADJ. beyond that which is normal in nature. John's mother's total ability to tell when he was lying struck him as almost *preternatural*.

pre-text\ʲprē-͵tekst\N. excuse. He looked for a good *pretext* to get out of paying a visit to his aunt.

pre-vail\pri-ʲvā(e)l\V. induce; triumph over. He tried to *prevail* on her to type his essay for him.

---

prev-a-lent\\'prev(-ə)-lənt\\ADJ. widespread; generally accepted. A radical committed to social change, Reed had no patience with the conservative views *prevalent* in the America of his day.

pre-var-i-cate\\pri-'var -ə̩kāt\\ v. lie. Some people believe that to *prevaricate* in a good cause is justifiable and regard the statement as a "white lie." **pre-var-i-ca-tion**\\pri-̩var -ə-'kā -shən\\N.—**pre-var-i-ca-tor**\\pri-'var -ə̩kāt -ər\\N.

prim \\'prim\\ ADJ. very precise and formal; exceedingly proper. Many people commented on the contrast between the *prim* attire of the young lady and the inappropriate clothing worn by her escort. **prim-ly** \\'prim -lē\\ ADV.—**prim-ness**\\'prim -nəs\\N.

pri-mo-gen-i-ture \\prī-mō-'jen-ə̩chu(ə)r\\ N. seniority by birth. By virtue of *primogeniture*, the first-born child has many privileges denied his brothers and sisters.

pri-mor-di-al\\prī-'mȯrd -ē-əl\\ADJ. existing at the beginning (of time); rudimentary. The Neanderthal Man is one of our *primordial* ancestors.

primp\\'primp\\v. dress or groom oneself with care. She *primps* for hours before a dance.

pris-tine \\'pris ̩tēn\\ ADJ. characteristic of earlier times; primitive; unspoiled. This area has been preserved in all its *pristine* wildness.

pri-va-tion\\prī-'vā-shən\\N. hardship; want. In his youth, he knew hunger and *privation*.

privy\\'priv -ē\\ADJ. secret; hidden; not public. We do not care for *privy* chamber government. **priv-i-ly**\\'priv -ə-lē\\ ADV.

probe\\'prōb\\ v. explore with tools. The surgeon *probed* the wound for foreign matter before suturing it. also N.

pro-bi-ty \\'prō -bət-ē\\ N. uprightness; incorruptibility. Everyone took his *probity* for granted; his defalcations, therefore, shocked us all.

prob-lem-at-ic\\̩präb-lə-'mat-ik\\ADJ. perplexing; unsettled; questionable. Given the many areas of conflict still awaiting resolution, the outcome of the peace talks remains *problematic*.

---

pro-bos-cis \prə-ˈbäs -əs\ N. long snout; nose. The elephant uses his *proboscis* to handle things and carry them from place to place.

pro-cliv-i-ty \prō-ˈkliv -ət-ē\ N. inclination; natural tendency. He has a *proclivity* to grumble.

pro-cras-ti-nate \p(r)ə-ˈkras-tə₋nāt\ V. postpone; delay. It is wise not to *procrastinate;* otherwise, we find ourselves bogged down in a mass of work which should have been finished long ago. **pro-cras-ti-na-tion** \p(r)ə₋kras -tə-ˈnā -shən\ N.—**pro-cras-ti-na-tor** \p(r)ə-ˈkras -tə₋nāt -ər\ N.

prod \ˈpräd\ V. poke; stir up; urge. If you *prod* him hard enough, he'll eventually clean his room.

prod-i-gal \ˈpräd -i-gəl\ ADJ. wasteful; reckless with money. The *prodigal* son squandered his inheritance. also N. **prod-i-gal-i-ty** \präd -ə-ˈgal -ət-ē\ N.

pro-di-gious \prə-ˈdij -əs\ ADJ. marvelous; enormous. He marveled at her *prodigious* appetite. **pro-di-gious-ly** \prə-ˈdij -əs-lē\ ADV.

prod-i-gy \ˈpräd-ə-jē\ N. marvel; highly gifted child. Menuhin was a *prodigy,* performing wonders on his violin when he was barely eight years old.

pro-fane \prō-ˈfān\ V. violate; desecrate. Tourists are urged not to *profane* the sanctity of holy places by wearing improper garb. also ADJ. **prof-a-na-tion** \ˌpräf -ə-ˈnā -shən\ N.

prof-li-gate \ˈpräf -li-gət\ ADJ. dissipated; wasteful; licentious. In this *profligate* company, he lost all sense of decency. also N. **prof-li-ga-cy** \ˈpräf -li-gə-sē\ N.—**prof-li-gate-ly** \ˈpräf -li-gət-lē\ ADV.

pro-fu-sion \prə-ˈfyü-zhən\ N. lavish expenditure; overabundant condition. Seldom have I seen food and drink served in such *profusion.* **pro-fuse** \prə-ˈfyüs\ ADJ.—**pro-fuse-ly** \prə-ˈfyüs -lē\ ADV.

pro-gen-i-tor \prō-ˈjen -ət-ər\ N. ancestor. We must not forget the teachings of our *progenitors* in our desire to appear modern.

prog-e-ny \ˈpräj -(ə-)nē\ N. children; offspring. He was proud of his *progeny* but regarded George as the most promising of all his children.

prog-no-sis \präg-'nō -səs\ N. forecasted course of a disease; prediction. If the doctor's *prognosis* is correct, the patient will be in a coma for at least twenty-four hours.

prog-nos-ti-cate \präg-'näs -tə¡kāt\ V. predict. I *prognosticate* disaster unless we change our wasteful ways. **prog-nos-ti-ca-tion** \(¡)präg¡näs -tə-'kā -shən\N.-**prog-nos-ti-ca-tor** \präg-'näs -tə¡kāt -ər\N.

pro-jec-tile \prə-'jek -t²l\N. missile. Man has always hurled *projectiles* at his enemy whether in the form of stones or of highly explosive shells.

pro-le-tar-i-an \prō -lə-'ter -ē-ən\N. member of the working class. The aristocrats feared mob rule and gave the right to vote only to the wealthy, thus depriving the *proletarians* of a voice in government. also ADJ.

pro-lif-ic \prə-'lif -ik\ADJ. abundantly fruitful. He was a *prolific* writer and wrote as many as three books a year. **pro-lif-i-cal-ly** \prə-'lif -i-k(ə-)lē\ADV.

pro-lix \prō-'liks\ ADJ. verbose; drawn out. His *prolix* arguments irritated the jury. **pro-lix-i-ty** \prō-'lik -sət-ē\N.

pro-mis-cu-ous \prə-'mis -kyə-wəs\ADJ. mixed indiscriminately; haphazard; irregular. In the opera *La Boheme,* we get a picture of the *promiscuous* life led by the young artists of Paris. **pro-mis-cu-i-ty** \präm- əs-'kyü -ət-ē\N.—**pro-mis-cu-ous-ly** \prə-'mis -kyə-wəs-lē\ADV.—**pro-mis-cu-ous-ness** \prə-'mis -kyə-wəs-nəs \N.

prom-on-to-ry \'präm -ən¡tōr -ē\N. headland. They erected a lighthouse on the *promontory* to warn approaching ships of their nearness to the shore.

pro-mul-gate \'präm -əl¡gāt\ V. make known by official proclamation or publication. As soon as the Civil Service Commission *promulgates* the names of the successful candidates, we shall begin to hire members of our staff. **pro-mul-ga-tion** \präm -əl-'gā -shən\N.

prone \'prōn \ ADJ. inclined to; prostrate. She was *prone* to sudden fits of anger.

prop-a-gate \'präp -ə¡gāt \ V. multiply; spread. I am sure disease must *propagate* in such unsanitary and crowded areas. **prop-a-ga-tion** \präp -ə-'gā -shən\N.

---

pro-pel-lants\prə-'pel -ənts\ N. substances which propel or drive forward. The development of our missile program has forced our scientists to seek more powerful *propellants*.

pro-pen-si-ty\prə-'pen(t)-sət-ē\N. natural inclination. I dislike your *propensity* to belittle every contribution he makes to our organization.

pro-phy-lac-tic\prō -fə-'lak -tik\ ADJ. used to prevent disease. Despite all *prophylactic* measures introduced by the authorities, the epidemic raged until cool weather set in. also N.

pro-pin-qui-ty\prə-'piŋ -kwət-ē\N. nearness; kinship. Their relationship could not be explained as being based on mere *propinquity;* they were more than relatives; they were true friends.

pro-pi-ti-ate\prō-'pish -ē-ͺāt\ V. appease. The natives offered sacrifices to *propitiate* the gods. **pro-pi-ti-a-tion**\prō-ͺpis(h) -ē-'ā -shən\ N.—**pro-pi-tia-to-ry** \prō-'pish -(ē-)ə-ͺtōr -ē\ADJ.

pro-pi-tious\prə-'pish -əs\ADJ. favorable; kindly. I think it is advisable that we wait for a more *propitious* occasion to announce our plans.

pro-pound\prə-'paund\ V. put forth for analysis. In your discussion, you have *propounded* several questions; let us consider each one separately.

pro-pri-et y\p(r)ə-'pri-ət-ē\ N. fitness; correct conduct. I want you to behave at this dinner with *propriety;* don't embarrass me.

pro-pul-sive\prə-'pel -siv\ ADJ. driving forward. The jet plane has a greater *propulsive* power than the engine-driven plane. **pro-pul-sion**\prə-'pel -shən\N.

pro-sa-ic\prō-'zā -ik\ADJ. commonplace; dull. I do not like this author because he is so unimaginative and *prosaic*.

pro-scribe\prō-'skrīb\ V. ostracize; banish; outlaw. Antony, Octavius, and Lepidus *proscribed* all those who had conspired against Julius Caesar. **pro-scrip-tion**\prō-'skrip -shən\N.

pros-e-ly-tize\'präs -(ə-)lə-ͺtīz\ V. convert to a religion or belief. In these interfaith meetings, there must be no attempt to *proselytize;* we must respect all points of view.

pros·o·dy \\'präs -əd-ē\\ N. the art of versification. This book on *prosody* contains a rhyming dictionary as well as samples of the various verse forms.

pros·trate \\'präs ˌtrāt \\ V. stretch out full on ground. He *prostrated* himself before the idol. also ADJ. **pros·tra·tion** \\prä-'strä -shən\\ N.

pro·té·gé \\'prōt -əˌzhā\\ N. person under the protection and support of a patron. Cyrano de Bergerac refused to be a *protégé* of Cardinal Richelieu. **pro·té·gée** \\'prōt-əˌzhā\\ N.

pro·to·col \\'prōt -əˌkȯl \\ N. diplomatic etiquette. We must run this state dinner according to *protocol* if we are to avoid offending any of our guests.

pro·to·type \\'prōt -əˌtīp \\ N. original work used as a model by others. The crude typewriter on display in this museum is the *prototype* of the elaborate machines in use today.

pro·tract \\prō-'trakt \\ V. prolong. Do not *protract* this phone conversation as I expect an important business call within the next few minutes.

pro·trude \\prō-'trüd\\ V. stick out. His fingers *protruded* from the holes in his gloves. **pro·tru·sion** \\prō-'trü -zhən\\ N.— **pro·tru·sive** \\prō-'trü -siv\\ ADJ.

prov·e·nance \\'präv(-ə)-nən(t)s\\ N. origin or source of something. I am not interested in its *provenance;* I am more concerned with its usefulness than with its source.

prov·en·der \\'präv -ən-dər\\ N. dry food; fodder. I am not afraid of a severe winter because I have stored a large quantity of *provender* for the cattle.

prov·i·dent \\'präv -əd-ənt\\ ADJ. displaying foresight; thrifty; preparing for emergencies. In his usual *provident* manner, he had insured himself against this type of loss. **prov·i·dent·ly** \\'präv -əd-ənt-lē\\ ADV.

pro·vin·cial \\prə-'vin -chəl\\ ADJ. pertaining to a province; limited. We have to overcome their *provincial* attitude and get them to become more cognizant of world problems. **pro·vin·cial·ism** \\prə-'vin -chəlˌiz´ -əm\\ N.

pro·vi·so \\prə-'vī-(ˌ)zō\\ N. stipulation. I am ready to accept your proposal with the *proviso* that you meet your obligations within the next two weeks.

\n\ **sing**	\ō\ **go**	\ȯ\ **law**	\ȯi\ **boy**	\th\ **thin**	\t̲h̲\ **the**	\ü\ **loot**	\u̇\ **foot**
\y\ **yet**	\zh\ **vision**	\à, k̲, ⁿ, œ, ō̄e, ue, ūe̲, ʸ\ *see* Pronunciation Symbols

prov-o-ca-tion \ˌpräv -ə-ˈkā -shən\ N. cause for anger or retaliation. In order to prevent a sudden outbreak of hostilities, we must give our foe no *provocation*. **pro-voc-a-tive**\prə-ˈväk -ət-iv\N.

prox-im-i-ty\präk-ˈsim -ət-ē\ N. nearness. The deer sensed the hunter's *proximity* and bounded away.

prox-y \ˈpräk -sē\ N. authorized agent. Please act as my *proxy* and vote for this slate of candidates. also ADJ.

pru-dent\ˈprüd-ᵊnt\ADJ. cautious; careful. A miser hoards money not because he is *prudent* but because he is greedy. **pru-dence**\ˈprüd-ᵊn(t)s\N.

prune\ˈprün\v. cut away; trim. With the help of her editor, she was able to *prune* her manuscript into publishable form.

pru-ri-ent\ˈprur -ē-ənt\ADJ. based on lascivious thoughts. The police attempted to close the theater where the *prurient* film was being presented. **pru-ri-ence**\ˈprur-ē-ən(t)s\ N.

pseud-o-nym\ˈsüd -ᵊn-ˌim\N. pen name. Samuel Clemens' *pseudonym* was Mark Twain. **pseud-on-y-mous**\sü-ˈdän -ə-məs\ADJ.

psy-che\ˈsī -kē\N. soul; mind. It is difficult to delve into the *psyche* of a human being.

psy-chi-a-trist\sə-ˈkī -ə-trəst\N. a doctor who treats mental diseases. A *psychiatrist* often needs long conferences with his patient before a diagnosis can be made. **psy-chi-a-try**\sə-ˈkī -ə-trē\N.—**psy-chi-at-ric**\ˌsī -kē-ˈa -trik\ADJ.

psy-cho-path-ic\ˌsī -kə-ˈpath -ik\ADJ. pertaining to mental derangement. The *psychopathic* patient suffers more frequently from a disorder of the nervous system than from a diseased brain. **psy-cho-path**\ˈsī-kə-ˌpath\ N.

psy-cho-sis\sī-ˈkō -səs\ N. mental disorder. We must endeavor to find an outlet for the patient's repressed desires if we hope to combat this *psychosis*.

pu-er-ile \ˈpyù(-ə)r-al\ ADJ. childish. His *puerile* pranks sometimes offended his serious-minded friends. **pu-er-il-i-ty**\ˌpyù(-ə) r-ˈil -ət-ē\N.

\ə\ abut \ᵊ\ kitten, F table \ər\ further \a\ ash \ā\ ace \ä\ cot, cart
\aù\ out \ch\ chin \e\ bet \ē\ easy \g\ go \i\ hit \ī\ ice \j\ job

pu-gi-list\\'pyü-jə-ləst\\ N. boxer. The famous *pugilist* Cassius Clay changed his name to Muhammed Ali.

pug-na-cious\\pəg -'nā -shəs\\ ADJ. combative; disposed to fight. As a child he was *pugnacious* and fought with everyone. **pug-nac-i-ty**\\pəg -'nas -ət-ē\\ N.

puis-sant\\'pwis -³nt\\ ADJ. powerful; strong; potent. We must keep his friendship for he will make a *puissant* ally. **puis-sance**\\'pwis -³n(t) s\\ N.

pul-chri-tude\\'pəl -krə-̩t(y)üd\\ N. beauty; comeliness. I do not envy the judges who have to select this year's Miss America from this collection of female *pulchitrude*. **pul-chri-tu-di-nous**\\pəl -krə-̩t(y)üd -nəs\\ ADJ.

pul-mo-nary\\'pùl -mə-̩ner -ē\\ ADJ. pertaining to the lungs. In his research on *pulmonary* diseases, he discovered many facts about the lungs of animals and human beings.

pul-sate\\'pəl -̩sāt\\ V. throb. We could see the blood vessels in his temple *pulsate* as he became more angry. **pul-sa-tion**\\pəl -'sā -shən\\ N.

pum-mel\\'pəm-əl\\ V. beat. The severity with which he was *pummeled* was indicated by the bruises he displayed on his head and face.

punc-til-i-ous\\pəŋ(k) -'til-ē-əs\\ ADJ. laying stress on niceties of conduct, form; precise. We must be *punctilious* in our planning of this affair, for any error may be regarded as a personal affront.

pun-dit\\'pən -dət\\ N. learned Hindu; any learned man; authority on a subject. Even though he discourses on the matter like a *pundit,* he is actually rather ignorant about this topic.

pun-gent\\'pən -jənt\\ ADJ. stinging; caustic. The *pungent* aroma of the smoke made me cough. **pun-gen-cy**\\'pən -jən-sē\\ N.—**pun-gent-ly**\\'pən -jənt-lē\\ ADV.

pu-ni-tive\\'pyü -nət -iv\\ ADJ. punishing. He asked for *punitive* measures against the offender.

pu-ny\\'pyü -nē\\ ADJ. insignificant; tiny; weak. Our *puny* efforts to stop the flood were futile.

pur-ga-to-ry\\'pər -gə-̩tōr -ē\\ N. place of spiritual expiation. In this *purgatory,* he could expect no help from his comrades. **pur-ga-tor-i-al**\\pər -gə-'tōr -ē-əl\\ ADJ.

\\ŋ\\ sing \\ō\\ go \\ȯ\\ law \\ȯi\\ boy \\th\\ thin \\th\\ the \\ü\\ loot \\ù\\ foot
\\y\\ yet \\zh\\ vision \\à, k, ⁿ, œ, œ̄, ue, ūe, ʼ\\ *see* Pronunciation Symbols

purge\\'pərj\ v. clean by removing impurities; to clear of charges. If you are to be *purged* of the charge of contempt of Congress, you must be willing to answer the questions previously asked. also N.

pur-loin \\(ₗ)pər-'lòin\ v. steal. In the story, "The *Purloined* Letter," Poe points out that the best hiding place is often the most obvious place.

pur-port\\'pər¡pō(ə)rt\ N. intention; meaning. If the *purport* of your speech was to arouse the rabble, you succeeded admirably. also V.

pur-vey-or \\(ₗ)pər-'vā -ər\ N. furnisher of foodstuffs; caterer. As *purveyor* of rare wines and viands, he traveled through France and Italy every year in search of new products to sell. **pur-vey** \\(ₗ)pər-'vā\ V.—**pur-vey-ance** \\(ₗ)pər-'vā -ən(t)s\ N.

pur-view \\'pər ¡vyü\ N. scope. The sociological implications of these inventions are beyond the *purview* of this book.

pu-sil-lan-i-mous \\ₗpyü -sə-'lan -ə-məs\ ADJ. cowardly; fainthearted. You should be ashamed of your *pusillanimous* conduct during this dispute. **pu-sil-la-nim-i-ty**\\ₗpyü -sə-lə-'nim -ət-ē\ N.

pu-ta-tive\\'pyüt -ət-iv\ADJ. supposed; reputed. Although there are some doubts, the *putative* author of this work is Massinger.

pu-trid \\'pyü -trəd\ ADJ. foul; rotten; decayed. The gangrenous condition of the wound was indicated by the *putrid* smell when the bandages were removed. **pu-trid-i-ty**\\pyü-'trid -ət-ē\ N.

py-ro-ma-ni-ac\\ₗpī -rō-'mā -nē¡ak\ N. person with an irrestible desire to set things on fire. The detectives searched the area for the *pyromaniac* who had set these costly fires. **py-ro-ma-ni-a**\\ₗpi-rō-'mā -nē-ə\ N.

–q–

quack\ˈkwak \N. charlatan; imposter. Do not be misled by the exorbitant claims of this *quack*. also ADJ.

quad-ru-ped\ˈkwäd -rə-ped \N. four-footed animal. Most mammals are *quadrupeds*.

quaff\ˈkwäf \V. drink with relish. As we *quaffed* our ale, we listened to the gay songs of the students in the tavern. also N.

quag-mire\ˈkwag ‚mī(ə)r \N. bog; marsh. Our soldiers who served in Vietnam will never forget the drudgery of marching through the *quagmires* of the delta country.

quail\ˈkwā(ə)l \V. cower; lose heart. He was afraid that he would *quail* in the face of danger.

qual-i-fied\ˈkwäl-ə-‚fīd \ADJ. limited; restricted. Unable to give the candidate full support, the mayor gave him only a *qualified* endorsement. (secondary meaning) **qual-i-fy**\ˈkwäl-ə-‚fī \V.

qualm\ˈkwäm \N. misgiving. His *qualms* of conscience had become so great that he decided to abandon his plans.

quan-da-ry\ˈkwän -d(ə-)rē\N. dilemma. When the two colleges to which he had applied accepted him, he was in a *quandary* as to which one he should attend.

quar-an-tine\ˈkwȯr -ən‚tēn \N. isolation of person or ship to prevent spread of infection. We will have to place this house under *quarantine* until we determine the exact nature of the disease, also V.

quar-ry\ˈkwȯr-ē\N. victim; object of a hunt. The police closed in on their *quarry*.

quar-ry\ˈkwȯr-ē\V. dig into. They *quarried* blocks of marble out of the hillside. also N.

quay\ˈkē \N. dock; landing place. Because of the captain's carelessness, the ship crashed into the *quay*.

quea-sy\ˈkwē -zē\ADJ. easily nauseated; squeamish. As the ship left the harbor, he became *queasy* and thought that he was going to suffer from seasickness.

quell\ˈkwel \V. put down; quiet. The police used fire hoses and tear gas to *quell* the rioters.

\ŋ\ **sing** \ō\ **go** \ȯ\ **law** \ȯi\ **boy** \th\ **thin** \t͟h\ **the** \ü\ **loot** \u̇\ **foot**
\y\ **yet** \zh\ **vision** \à, k̲, ⁿ, œ, œ̄, ue, ūe, ʸ\ *see* Pronunciation Symbols

quer-u-lous \\'kwer -(y)ə-ləs\\ ADJ. fretful; whining. His classmates were repelled by his *querulous* and complaining statements.

queue \\'kyü\\ N. line. They stood patiently in the *queue* outside the movie theater.

quib-ble \\'kwib -əl\\ V. equivocate; play on words. Do not *quibble;* I want a straightforward and definite answer. also N.

qui-es-cent \\kwī'es -ᵊnt\\ ADJ. at rest; dormant. After this geyser erupts, it will remain *quiescent* for twenty-four hours.

qui-e-tude \\'kwī -ə₁t(y)üd\\ N. tranquillity. He was impressed by the air of *quietude* and peace that pervaded the valley.

quin-tes-sence \\kwin'tes -ᵊn(t)s\\ N. purest and highest embodiment. These books display the *quintessence* of wit.

quip \\'kwip\\ N. taunting remark. You are unpopular because you are too free with your *quips* and sarcastic comments. also V.

quirk \\'kwərk\\ N. startling twist; caprice. By a *quirk* of fate, he found himself working for the man whom he had discharged years before.

quix-ot-ic \\kwik'sät -ik\\ ADJ. idealistic but impractical. He is constantly presenting these *quixotic* schemes.

quiz-zi-cal \\'kwiz -i-kəl\\ ADJ. bantering; comical; humorously serious. Will Rogers' *quizzical* remarks endeared him to his audiences.

quo-rum \\'kwōr -əm\\ N. number of members necessary to conduct a meeting. The senator asked for a roll call to determine whether a *quorum* was present.

—r—

ra-bid\\'rab -əd\\ADJ. like a fanatic; furious. He was a *rabid* follower of the Dodgers and watched them play whenever he could go to the ball park.

ra-con-teur\\ˌrak-ˌän-'tər\\N. storyteller. My father was a gifted *raconteur* with an unlimited supply of anecdotes.

rag-a-muf-fin\\'rag -əˌməf -ən\\N. person wearing tattered clothes. He felt sorry for the *ragamuffin* who was begging for food and gave him money to buy a meal.

rail\\'rā(ə)l\\v. scold; rant. You may *rail* at him all you want; you will never change him.

rai-ment\\'rā-mənt\\N. clothing. "How can I go to the ball?" asked Cinderella. "I have no *raiment* to wear."

rak-ish\\'rā-kish\\ADJ. stylish; sporty. He wore his hat at a *rakish* and jaunty angle.

ram-i-fi-ca-tion\\ˌram -ə-fə'kā -shən\\N. branching out; subdivision. We must examine all the *ramifications* of this problem.

ram-i-fy\\'ram -əˌfī\\v. divide into branches or subdivisions. When the plant begins to *ramify,* it is advisable to nip off most of the new branches.

ramp\\'ramp\\N. slope; inclined plane. The house was built with *ramps* instead of stairs in order to enable the man in the wheelchair to move easily from room to room and floor to floor.

ram-pant\\'ram -pənt\\ADJ. rearing up on hind legs; unrestrained. The *rampant* weeds in the garden killed all the flowers which had been planted in the spring.

ram-part\\'ram -ˌpärt\\N. defensive mound of earth. "From the *ramparts* we watched" as the fighting continued.

ran-cid\\'ran(t) -səd\\ADJ. having the odor of stale fat. A *rancid* odor filled the ship's galley.

ran-cor\\'raŋ -kər\\N. bitterness; hatred. Let us forget our *rancor* and cooperate in this new endeavor.

ran-kle\\'raŋ-kəl\\v. irritate; fester. The memory of having been jilted *rankled* him for years.

rant\\'rant\\v. rave; speak bombastically. As we heard him *rant* on the platform, we could not understand his strange popularity with many people. also N.

---

ra·pa·cious \rə-'pā -shəs\ ADJ. excessively grasping; plundering. Hawks and *rapacious* birds play an important role in the "balance of nature"; therefore, they are protected throughout North America.

rap·proche·ment \rap ˌrōsh -'mäⁿ \ N. reconciliation. Both sides were eager to effect a *rapprochement* but did not know how to undertake a program designed to bring about harmony.

rar·e·fied \'rar -əˌfīd \ADJ. made less dense [of a gas]. The mountain climbers had difficulty breathing in the *rarefied* atmosphere.

raspy \'ras-pē\ADJ. grating; harsh. The sergeant's *raspy* voice grated on the recruits' ears.

ra·ti·o·ci·na·tion \ˌrat -ē-ōs -'ⁿ'ā -shən\ N. reasoning; act of drawing conclusions from premises. Poe's "The Gold Bug" is a splendid example of the author's use of *ratiocination*.

ra·tio·nal·i·za·tion \ˌrash -nə-lə-'zā-shən\ N. bringing into conformity with reason. All attempts at *rationalization* at this time are doomed to failure; tempers and emotions run too high for intelligent thought to prevail.

ra·tio·na·lize \'rash -nəˌlīz \v. reason; justify an improper act. Do not try to *rationalize* your behavior by blaming your companions.

rau·cous \'rȯ -kəs\ADJ. harsh and shrill. His *raucous* laughter irritated me.

rav·age \'rav -ij\v. plunder; despoil. The marauding army *ravaged* the countryside. also N.

rav·en·ous \'rav -(ə-)nəs\ADJ. extremely hungry. The *ravenous* dog upset several garbage pails in its search for food.

raze \'rāz \v. destroy completely. The owners intend to *raze* the hotel and erect an office building on the site.

re·ac·tion·ar·y \rē-'ak -shəˌner -ē\ ADJ. recoiling from progress; retrograde. His program was *reactionary* since it sought to abolish many of the social reforms instituted by the previous administration. also N.

realm \'relm \N. kingdom; sphere. The *realm* of possibilities for the new invention was endless.

re-bate\\'re ͵bāt \\ N. discount. We offer a *rebate* of ten percent to those who pay cash. also V.

re-buff\\ri-'bəf\\V. reject sharply; snub. She *rebuffed* his invitation so smoothly that he did not realize he had been snubbed.

re-cal-ci-trant\\ri-'kal -sə-trənt\\ADJ. obstinately stubborn. Donkeys are reputed to be the most *recalcitrant* of animals.

re-cant \\ri-'kant \\ V. repudiate; withdraw previous statement. Unless you *recant* your confession, you will be punished severely.

re-ca-pit-u-late\\͵rē -kə-'pich -ə͵lāt \\ V. summarize. Let us *recapitulate* what has been said thus far before going ahead.

re-ces-sion\\ri-'sesh -ən\\N. withdrawal; retreat. The *recession* of the troops from the combat area was completed in an orderly manner.

re-cid-i-vism\\ri-'sid -ə͵viz -əm\\N. habitual return to crime. Prison reformers in the United States are disturbed by the high rate of *recidivism;* the number of men serving second and third terms in prison indicates the failure of the prisons to rehabilitate the inmates.

re-cip-i-ent\\ri-'sip -ē-ənt\\N. receiver. Although he had been the *recipient* of many favors, he was not grateful to his benefactor.

re-cip-ro-cal \\ri-'sip -rə-kəl\\ ADJ. mutual; exchangeable; interacting. The two nations signed a *reciprocal* trade agreement. also N.

re-cip-ro-cate\\ri-'sip -rə͵kāt \\V. repay in kind. If they attack us, we shall be compelled to *reciprocate* and bomb their territory.

re-cluse\\'rek ͵lüs \\N. hermit. The *recluse* lived in a hut in the forest. also ADJ.

rec-on-cile \\'rek -ən͵sīl \\ V. make friendly after quarrel; correct inconsistencies. Each month we *reconcile* our checkbook with the bank statement.

re-con-dite\\'rek -ən͵dīt \\ADJ. abstruse; profound; hidden from view. He read many *recondite* books in order to obtain the material for his scholarly thesis.

re-con-nais-sance\ri-'kän -ə-zən(t)s\N. survey of enemy by soldiers; reconnoitering. If you encounter any enemy soldiers during your *reconnaissance*, capture them for questioning.

re-course\'rē ˌkō(ə)rs \N. resorting to help when in trouble. The boy's only *recourse* was to appeal to his father for aid.

rec-re-ant\'rek -rē-ənt\N. coward; betrayer of faith. The religious people ostracized the *recreant* who had abandoned their faith. also ADJ.

re-crim-i-na-tion\ri͜krim -ə-'nā -shən\N. countercharges. Loud and angry *recriminations* were her answer to his accusations.

rec-ti-fy\'rek -təˌfī \ V. correct. I want to *rectify* my error before it is too late.

rec-ti-tude \'rek -təˌt(y)üd \ N. uprightness. He was renowned for his *rectitude* and integrity.

re-cum-bent \ri-'kəm -bənt\ ADJ. reclining; lying down completely or in part. The command "AT EASE" does not permit you to take a *recumbent* position.

re-cu-per-ate\ri-'k(y)ü -pəˌrāt \V. recover. The doctors were worried because the patient did not *recuperate* as rapidly as they had expected.

re-cur-rent \ri-'kər -ənt\ ADJ. occurring again and again. These *recurrent* attacks disturbed us and we consulted a physician.

re-cu-sant\'rek -yə-zənt\N. person who refuses to comply; applied specifically to those who refused to attend Anglican services. In that religious community, the *recusant* was shunned as a pariah. also ADJ.—**re-cu-san-cy**\'rek -yə-zən-sē\N.

red-o-lent\'red -ᵊl-ənt\ADJ. fragrant; odorous; suggestive of an odor. Even though it is February, the air is *redolent* of spring.

re-doubt-a-ble\ri-'daủt -ə-bəl\ADJ. formidable; causing fear. The neighboring countries tried not to offend the Russians because they could be *redoubtable* foes.

re-dress\ri-'dres \N. remedy; compensation. Do you mean to tell me that I can get no *redress* for my injuries? also V.

\ə\ abut	\ᵊ\ kitten, F table	\ər\ further	\a\ ash	\ā\ ace	\ä\ cot, cart
\aủ\ out	\ch\ chin	\e\ bet	\ē\ easy	\g\ go	\i\ hit	\ī\ ice	\j\ job

re-dun-dant \ri-'dən -dənt\ ADJ. superfluous; excessively wordy; repetitious. Your composition is *redundant;* you can easily reduce its length.

reek \'rēk \ V. emit (odor). The room *reeked* with stale tobacco smoke. also N.

re-fec-tion \ri-'fek -shən\ N. slight refreshment. In our anxiety to reach our destination as rapidly as possible, we stopped on the road for only a quick *reflection.*

re-fec-to-ry \ri-'fek -t(ə-)rē\ N. dining hall. In this huge *refectory,* we can feed the entire monastic order at one sitting.

re-frac-tion \ri-'frak -shən\ N. bending of a ray of light. When you look at a stick inserted in water, it looks bent because of the *refraction* of the light by the water.

re-frac-to-ry \ri-'frak -t(ə-)rē\ ADJ. stubborn; unmanageable. The *refractory* horse was eliminated from the race.

re-fur-bish \ri-'fər -bish\ V. renovate; make bright by polishing. The flood left a deposit of mud on everything; it was necessary to *refurbish* our belongings.

ref-u-ta-tion \ref -yù-'tā -shən\ N. disproof of opponents' arguments. I will wait until I hear the *refutation* before deciding whom to favor.

re-fute \ri-'fyüt \ V. disprove. The defense called several respectable witnesses who were able to *refute* the false testimony of the prosecution's only witness.

re-gal \'rē -gəl\ ADJ. royal. He has a *regal* manner.

re-gale \ri-'gā(ə)l \ V. entertain. John *regaled* us with tales of his adventures in Africa.

re-gat-ta \ri-'gät -ə\ N. boat or yacht race. Many boating enthusiasts followed the *regatta* in their own yachts.

re-gen-er-a-tion \ri-jen -ə-'rā -shən\ N. spiritual rebirth. Modern penologists strive for the *regeneration* of the prisoners.

reg-i-cide \'rej-ə-sīd \ N. murder of a king or queen. The death of Mary Queen of Scots was an act of *regicide.*

re-gime \rā-'zhēm \ N. method or system of government. When a Frenchman mentions the Old *Regime,* he refers to the government existing before the revolution.

reg-i-men \\'rej -ə-mən\\ N. systematic plan, especially for improving health. I hope the results warrant our living under this strict and inflexible *regimen* of exercise.

re-ha-bil-i-tate \\ˌrē -(h)ə-'bil -ə-ˌtāt \\ V. restore to proper condition. We must *rehabilitate* those whom we send to prison.

re-im-burse \\ˌrē -əm-'bərs \\ V. repay. Let me know what you have spent and I will *reimburse* you.

re-it-er-ate \\rē-'it -ə-ˌrāt \\V. repeat. I shall *reiterate* this message until all have understood it.

re-ju-ve-nate \\ri-'jü-və-ˌnāt \\ V. make young again. The charlatan claimed that his elixir would *rejuvenate* the aged and weary.

rel-e-gate \\'rel -ə-ˌgāt \\ V. banish; consign to inferior position. If we *relegate* these experienced people to positions of unimportance because of their political persuasions, we shall lose the services of valuably trained personnel.

rel-e-van-cy \\'rel -ə-vən-sē\\N. pertinence; reference to the case in hand. I was impressed by the *relevancy* of your remarks. **rel-e-vant** \\'rel -ə-vənt\\ADJ.

re-lin-quish \\ri-'liŋ -kwish\\V. abandon. I will *relinquish* my claims to this property if you promise to retain my employees.

rel-ish \\'rel -ish\\V. savor; enjoy. I *relish* a good joke as much as anyone else. also N.

re-me-di-a-ble \\ri-'mēd -ē-ə-bəl\\ADJ. reparable. Let us be grateful that the damage is *remediable*.

re-me-di-al \\ri-'mēd -ē-əl\\ ADJ. curative; corrective. Because he was a slow reader, he decided to take a course in *remedial* reading.

rem-i-nis-cence \\ˌrem -ə-'nis -ᵊn(t)s\\ N. recollection. Her *reminiscences* of her experiences are so fascinating that she ought to write a book.

re-miss \\ri-'mis \\ADJ. negligent. He was accused of being *remiss* in his duty.

rem-nant \\'rem -nənt\\N. remainder. I suggest that you wait until the store places the *remnants* of these goods on sale.

re-mon-strate \\ri-'män ˌstrāt \\V. protest. I must *remonstrate* about the lack of police protection in this area.

---

re-morse\ri-'mȯ(ə)rs\ N. guilt; self-reproach. The murderer felt no *remorse* for his crime.

re-mu-ner-a-tive \ri⸱'myü -nə-rət-iv\ ADJ. compensating; rewarding. I find my new work so *remunerative* that I may not return to my previous employment. **re-mu-ner-a-tion** \ri⸱myü -nə⸱'rā -shən\ N.

rend\'rend \ V. split; tear apart. In his grief, he tried to *rend* his garments.

ren-der \'ren -dər\ V. deliver; provide; represent. He *rendered* aid to the needy and indigent.

ren-dez-vous \'rän -di⸱vü \ N. meeting place. The two fleets met at the *rendezvous* at the appointed time. also V.

ren-di-tion \ren-'dish -ən\ N. translation; artistic interpretation of a song, etc. The audience cheered enthusiastically as she completed her *rendition* of the aria.

ren-e-gade \'ren -i⸱gād \ N. deserter; apostate. Because he refused to support his fellow members in their drive, he was shunned as a *renegade*.

re-nounce\ri-'naún(t)s \ V. abandon; discontinue; disown; repudiate. Joan of Arc refused to *renounce* her statements even though she knew she would be burned at the stake as a witch.

ren-o-vate \'ren -ə⸱vāt \ V. restore to good condition; renew. They claim that they can *renovate* worn shoes so that they look like new ones.

re-nun-ci-a-tion \ri⸱nən(t) -sē⸱'ā-shən\ N. giving up; renouncing. Do not sign this *renunciation* of your right to sue until you have consulted a lawyer.

rep-a-ra-ble \'rep -(ə-)rə-bəl\ ADJ. capable of being repaired. Fortunately, the damages we suffered in the accident were *reparable*.

rep-a-ra-tion\⸱rep -ə⸱'rā -shən\ N. amends; compensation. At the peace conference, the defeated country promised to pay *reparations* to the victors.

rep-ar-tee\⸱rep -ər⸱'tē \ N. clever reply. He was famous for his witty *repartee* and his sarcasm.

re-pel-lent \ri⸱'pel -ənt\ ADJ. driving away; unattractive. Mosquitoes find the odor so *repellent* that they leave any spot where this liquid has been sprayed. also N.

\ŋ\ **sing**   \ō\ **go**   \ȯ\ **law**   \ȯi\ **boy**   \th\ **thin**   \t͟h\ **the**   \ü\ **loot**   \ u̇\ **foot**
\y\ **yet**   \zh\ **vision**   \à, k̲, ⁿ, œ, ōē, ue, ūē, ʳ\ *see* Pronunciation Symbols

re·per·cus·sion \rē -pər-ʲkəsh -ən\ N. rebound; reverberation; reaction. I am afraid that this event will have serious *repercussions*.

rep·er·toire\ʹrep -ə(r)ˌtwär \ N. list of works of music, drama, etc., a performer is prepared to present. The opera company decided to include *Madame Butterfly* in its *repertoire* for the following season.

re·plen·ish \ri-ʲplen -ish\ v. fill up again. The end of rationing enabled us to *replenish* our supply of canned food.

re·plete \ri-ʲplēt \ ADJ. filled to capacity; abundantly supplied. This book is *replete* with humorous situations.

rep·li·ca\ʹrep -li-kə\ N. copy. Are you going to hang this *replica* of the Declaration of Independence in the classroom or in the auditorium?

re·pos·i·to·ry \ri-ʲpäz -ə-ˌtōr -ē\ N. storehouse. Libraries are *repositories* of the world's best thoughts.

rep·re·hen·si·ble \rep -ri-ʲhen(t) -sə-bəl\ ADJ. deserving blame. Your vicious conduct in this situation is *reprehensible*.

re·prieve\ri-ʲprēv \ N. temporary stay. During the twenty-four-hour *reprieve*, the lawyers sought to make the stay of execution permanent, also v.

rep·ri·mand \ʹrep -rə-ˌmand \ v. reprove severely. I am afraid that my parents will *reprimand* me when I show them my report card. also N.

re·pri·sal\ri-ʲprī-zəl\ N. retaliation. I am confident that we are ready for any *reprisals* the enemy may undertake.

rep·ro·bate\ʹrep -rə-ˌbāt \ N. person hardened in sin, devoid of a sense of decency. I cannot understand why he has so many admirers if he is the *reprobate* you say he is. also ADJ.

rep·ro·ba·tion\rep -rə-ʲbā -shən\ N. severe disapproval. The students showed their *reprobation* of his act by refusing to talk with him.

re·prove\ri-ʲprüv \ v. censure; rebuke. The principal *reproved* the students when they became unruly in the auditorium.

\ə\ abut \ᵊ\ kitten, F table \ər\ further \a\ ash \ā\ ace \ä\ cot, cart
\aᵰ\ out \ch\ chin \e\ bet \ē\ easy \g\ go \i\ hit \ī\ ice \j\ job

re-pu-di-ate \ri-'pyüd -ē₁āt \ v. disown; disavow. He announced that he would *repudiate* all debts incurred by his wife.

re-pug-nance \ri-'pəg -nən(t)s\ n. loathing. She looked at the snake with *repugnance*.

re-qui-em \'rek -wē-əm\ n. mass for the dead; dirge. They played Mozart's *Requiem* at the funeral.

req-ui-site \'rek -wə-zət\ n. necessary requirement. Many colleges state that a student must offer three years of a language as a *requisite* for admission. also ADJ.

re-quite \ri-'kwīt \ v. repay; revenge. The wretch *requited* his benefactors by betraying them.

re-scind \ri-'sind \ v. cancel. Because of public resentment, the king had to *rescind* his order.

re-scis-sion \ri-'sizh -ən\ n. abrogation; annulment. The *rescission* of the unpopular law was urged by all political parties.

re-serve \ri-'zərv\ n. self-control; care in expressing oneself. She was outspoken and uninhibited; he was cautious and inclined to *reserve*. (secondary meaning) **re-served** \ri-'zərvd\ ADJ.

res-i-due \'rez -ə₁d(y)ü \ n. remainder; balance. In his will, he requested that after payment of debts, taxes, and funeral expenses, the *residue* be given to his wife.

re-signed \ri-'zīnd\ ADJ. unresisting; patiently submissive. Bob Cratchit was too *resigned* to his downtrodden existence to protest Scrooge's bullying. **res-ig-na-tion** \₁rez-ig-'nā-shən\ n.

re-sil-ient \ri-'zil -yənt\ ADJ. elastic; having the power of springing back. Steel is highly *resilient* and therefore is used in the manufacture of springs.

res-o-nant \'rez -ᵊn-ənt\ ADJ. echoing; resounding; possessing resonance. His *resonant* voice was particularly pleasing.

re-spite \'res -pət\ n. delay in punishment; interval of relief; rest. The judge granted the condemned man a *respite* to enable his attorneys to file an appeal.

---

re-splen-dent\ri-ˈsplen-dənt\ADJ. brilliant; lustrous. The toreador wore a *resplendent* costume.

re-spon-sive-ness\ri-ˈspän(t)-siv-nəs\N. state of reacting readily to appeals, orders, etc. The audience cheered and applauded, delighting the performers by its *responsiveness*.

res-ti-tu-tion\ˌres-tə-ˈt(y)ü-shən\N. reparation; indemnification. He offered to make *restitution* for the window broken by his son.

res-tive\ˈres-tiv\ADJ. unmanageable; fretting under control. We must quiet the *restive* animals.

re-sur-gent\ri-ˈsər-jənt\ADJ. rising again after defeat, etc. The *resurgent* nation surprised everyone by its quick recovery after total defeat.

re-sus-ci-tate\ri-ˈsəs-ə-ˌtāt\V. revive. The lifeguard tried to *resuscitate* the drowned child by applying artificial respiration.

re-tal-i-ate\ri-ˈtal-ē-ˌāt\V. repay in kind (usually for bad treatment). Fear that we will *retaliate* immediately deters our foe from attacking us.

re-ten-tive\ri-ˈtent-iv\ADJ. holding; having a good memory. The pupil did not need to spend much time in study as he had a *retentive* mind.

ret-i-cence\ˈret-ə-sən(t)s\N. reserve; uncommunicativeness; inclination to be silent. Because of the *reticence* of the key witness, the case against the defendant collapsed.

ret-i-nue\ˈret-ᵊn-ˌ(y)ü\N. following; attendants. The queen's *retinue* followed her down the aisle.

re-tort\ri-ˈtȯ(ə)rt\N. quick, sharp reply. Even when it was advisable for her to keep her mouth shut, she was always ready with a quick *retort*. also v.

re-trac-tion\ri-ˈtrak-shən\N. withdrawal. He dropped his libel suit after the newspaper published a *retraction* of its statement.

re-trench\ri-ˈtrench\V. cut down; economize. If they were able to send their children to college, they would have to *retrench*.

---

ret-ri-bu-tion \‚re -trə-ꞏbyü -shən\ N. vengeance; compensation; punishment for offenses. The evangelist maintained that an angry deity would exact *retribution* from the sinners.

re-trieve \ri-ꞏtrēv \ V. recover; find and bring in. The dog was intelligent and quickly learned to *retrieve* the game killed by the hunter. also N.

ret-ro-ac-tive \‚re -trō-ꞏak -tiv\ ADJ. of a law which dates back to a period before its enactment. Because the law was *retroactive* to the first of the year, we found he was eligible for the pension.

ret-ro-grade \‚re -trə-grād \ V. go backwards; degenerate. Instead of advancing, our civilization seems to have *retrograded* in ethics and culture. also ADV., ADJ.

ret-ro-spec-tive \‚re -trə-ꞏspek -tiv\ ADJ. looking back on the past. It is only when we become *retrospective* that we can appreciate the tremendous advances made during this century. also N.

rev-el-ry \ꞏrev -əl-rē\ N. boisterous merrymaking. New Year's Eve is a night of *revelry*.

re-ver-ber-ate \ri-ꞏvər -bə‚rāt \ V. echo; resound. The entire valley *reverberated* with the sound of the church bells.

re-vere \ri-'vi(ə)r\ V. respect; honor. In Asian societies, people *revere* their elders.

rev-er-ie \ꞏrev -(ə-)rē\ N. daydream; musing. He was awakened from his *reverie* by the teacher's question.

re-vile \ri-ꞏvī(ə)l \ V. slander; use verbal abuse. He was avoided by all who feared that he would *revile* and abuse them if they displeased him.

re-vul-sion \ri-ꞏvəl -shən\ N. sudden violent change of feeling; reaction. Many people in this country who admired dictatorships underwent a *revulsion* when they realized what Hitler and Mussolini were trying to do.

rhap-so-dize \ 'rap-sə-‚dīz \ V. to speak or write in an exaggeratedly enthusiastic manner. She greatly enjoyed her Hawaiian vacation and *rhapsodized* about it for weeks.

rhet-o-ric \ꞏret -ə-rik\ N. art of effective communication; insincere language. All writers, by necessity, must be skilled in *rhetoric*. **rhe-tor-i-cal** \ri-ꞏtȯr -i-kəl\ADJ.

\ŋ\ sing   \ō\ go   \ȯ\ law   \ȯi\ boy   \th\ thin   \t͟h\ the   \ü\ loot   \u̇\ foot
\y\ yet   \zh\ vision   \à, k̲, ⁿ, œ, œ̄, ue, u̅e̅, ʸ\ *see* Pronunciation Symbols

rheum-y\\'rü -mē\\ADJ. pertaining to a discharge from nose and eyes. His *rheumy* eyes warned us that he was coming down with a cold.

rib-ald \\'rib -əld\\ ADJ. wanton; profane. He sang a *ribald* song which offended many of us.

rife\\'rīf \\ADJ. abundant; current. In the face of the many rumors of scandal, which are *rife* at the moment, it is best to remain silent.

rift \\'rift \\ N. opening; break. The plane was lost in the stormy sky until the pilot saw the city through a *rift* in the clouds.

rig-or \\'rig -ər\\ N. severity. Many settlers could not stand the *rigors* of the New England winters.

rime \\'rīm \\ N. white frost. The early morning dew had frozen and everything was covered with a thin coat of *rime*.

ris-i-ble \\'riz -ə-bəl\\ ADJ. inclined to laugh; ludicrous. His remarks were so *risible* that the audience howled with laughter. **ris-i-bil-i-ty**\\riz -ə-'bil -ət-ē\\N.

ris-qué\\ri-'skā \\ADJ. verging upon the improper; off-color. Please do not tell your *risqué* anecdotes at this party.

roan\\'rōn \\ADJ. brown mixed with gray or white. You can distinguish this horse in a race because it is *roan* while all the others are bay or chestnut. also N.

ro-bust\\rō-'bəst \\ADJ. vigorous; strong. The candidate for the football team had a *robust* physique.

ro-co-co\\rə-'kō -ₒkō\\ADJ. ornate; highly decorated. The *rococo* style in furniture and architecture, marked by scrollwork and excessive decoration, flourished during the middle of the eighteenth century. also N.

ro-se-ate\\'rō -zē-ət\\ADJ. rosy; optimistic. I am afraid you will have to alter your *roseate* views in the light of the distressing news that has just arrived.

ros-ter\\ 'räs-tər \\ N. list. They print the *roster* of players in the season's program.

ros-trum\\'räs -trəm\\N. platform for speech-making; pulpit. The crowd murmured angrily and indicated that they did not care to listen to the speaker who was approaching the *rostrum*.

\\ə\\ abut \\ᵊ\\ kitten, F table \\ər\\ further \\a\\ ash \\ā\\ ace \\ä\\ cot, cart
\\aᵘ\\ out \\ch\\ chin \\e\\ bet \\ē\\ easy \\g\\ go \\i\\ hit \\ī\\ ice \\j\\ job

rote\\'rōt \\N. repetition. He recited the passage by *rote* and gave no indication he understood what he was saying.

ro-tun-da\\rō-'tən -də\\N. circular building or hall covered with a dome. His body lay in state in the *rotunda* of the Capitol.

ro-tun-di-ty\\rō-'tən -dət-ē\\N. roundness; sonorousness of speech. Washington Irving emphasized the *rotundity* of the governor by describing his height and circumference. **ro-tund**\\rō-'tənd \\ADJ.

rout\\'raüt\\v. stampede; drive out; defeat decisively. The reinforcements were able to *rout* the enemy. also N.

rub-ble\\'rəb -əl\\N. fragments. Ten years after World War II, some of the *rubble* left by enemy bombings could still be seen.

ru-bi-cund\\'rü -bi-₍ₒ₎kənd\\ADJ. having a healthy reddish color; ruddy; florid. His *rubicund* complexion was the result of an active outdoor life.

rud-dy \\'rəd -ē\\ ADJ. reddish; healthy-looking. His *ruddy* features indicated that he had spent much time in the open.

ru-di-men-ta-ry \\,rüd -ə-'ment -ə-rē\\ ADJ. not developed; elementary. His dancing was limited to a few *rudimentary* steps.

rue-ful\\'rü -fəl\\ ADJ. regretful; sorrowful; dejected. The artist has captured the sadness of childhood in his portrait of the boy with the *rueful* countenance.

ruf-fi-an\\'rəf-ē-ən\\N. bully; scoundrel. The *ruffians* threw stones at the police.

ru-mi-nate \\'rü -mə¸nāt \\ v. chew the cud; ponder. We cannot afford to wait while you *ruminate* upon these plans.

rum-mage\\'rəm -ij\\v. ransack; thoroughly search. When we *rummaged* through the trunks in the attic, we found many souvenirs of our childhood days. also N.

ruse\\'rüs \\N. trick; stratagem. You will not be able to fool your friends with such an obvious *ruse*.

rus-tic \\'rəs -tik\\ ADJ. pertaining to country people; uncouth. The backwoodsman looked out of place in his *rustic* attire. also N.

rus·ti·cate\\'rəs -ti₁kāt \\ v. banish to the country; dwell in the country. I like city life so much that I can never understand how people can *rusticate* in the suburbs.

ruth·less\\'rüth -ləs\\ ADJ. pitiless. The escaped convict was a dangerous and *ruthless* murderer.

—S—

sac-cha-rine \ 'sak-(ə-)rən \ ADJ. cloyingly sweet. She tried to ingratiate herself, speaking sweetly and smiling a *saccharine* smile.

sac-er-do-tal \ ˌsas -ər-ˈdōt -ᵊl \ ADJ. priestly. The priest decided to abandon his *sacerdotal* duties and enter the field of politics.

sac-ri-le-gious \ ˌsak -rə-ˈlij -əs \ ADJ. desecrating; profane. His stealing of the altar cloth was a very *sacrilegious* act.

sac-ro-sanct \ 'sak -rō-ˌsaŋ(k)t \ ADJ. most sacred; inviolable. The brash insurance salesman invaded the *sacrosanct* privacy of the office of the president of the company.

sa-dis-tic \ sə-ˈdis -tik \ ADJ. inclined to cruelty. If we are to improve conditions in this prison, we must first get rid of the *sadistic* warden. **sa-dism** \ 'sā-ˌdiz -əm \ N.

saf-fron \ 'saf -rən \ ADJ. orange-colored; colored like the autumn crocus. The Halloween cake was decorated with *saffron*-colored icing.

sa-ga \ 'säg -ə \ N. Scandinavian myth; any legend. This is a *saga* of the sea and the men who risk their lives on it.

sa-ga-cious \ sə-ˈgā -shəs \ ADJ. keen; shrewd; having insight. He is much too *sagacious* to be fooled by a trick like that.

sa-lient \ 'sā -lyənt \ ADJ. prominent. One of the *salient* features of that newspaper is its excellent editorial page. also N.

sa-line \ 'sā -ˌlēn \ ADJ. salty. The slighty *saline* taste of this mineral water is pleasant. also N.

sal-low \ 'sal -(ˌ)ō \ ADJ. yellowish; sickly in color. We were disturbed by his *sallow* complexion.

sa-lu-bri-ous \ sə-ˈlü -brē-əs \ ADJ. healthful. Many people with hay fever move to more *salubrious* sections of the country during the months of August and September.

sal-u-ta-ry \ 'sal -yə -ˌter -ē \ ADJ. tending to improve; beneficial; wholesome. The punishment had a *salutary* effect on the boy, as he became a model student. also N.

sal-vage \ 'sal -vij \ V. rescue from loss. All attempts to *salvage* the wrecked ship failed. also N.

sal-ver \ 'sal -vər \ N. tray. The food was brought in on silver *salvers* by the waiters.

\ŋ\ **sing**	\ō\ **go**	\o\̇ **law**	\oi\̇ **boy**	\th\ **thin**	\t̲h̲\ **the**	\ü\ **loot**	\u\̇ **foot**
\y\ **yet**	\zh\ **vision**	\ə, k̲,̲ ⁿ, œ, œ̄, ue, ūe, ʳ\ *see* Pronunciation Symbols

sanc·ti·mo·ni·ous \ˌsaŋ(k) -tə-'mō -nē-əs\ ADJ. displaying ostentatious or hypocritical devoutness. You do not have to be so *sanctimonious* to prove that you are devout.

sanc·tion \ 'saŋ(k)-shən \ V. approve; ratify. Nothing will convince me to *sanction* the engagement of my daughter to such a worthless young man.

sang·froid \ 'sänⁿ -'f(r)wä \ N. coolness in a trying situation. The captain's *sangfroid* helped to allay the fears of the passengers.

san·gui·nar·y \ 'saŋ -gwə-ˌner -ē\ ADJ. bloody. The battle of Iwo Jima was unexpectedly *sanguinary*.

san·guine \ 'saŋ -gwən\ ADJ. cheerful; hopeful. Let us not be too *sanguine* about the outcome.

sa·pi·ent \ 'sā -pē-ənt\ ADJ. wise; shrewd. The students enjoyed the professor's *sapient* digressions more than his formal lectures.

sar·casm \ 'sär-ˌkaz-əm \ N. scornful remarks; stinging rebuke. His feelings were hurt by the *sarcasm* of his supposed friends. **sar·cas·tic** \ sär-'kas-tik \ ADJ.

sar·coph·a·gus \ sär-'käf -ə-gəs\ N. stone coffin, often highly decorated. The display of the *sarcophagus* in the art museum impresses me as a morbid exhibition.

sar·don·ic \ sär -'dän -ik\ ADJ. disdainful; sarcastic; cynical. The *sardonic* humor of nightclub comedians who satirize or ridicule patrons in the audience strikes some people as amusing and others as rude.

sar·to·ri·al \ sär-'tōr -ē-əl\ ADJ. pertaining to tailors or tailored clothes. He was as famous for the *sartorial* splendor of his attire as he was for his acting.

sate \ 'sāt \ V. satisfy to the full; cloy. Its hunger *sated*, the lion dozed.

sat·el·lite \ 'sat -ᵊlˌīt \ N. small body revolving around a larger one. During the first few years of the Space Age, hundreds of *satellites* were launched by Russia and the United States.

sa·ti·ate \ 'sā -shē-ˌāt \ V. surfeit; satisfy fully. The guests, having eaten until they were *satiated*, now listened inattentively to the speakers. **sa·tiate** \ 'sā-sh(ē-)ət\ ADJ.

\ə\ abut	\ᵊ\ kitten, F table	\ər\ **further**	\a\ **ash**	\ā\ **ace**	\ä\ **cot, cart**
\au̇\ **out**	\ch\ **chin**	\e\ **bet**	\ē\ **easy**	\g\ **go**	\i\ **hit** \ī\ **ice** \j\ **job**

sa-ti-e-ty \sə⸱tī ⸱-ət-ē\ N. condition of being crammed full; glutted state; repletion. The *satiety* of the guests at the sumptuous feast became apparent when they refused the delicious dessert.

sat-ire\'sa ˌtī(ə)r \ N. form of literature in which irony, sarcasm, and ridicule, are employed to attack vice and folly. *Gulliver's Travels*, which is regarded by many as a tale for children, is actually a bitter *satire* attacking man's folly.

sat-u-rate\'sach -əˌrāt \ v. soak. Their clothes were *saturated* by the rain. **sat-u-rate**\'sach ⸱-(ə-)rət\ADJ.

sat-ur-nine\'sat -ərˌnīn \ADJ. gloomy. Do not be misled by his *saturnine* countenance; he is not as gloomy as he looks.

sa-tyr\'sāt -ər\ N. half-human, half-bestial being in the court of Dionysos, portrayed as wanton and cunning. He was like a *satyr* in his lustful conduct.

saun-ter\'sȯnt -ər\ v. stroll slowly. As we *sauntered* through the park, we stopped frequently to admire the spring flowers.

sa-vant \sa⸱vänt \ N. scholar. Our faculty includes many world-famous *savants*.

sa-voir faire \ˌsav ˌwär ⸱fa(ə)r \ N. tact; poise; sophistication. I envy his *savoir faire;* he always knows exactly what to do and say.

sa-vor\'sā -vər\v. have a distinctive flavor, smell, or quality. I think your choice of a successor *savors* of favoritism. also N.

scanty\'skant-ē\ADJ. meager; insufficient. Thinking his helping of food was *scanty,* Oliver Twist asked for more.

scape-goat\'skāp-ˌgōt\N. someone who bears the blame for others. After the Challenger disaster, NASA searched for *scapegoats* on whom it could cast the blame.

scav-en-ger\'skav -ən-jər\N. collector and disposer of refuse; animal that devours refuse and carrion. The Oakland *Scavenger* Company is responsible for the collection and disposal of the community's garbage.

schism \'siz -əm\ N. division; split. Let us not widen the *schism* by further bickering.

scin-til-la\sin-ᵗtil -ə\N. shred; least bit. You have not produced a *scintilla* of evidence to support your argument.

scin-til-late\ˈsint -ᵊlˌāt \V. sparkle; flash. I enjoy her dinner parties because the food is excellent and the conversation *scintillates*.

sci-on\sī -ən\N. offspring. The farm boy felt out of place in the school attended by the *scions* of the wealthy and noble families.

scourge \ˈskərj \ N. lash; whip; severe punishment. They feared the plague and regarded it as a deadly *scourge*. also V.

scru-pu-lous\ˈskrü-pyə-ləs\ADJ. conscientious; extremely thorough. I can recommend him for a position of responsibility for I have found him a very *scrupulous* young man.

scru-ti-nize\ˈskrüt-ᵊn-ˌīz\V. examine closely and critically. Searching for flaws, the sergeant *scrutinized* every detail of the private's uniform.

scul-lion\ˈskəl -yən\N. menial kitchen worker. Lynette was angry because she thought she had been given a *scullion* to act as her defender.

scur-ri-lous \ˈskər -ə-ləs\ ADJ. obscene; indecent. Your *scurrilous* remarks are especially offensive because they are untrue.

scut-tle\ˈskət -ᵊl\ V. sink by cutting holes in. The sailors decided to *scuttle* their vessel rather than surrender it to the enemy. also N.

se-ba-ceous\si-ᵗbā -shəs\ADJ. oily; fatty. The *sebaceous* glands secrete oil to the hair follicles.

se-ces-sion\si-ˈsesh -ən\N. withdrawal. The *secession* of the Southern states provided Lincoln with his first major problem after his inauguration.

sec-u-lar\ˈsek -yə-lər\ADJ. worldly; not pertaining to church matters; temporal. The church leaders decided not to interfere in *secular* matters. also N.

se-date\si-ˈdāt \ADJ. composed; grave. The parents were worried because they felt their son was too quiet and *sedate*. also V.

\ə\ abut   \ᵊ\ kitten, F table   \ər\ further   \a\ ash   \ā\ ace   \ä\ cot, cart
\au̇\ out   \ch\ chin   \e\ bet   \ē\ easy   \g\ go   \i\ hit   \ī\ ice   \j\ job

sed-en-tar-y\\'sed -ᵊn̩ter -ē\\ADJ. requiring sitting. Because he had a *sedentary* occupation, he decided to visit a gymnasium weekly.

se-di-tion\\si-'dish-ən\\N. resistance to authority; insubordination. His words, though not treasonous in themselves, were calculated to arouse thoughts of *sedition*.

sed-u-lous\\'sej -ə-ləs\\ADJ. diligent. Stevenson said that he played the "*sedulous* ape" and diligently imitated the great writers of the past.

seethe\\'sē<u>th</u>\\V. be disturbed; boil. The nation was *seething* with discontent as the noblemen continued their arrogant ways.

seine\\'sān\\N. net for catching fish. When the shad run during the spring, you may see fishermen with *seines* along the banks of our coastal rivers.

sem-blance\\'sem -blən(t)s\\N. outward appearance; guise. Although this book has a *semblance* of wisdom and scholarship, a careful examination will reveal many errors and omissions.

se-nil-i-ty\\si-'nil -ət-ē\\N. old age; feeblemindedness of old age. Most of the decisions are being made by the junior members of the company because of the *senility* of the president.

sen-su-al\\'sench -(ə-)wəl\\ADJ. devoted to the pleasures of the senses; carnal; voluptuous. I cannot understand what caused him to drop his *sensual* way of life and become so ascetic.

sen-su-ous\\'sench -(ə-)wəs\\ADJ. pertaining to the physical senses; operating through the senses. He was stimulated by the sights, sounds and smells about him; he was enjoying his *sensuous* experience.

sen-ten-tious\\sen-'ten -chəs\\ADJ. terse; concise; aphoristic. After reading so many redundant speeches, I find his *sentetious* style particularly pleasing.

sep-tic\\'sep -tik\\ADJ. putrid; producing putrefaction. The hospital was in such a filthy state that we were afraid that many of the patients would suffer from *septic* poisoning.

sep-ul-cher\\'sep -əl-kər\\N. tomb. Annabel Lee was buried in the *sepulcher* by the sea.

\\ŋ\\ **sing** \\ō\\ **go** \\ȯ\\ **law** \\ȯi\\ **boy** \\th\\ **thin** \\<u>th</u>\\ **the** \\ü\\ **loot** \\u̇\\ **foot**
\\y\\ **yet** \\zh\\ **vision** \\à, <u>k</u>, ⁿ, œ, ō̄e, ue, ū̄e, ʸ\\ *see* Pronunciation Symbols

se·qua·cious \si⸱ʼkwā -shəs\ ADJ. eager to follow; ductile. The *sequacious* members of Parliament were only too willing to do the bidding of their leader.

se·ques·ter \si⸱ʼkwes -tər\ V. retire from public life; segregate; seclude. Although he had hoped for a long time to *sequester* himself in a small community, he never was able to drop his busy round of activities in the city.

ser·aph \ʼser -əf\ N. high-ranking, six-winged angel. In "Annabel Lee" Poe maintains that the "winged *seraphs* of Heaven" envied their great love.

ser·en·dip·i·ty \ˌser -ən-ʼdip -ət-ē\ N. gift for finding valuable things not searched for. Many scientific discoveries are a matter of *serendipity*.

se·ren·i·ty \sə⸱ʼren -ət-ē\ N. calmness; placidity. The *serenity* of the sleepy town was shattered by a tremendous explosion.

ser·pen·tine \ʼsər-pən-ˌtēn\ ADJ. winding; twisting. The car swerved at every curve in the *serpentine* road.

ser·rate \ʼse(ə)r ˌāt\ ADJ. having a sawtoothed edge. The beech tree is one of many plants that has *serrate* leaves. **ser·rate** \sə⸱ʼrāt\ V.

ser·vile \ʼsər -vəl\ ADJ. slavish; cringing. Uriah Heep was a very *servile* individual.

sev·er·ance \ʼsev -(ə-)rən(t)s\ N. the act of dividing or separating. A factory accident resulted in the *severance* of two of the worker's fingers. **sev·er** \ʼsev -ər\ V.

se·ver·i·ty \sə⸱ʼver-ət-ē\ N. harshness; plainness. The newspapers disapproved of the *severity* of the sentence.

shack·le \ʼshak -əl\ V. chain; fetter. The criminal's ankles were *shackled* to prevent his escape. also N.

sham \ʼsham\ V. pretend. He *shammed* sickness to get out of going to school. also N.

sham·bles \ʼsham -bəlz\ N. slaughterhouse; scene of carnage. By the time the police arrived, the room was a *shambles*.

sheaf \ʼshēf\ N. bundle of stalks of grain; any bundle of things tied together. The lawyer picked up a *sheaf* of papers as he rose to question the witness.

---

sheathe\\'shēth \ v. place into a case. As soon as he recognized the approaching men, he *sheathed* his dagger and hailed them as friends.

sher-bet\\'shər -bət\ n. flavored dessert ice. I prefer raspberry *sherbet* to ice cream since it is less fattening.

shib-bo-leth\\'shib -ə-ləth\ n. watchword; slogan. We are often misled by *shibboleths*.

shim-mer \\'shim -ər\ v. glimmer intermittently. The moonlight *shimmered* on the water as the moon broke through the clouds for a moment. also n.

shoal\\'shōl \ n. shallow place. The ship was stranded on a *shoal* and had to be pulled off by tugs. also v.

shod-dy \\'shäd -ē\ adj. sham; not genuine; inferior. You will never get the public to buy such *shoddy* material.

shrew\\ 'shrü \ n. scolding woman. No one wanted to marry Shakespeare's Kate because she was a *shrew.*

sib-ling\\ 'sib-ling\ n. brother or sister. We may not enjoy being *siblings,* but we cannot forget that we still belong to the same family.

sib-yl-line\\sib -ə͵līn \adj. prophetic; oracular. Until their destruction by fire in 83 B.C., the *sibylline* books were often consulted by the Romans.

si-de-re-al\\sī-'dir -ē-əl\adj. relating to the stars. The study of *sidereal* bodies has been greatly advanced by the new telescope.

silt \\'silt \ n. sediment deposited by running water. The harbor channel must be dredged annually to remove the *silt.* also v.

sim-i-an\\'sim -ē-ən\adj. monkeylike. Lemurs are nocturnal mammals and have many *simian* characteristics, although they are less intelligent than monkeys. also n.

sim-i-le\\'sim -ə͵lē \ n. comparison of one thing with another, using the word *like* or *as.* We are constantly using *similes* and metaphors to convey our thoughts to others.

si-mil-i-tude \\sə-'mil -ə-͵t(y)üd \ n. similarity; using comparisons such as similes, etc. Although the critics deplored his use of mixed metaphors, he continued to write in *similitudes.*

\ŋ\ sing   \ō\ go   \ȯ\ law   \ȯi\ boy   \th\ thin   \th\ the   \ü\ loot   \u̇\ foot
\y\ yet   · \zh\ vision   \à, k̲, ⁿ, œ, œ̄, ue, ūe̲, ᵛ\ *see* Pronunciation Symbols

sim-per-ing\\'sim -p(ə-)riŋ\\ ADJ. smirking. I can overlook his *simpering* manner, but I cannot ignore his stupidity.

sim-u-late\\'sim -yə-ˌlāt \\ V. feign. He *simulated* insanity in order to avoid punishment for his crime.

si-ne-cure\\'sī -ni-ˌkyu̇(ə)r \\ N. well-paid position with little responsibility. My job is no *sinecure;* I work long hours and have much responsibility.

sin-ewy\\'sin-yə-wē\\ ADJ. tough; strong and firm. The steak was too *sinewy* to chew.

sin-is-ter\\'sin -əs-tər\\ ADJ. evil. We must defeat the *sinister* forces that seek our downfall.

sin-u-ous\\'sin -yə-wəs\\ ADJ. winding; bending in and out; not morally honest. The snake moved in a *sinuous* manner.

si-roc-co \\sə-ˈräk -(ˌ)ō\\ N. warm, sultry wind blown from Africa to southern Europe. We can understand the popularity of the siesta in southern Spain; when the *sirocco* blows, the afternoon heat is unbearable.

skep-tic\\'skep -tik\\ N. doubter; person who suspends judgment until he has examined the evidence supporting a point of view. In this matter, I am a *skeptic;* I want proof.

skimp\\'skimp \\ V. provide scantily; live very economically. They were forced to *skimp* on necessities in order to make their limited supplies last the winter.

skit-tish\\'skit -ish\\ ADJ. lively; frisky. He is as *skittish* as a kitten playing with a piece of string.

skul-dug-gery\\ˌskəl-ˈdəg-(ə-)rē\\ N. dishonest behavior. The investigation into municipal corruption turned up new instances of *skulduggery* daily.

skulk\\'skəlk \\ V. move furtively and secretly. He *skulked* through the less fashionable sections of the city in order to avoid meeting any of his former friends. also N.

slack-en\\'slak-ən\\ V. slow up; loosen. As they passed the finish line, the runners *slackened* their pace.

slake\\'slāk \\ V. quench; sate. When we reached the oasis, we were able to *slake* our thirst.

slan-der\\'slan -dər\\ N. defamation; utterance of false and malicious statements. Unless you can prove your allegations, your remarks constitute *slander*. also V.

slat-tern\\'slat -ərn\\ N. untidy or slovenly person. If you persist in wearing such sloppy clothes, people will call you a *slattern*. also ADJ.

slea-zy\\'slē -zē\\ ADJ. flimsy; unsubstantial. This is a *sleazy* material; it will not wear well.

sleep-er\\'slē-pər\\ N. something originally of little value or importance that in time becomes very valuable. Unnoticed by the critics at its publication, the eventual Pulitzer Prize winner was a classic *sleeper*.

sleight\\'slīt \\ N. dexterity. The magician amazed the audience with his *sleight* of hand.

slith-er\\'slith -ər\\ V. slip or slide. After the mud slide, many people *slithered* down this hill as they left their homes.

sloth\\'slòth \\ N. laziness. Such *sloth* in a young person is deplorable.

slough\\'sləf \\ V. cast off. Each spring, the snake *sloughs* off its skin. also N.

slov-en-ly\\'sləv -ən-lē\\ ADJ. untidy; careless in work habits. Such *slovenly* work habits will never produce good products.

slug-gard\\'sləg -ərd\\ N. lazy person. "You are a *sluggard*, a drone, a parasite," the angry father shouted at his lazy son.

slug-gish\\'sləg-ish\\ ADJ. slow; lazy; lethargic. After two nights without sleep, she felt *sluggish* and incapable of exertion.

sluice\\'slüs \\ N. artificial channel for directing or controlling the flow of water. This *sluice* gate is opened only in times of drought to provide water for irrigation. also V.

smat-ter-ing\\'smat -ə-riŋ\\ N. slight knowledge. I don't know whether it is better to be ignorant of a subject or to have a mere *smattering* of information about it.

smirk\\'smərk \\ N. conceited smile. Wipe that *smirk* off your face! also V.

smol-der\\'smōl-dər\\ V. burn without flame; be liable to break out at any moment. The rags *smoldered* for hours before they burst into flame.

snick-er\\'snik-ər\\ N. half-stifled laugh. The boy could not suppress a *snicker* when the teacher sat on the tack. also V.

sniv-el\\'sniv-əl\\ v. run at the nose; snuffle; whine. Don't you come *sniveling* to me complaining about your big brother.

so-bri-e-ty\\sə-'brī -ət-ē\\ N. soberness. The solemnity of the occasion filled us with *sobriety*.

so-bri-quet\\'sō -bri¸kā \\ N. nickname. Despite all his protests, his classmates continued to call him by that unflattering *sobriquet*.

sod-den\\'säd-ən\\ ADJ. soaked; dull, as if from drink. He set his *sodden* overcoat near the radiator to dry.

so-journ\\'sō ¸jərn \\ N. temporary stay. After his *sojourn* in Florida, he began to long for the colder climate of his native New England home. also v.

so-lace\\'säl -əs\\ N. comfort in trouble. I hope you will find *solace* in the thought that all of us share your loss.

so-le-cism\\'säl -ə¸siz -əm\\ N. construction that is flagrantly incorrect grammatically. I must give this paper a failing mark because it contains many *solecisms*.

so-lem-ni-ty\\sə-'lem-nət-ē\\ N. seriousness; gravity. The minister was concerned that nothing should disturb the *solemnity* of the marriage service. **sol-emn**\\'säl-əm\\ ADJ.

so-lic-i-tous \\sə-'lis -ət-əs\\ ADJ. worried; concerned. The employer was very *solicitous* about the health of his employees as replacements were difficult to get.

so-lil-o-quy\\sə-'lil -ə-kwē\\ N. the act of talking to oneself. The *soliloquy* is a device used by the dramatist to reveal a character's innermost thoughts and emotions.

sol-stice\\'säl -stəs\\ N. point at which the sun is farthest from the equator. The winter *solstice* usually occurs on December 21.

sol-vent\\'säl -vənt\\ ADJ. able to pay all debts. By dint of very frugal living, he was finally able to become *solvent* and avoid bankruptcy proceedings. also N.

so-mat-ic\\sō-'mat -ik\\ ADJ. pertaining to the body; physical. Why do you ignore the spiritual aspects and emphasize only the corporeal and the *somatic*?

som-nam-bu-list\\säm¹nam -byə-ləst\\ N. sleepwalker. The most famous *somnambulist* in literature is Lady Macbeth; her monologue in the sleepwalking scene is one of the highlights of Shakespeare's play.

som-no-lent\\'säm -nə-lənt\\ADJ. half asleep. The heavy meal and the overheated room made us all *somnolent* and indifferent to the speaker.

so-no-rous \\sə-'nȯr -əs\\ ADJ. resonant. His *sonorous* voice resounded through the hall.

soph-ist\\'säf -əst\\N. quibbler; employer of fallacious reasoning. You are using all the devices of a *sophist* in trying to prove your case; your argument is specious.

so-phis-ti-ca-tion\\sə͵fis -tə-'kā -shən\\ N. artificiality; unnaturalness; act of employing sophistry in reasoning. *Sophistication* is an acquired characteristic, found more frequently among city dwellers than among residents of rural areas.

soph-ist-ry\\'säf-ə-strē\\N. seemingly plausible but fallacious reasoning. Instead of advancing valid arguments, he tried to overwhelm his audience with a flood of *sophistries*. **soph-ist**\\'säf-əst\\N.

soph-o-mor-ic \\͵säf -ə-'mȯr -ik\\ ADJ. immature; shallow. Your *sophomoric* remarks indicate that you have not given much thought to the problem.

so-po-ri-fic\\͵säp -ə-'rif -ik\\N. sleep producer. I do not need a *soporific* when I listen to one of his speeches. also ADJ.

sor-did\\'sȯrd-əd\\ADJ. filthy; base; vile. The social worker was angered by the *sordid* housing provided for the homeless.

soup-çon\\süp-'sōⁿ \\N. suggestion; hint; taste. A *soupçon* of garlic will improve this dish.

span-gle\\'spaŋ -gəl\\N. small metallic piece sewn to clothing for ornamentation. The thousands of *spangles* on her dress sparkled in the glare of the stage lights. also V.

sparse\\'spärs\\ADJ. not thick; thinly scattered; scanty. He had moved from the densely populated city to the remote countryside where the population was *sparse*.

spas-mod-ic\\spaz-'mäd -ik\\ADJ. fitful; periodic. The *spasmodic* coughing in the auditorium annoyed the performers.

spate\\'spāt \\N. large amount. She commented on the *spate* of exercise books now on the market.

spa-tial\\'spā -shəl\\ADJ. relating to space. It is difficult to visualize the *spatial* extent of our universe.

\\ŋ\ sing \\ō\ go \\ȯ\ law \\ȯi\ boy \\th\ thin \\<u>th</u>\ the \\ü\ loot \\u̇\ foot
\\y\ yet \\zh\ vision \\à, <u>k</u>, ⁿ, œ, œ̄, ue, ūe, ʸ\ *see* Pronunciation Symbols

spat-u-la \\'spach -(ə-)lə\ N. broad-bladed instrument used for spreading or mixing. The manufacturers of this frying pan recommend the use of a rubber *spatula* to avoid scratching the specially treated surface.

spawn \\'spȯn \ V. lay eggs. Fish ladders had to be built in the dams to assist the salmon returning to *spawn* in their native streams. also N.

spe-cious \\'spē -shəs\ ADJ. seemingly reasonable but incorrect. Let us not be misled by such *specious* arguments.

spec-tral \\'spek -trəl\ ADJ. ghostly. We were frightened by the *spectral* glow that filled the room.

spec-trum \\'spek -trəm\ N. colored band produced when beam of light passes through a prism. The visible portion of the *spectrum* includes red at one end and violet at the other.

sple-net-ic \spli-'net -ik\ ADJ. spiteful; irritable; peevish. People shunned him because of his *splenetic* temper. **spleen** \\'splēn \ N.

spo-li-a-tion \,spō -lē-'ā -shən\ N. pillaging; depredation. We regard this unwarranted attack on a neutral nation as an act of *spoliation* and we demand that it cease at once and that proper restitution be made.

spoo-ner-ism \\'spü -nə,riz -əm\ N. accidental transposition of sounds in successive words. When the radio announcer introduced the President as Hoobert Herver, he was guilty of a *spoonerism*.

spo-rad-ic \spə-'rad -ik\ ADJ. occurring irregularly. Although there are *sporadic* outbursts of shooting, we may report that the major rebellion has been defeated.

sport-ive \\'spȯrt -iv\ ADJ. playful. Such a *sportive* attitude is surprising in a person as serious as you usually are.

spume \\'spyüm \ N. froth; foam. The *spume* at the base of the waterfall extended for a quarter of a mile downriver. also V.

spu-ri-ous \\'spyu̇r -ē-əs\ ADJ. false; counterfeit. He tried to pay the check with a *spurious* ten-dollar bill.

spurn \\'spərn \ V. reject; scorn. The heroine *spurned* the villain's advances.

squal-id \\'skwäl -əd\\ ADJ. dirty; neglected; poor. It is easy to see how crime can breed in such a *squalid* neighborhood.

squan-der \\'skwän -dər\\ V. waste. The prodigal son *squandered* the family estate. also N.

stac-ca-to \\stə-'kät -(ˌ)ō\\ ADJ. played in an abrupt manner; marked by abrupt sharp sound. His *staccato* speech reminded one of the sound of a machine gun.

stag-nant \\'stag -nənt\\ ADJ. motionless; stale; dull. The *stagnant* water was a breeding ground for disease. **stag-nate** \\'stag ˌnāt\\, V.

staid \\'stād\\ ADJ. sober; sedate. His conduct during the funeral ceremony was *staid* and solemn.

stale-mate \\'stā(ə)l ˌmāt\\ N. deadlock. Negotiations between the union and the employers have reached a *stalemate;* neither side is willing to budge from previously stated positions. also V.

stal-wart \\'stȯl -wərt\\ ADJ. strong, brawny; steadfast. His consistent support of the party has proved that he is a *stalwart* and loyal member. also N.

stam-i-na \\'stam -ə-nə\\ N. strength; staying power. I doubt that he has the *stamina* to run the full distance of the marathon race.

stanch \\'stȯnch\\ V. check flow of. It is imperative that we *stanch* the gushing wound before we attend to the other injuries.

stat-ic \\'stat-ik\\ ADJ. unchanging; lacking development. Nothing had changed at home; things were *static*. **sta-sis** \\'stā-səs\\ N.

stat-ute \\'stach -(ˌ)üt\\ N. law. We have many *statutes* in our law books which should be repealed.

stat-u-to-ry \\'stach -əˌtȯr -ē\\ ADJ. created by statute or legislative action. This is a *statutory* crime.

stead-fast \\'sted-ˌfast\\ ADJ. loyal. I am sure you will remain *steadfast* in your support of the cause.

stein \\'stīn\\ N. beer mug. He thought of college as a place where one drank beer from *steins* and sang songs of lost lambs.

\\ŋ\\ sing	\\ō\\ go	\\ȯ\\ law	\\ȯi\\ boy	\\th\\ thin	\\th\\ the	\\ü\\ loot	\\u̇\\ foot
\\y\\ yet	\\zh\\ vision	\\à, k̲, ⁿ, œ, œ̄, ue, ūe, ʸ\\ *see* Pronunciation Symbols

stel·lar\\'stel -ər\\ ADJ. pertaining to the stars, outstanding. He was the *stellar* attraction of the entire performance.

sten·to·ri·an\\sten·'tōr -ē-ən\\ ADJ. éxtremely loud. The town crier had a *stentorian* voice.

ste·re·o·typed \\'ster -ē-ə₋tīpt \\ ADJ. fixed and unvarying representation. My chief objection to the book is that the characters are *stereotyped*.

stig·ma \\'stig -mə\\ N. token of disgrace; brand. I do not attach any *stigma* to the fact that you were accused of this crime; the fact that you were acquitted clears you completely.

stig·ma·tize\\'stig -mə ₋tīz \\ V. brand; mark as wicked. I do not want to *stigmatize* this young offender for life by sending him to prison.

stilt·ed\\'stil -təd\\ ADJ. bombastic; inflated. His *stilted* rhetoric did not impress the college audience; they were immune to bombastic utterances.

stint\\'stint \\ N. supply; allotted amount; assigned portion of work. After his *stint* in the Army he will join his father's company. also V.

sti·pend\\'stī ₋pend \\N. pay for services. There is a nominal *stipend* attached to this position.

sto·ic\\'stō -ik\\N. person who is indifferent to pleasure or pain. The doctor called her patient a *stoic* because he had borne the pain of the examination without whimpering. also ADJ.

stoke\\'stōk\\V. provide with fuel; feed abundantly. They swiftly *stoked* themselves, knowing they would not have another meal until they reached camp.

stol·id\\'stäl -əd\\ADJ. dull; impassive. I am afraid that this imaginative poetry will not appeal to such a *stolid* person.

strat·a·gem \\'strat -ə-jəm\\ N. deceptive scheme. We saw through his clever *stratagem*.

stra·tum \\'strāt -əm\\ N. layer of earth's surface; layer of society. Unless we alleviate conditions in the lowest *stratum* of our society, we may expect grumbling and revolt.

stri·at·ed\\'strī ₋āt -əd\\ADJ. marked with parallel bands. The glacier left many *striated* rocks.

\\ə\\ abut   \\ᵊ\\ kitten, F table   \\ər\\ further   \\a\\ ash   \\ā\\ ace   \\ä\\ cot, cart
\\aů\\ out   \\ch\\ chin   \\e\\ bet   \\ē\\ easy   \\g\\ go   \\i\\ hit   \\ī\\ ice   \\j\\ job

stric-ture\\'strik -chər\N. critical comments; severe and adverse criticism. His *strictures* on the author's style are prejudiced and unwarranted.

stri-dent\\'strīd -ᵊnt\ADJ. loud and harsh. She scolded him in a *strident* voice.

strin-gent \\'strin -jənt\ ADJ. binding; rigid. I think these regulations are too *stringent*.

strut\\'strət\N. pompous walk. His *strut* as he marched about the parade ground revealed him for what he was: a pompous buffoon. also v.

strut\\'strət\N. supporting bar. The engineer calculated that the *strut* supporting the rafter needed to be reinforced. (secondary meaning)

stul-ti-fy\\'stəl -tə₋fī \ V. cause to appear foolish or inconsistent. By changing your opinion at this time, you will *stultify* yourself.

stu-por\\'st(y)ü -pər\N. state of apathy; daze; lack of awareness. In his *stupor*, the addict was unaware of the events taking place around him.

sty-gian\\'stij-(ē-)ən\ADJ. gloomy; hellish; deathly. They descended into the *stygian*, half-lit subbasement.

sty-mie\\'stī -mē\ V. present an obstacle; stump. The detective was *stymied* by the contradictory evidence in the robbery investigation. also N.

suave\\'swäv \ADJ. smooth; bland. He is the kind of individual who is more easily impressed by a *suave* approach than by threats or bluster.

sua-vi-ty\\'swäv -ət-ē\N. urbanity; polish. He is particularly good in roles that require *suavity* and sophistication.

sub-al-tern\sə-'bòl -tərn\N. subordinate. The captain treated his *subalterns* as though they were children rather than commissioned officers. also ADJ.

sub-jec-tive\₍ₗ₎səb-'jek -tiv\ADJ. occurring or taking place within the subject; unreal. Your analysis is highly *subjective;* you have permitted your emotions and your opinions to color your thinking.

sub-ju-gate\\'səb -ji₋gāt \ V. conquer; bring under control. It is not our aim to *subjugate* our foe; we are interested only in establishing peaceful relations.

sub·li·mate\\'səb -lə₁māt \\v. refine; purify. We must strive to *sublimate* these desires and emotions into worthwhile activities. also N.

sub·lime\\sə-'blīm \\ADJ. exalted; noble; uplifting. We must learn to recognize *sublime* truths. also V.

sub·lim·i·nal \\(₁)səb-'lim -ən-ᵊl\\ ADJ. below the threshold. We may not be aware of the *subliminal* influences which affect our thinking.

sub·se·quent\\'səb -si-kwənt\\ ADJ. following; later. In *subsequent* lessons, we take up more difficult problems.

sub·ser·vi·ent\\səb-'sər -vē-ənt\\ADJ. behaving like a slave; servile; obsequious. He was proud and dignified; he refused to be *subservient* to anyone.

sub·sid·i·ar·y\\səb-'sid -ē₁er -ē\\ ADJ. subordinate; secondary. This information may be used as *subsidiary* evidence but is not sufficient by itself to prove your argument. also N.

sub·si·dy \\'səb -səd-ē\\ N. direct financial aid by government, etc. Without this *subsidy*, American ship operators would not be able to compete in world markets.

sub·sis·tence\\səb-'sis -tən(t)s\\N. existence; means of support; livelihood. In these days of inflated prices, my salary provides a mere *subsistence*.

sub·stan·ti·ate\\səb-'stan -chē₁āt \\v. verify; support. I intend to *substantiate* my statement by producing witnesses.

sub·stan·tive\\'səb -stən-tiv\\ ADJ. essential; pertaining to the substance. Although the delegates were aware of the importance of the problem, they could not agree on the *substantive* issues.

sub·ter·fuge\\'səb -tər₁fyüj \\N. pretense; evasion. As soon as we realized that you had won our support by *subterfuge*, we withdrew our endorsement of your candidacy.

sub·tle·ty\\'sət -ᵊl-tē\\N. nicety; cunning; guile; delicacy. The *subtlety* of his remarks was unnoticed by most of his audience.

sub·ver·sive \\səb-'vər -siv\\ ADJ. tending to overthrow or ruin. We must destroy such *subversive* publications. also N.

---

suc-cinct\ $_{(,)}$sək-'siŋ(k)t \ADJ. brief; terse; compact. His remarks are always *succinct* and pointed.

suc-cor\ 'sək -ər\N. aid; assistance; relief. We shall be ever grateful for the *succor* your country gave us when we were in need. also V.

suc-cu-lent\ 'sək -yə-lənt\ADJ. juicy; full of richness. The citrus foods from Florida are more *succulent* to some people than those from California. also N.

suc-cumb\ sə-'kəm \v. yield; give in; die. I *succumb* to temptation whenever it comes my way.

suf-fuse\ sə-'fyüz \v. spread over. A blush *suffused* her cheeks when we teased her about her love affair.

sul-ly\ 'səl -ē\ v. tarnish; soil. He felt that it was beneath his dignity to *sully* his hands in such menial labor.

sul-try\ 'səl -trē\ADJ. sweltering. He could not adjust himself to the *sultry* climate of the tropics.

sum-ma-tion\ $_{(,)}$sə-'mā -shən\ N. act of finding the total; summary. In his *summation*, the lawyer emphasized the testimony given by the two witnesses.

sump-tu-ous\ 'səm(p) -ch(ə-w)əs\ADJ. lavish; rich. I cannot recall when I have had such a *sumptuous* feast.

sun-der\ 'sən -dər\v. separate; part. Northern and southern Ireland are politically and religiously *sundered*.

sun-dry\ 'sən -drē\ADJ. various; several. My suspicions were aroused when I read *sundry* items in the newspapers about your behavior.

su-per-an-nu-at-ed \ ˌsü -pə-'ran -yə-ˌwāt -əd\ ADJ. retired on pension because of age. The *superannuated* man was indignant because he felt that he could still perform a good day's work.

su-per-cil-i-ous \ ˌsü -pər-'sil -ē-əs\ ADJ. contemptuous; haughty. I resent your *supercilious* and arrogant attitude.

su-per-fi-cial\ ˌsü -pər-'fish -əl\ADJ. trivial; shallow. Since your report gave only a *superficial* analysis of the problem, I cannot give you more than a passing grade.

su-per-flu-it-y \ ˌsü -per-'flü -ət-ē\ N. excess; overabundance. We have a definite lack of sincere workers and a *superfluity* of leaders.

\ŋ\ sing	\ō\ go	\ȯ\ law	\ȯi\ boy	\th\ thin	\t͟h\ the	\ü\ loot	\u̇\ foot
\y\ yet	\zh\ vision	\à, k̲, ⁿ, œ, œ̄, ue, ue̅, ʸ\ *see* Pronunciation Symbols					

su·per·im·pose \ˌsü -pə-rim-ˈpōz \ v. place over something else. Your attempt to *superimpose* another agency in this field will merely increase the bureaucratic nature of our government.

su·per·nal \sü-ˈpərn -ᵊl\ ADJ. heavenly; celestial. His tale of *supernal* beings was skeptically received.

su·per·nu·mer·ar·y \ˌsü -pər-ˈn(y)ü -mə₁rer -ē\ N. person or thing in excess of what is necessary; extra. His first appearance on the stage was as a *supernumerary* in a Shakespearean tragedy.

su·per·sede \ˌsü -pər-ˈsēd \ v. cause to be set aside; replace. This regulation will *supersede* all previous rules.

su·pine \sü-ˈpīn \ ADJ. lying on back. The defeated pugilist lay *supine* on the canvas.

sup·plant \sə-ˈplant\ v. replace; usurp. Richard II was *supplanted* by Bolingbroke, who later became King Henry IV.

sup·ple \ˈsəp -əl\ ADJ. flexible; pliant. The angler found a *supple* limb and used it as a fishing rod. also v.

sup·pli·ant \ˈsəp -lē-ənt\ ADJ. entreating; beseeching. He could not resist the dog's *suppliant* whimpering, and he gave it some food. also N.

sup·pli·cate \ˈsəp -lə₁kāt \ v. petition humbly; pray to grant a favor. We *supplicate* your majesty to grant him amnesty.

sup·pos·i·ti·tious \sə₁päz -ə-ˈtish -əs\ ADJ. assumed; counterfeit; hypothetical. I find no similarity between your *supposititious* illustration and the problem we are facing.

sup·press \sə-ˈpres\ v. crush; subdue; inhibit. After the armed troops had *suppressed* the rebellion, the city was placed under martial law.

sur·cease \ˈsər ₁sēs \ N. cessation. He begged the doctors to grant him *surcease* from his suffering. **sur·cease** \ₗₜ₁sər-ˈsēs \ V.

sur·feit \ˈsər -fət\ v. cloy; overfeed. I am *surfeited* with the sentimentality of the average motion picture film. also N.

sur·ly \ˈsər -lē\ ADJ. rude; cross. Because of his *surly* attitude, many people avoided his company.

sur·mise \sər-ˈmīz \ v. guess. I *surmise* that he will be late for this meeting. also N.

\ə\ abut   \ᵊ\ kitten, F table   \ər\ **further**   \a\ ash   \ā\ ace   \ä\ cot, cart
\aů\ out   \ch\ chin   \e\ bet   \ē\ **easy**   \g\ **go**   \i\ hit   \ī\ ice   \j\ job

sur-mount\sər-'maùnt\v. overcome. He had to *surmount* many obstacles in order to succeed.

sur-rep-ti-tious\sər -əp-'tish -əs\ADJ. secret. News of their *surreptitious* meeting gradually leaked out.

sur-ro-gate\'sər-ə-,gät\N. substitute. For a fatherless child, a male teacher may become a father *surrogate*.

sur-veil-lance\sər-'vā -lən(t)s\N. watching; guarding. The FBI kept the house under constant *surveillance* in the hope of capturing all the criminals at one time.

sus-te-nance \'səs -tə-nən(t)s\ N. means of support, food, nourishment. In the tropics, the natives find *sustenance* easy to obtain.

su-ture\'sü -chər\N. stitches sewn to hold the cut edges of a wound or incision; material used in sewing. We will remove the *sutures* as soon as the wound heals. also v.

swar-thy\'swòr-thē\ADJ. dark; dusky. Despite the stereo-types, not all Italians are *swarthy;* many are fair-skinned and blond-haired.

swathe\'swäth \v. wrap around; bandage. When I visited him in the hospital, I found him *swathed* in bandages.

swel-ter\'swel -tər\v. be oppressed by heat. I am going to buy an air conditioning unit for my apartment as I do not intend to *swelter* through another hot and humid summer. also N.

swin-dler\'swin-(d)lər\N. cheat. She was gullible and trusting, an easy victim for the first *swindler* who came along.

syb-a-rite\'sib-ə-,rīt\N. lover of luxury. Rich people are not always *sybarites;* some of them have little taste for a life of luxury.

sy-co-phan-tic\,sik -ə-'fant -ik\ADJ. servilely flattering. The king enjoyed the *sycophantic* attentions of his followers.

syl-lo-gism\'sil -ə-,jiz -əm\N. logical formula utilizing a major premise, a minor premise and a conclusion. There must be a fallacy in this *syllogism;* I cannot accept the conclusion.

syl-van \'sil -vən\ADJ. pertaining to the woods; rustic. His paintings of nymphs in *sylvan* backgrounds were criti-cized as overly sentimental. also N.

\ŋ\ sing   \ō\ go   \ò\ law   \òi\ boy   \th\ thin   \th\ the   \ü\ loot   \ù\ foot
\y\ yet   \zh\ vision   \à, k̲, ⁿ, œ, œ̄, ue, ūe, r\ *see* Pronunciation Symbols

sym-me-try \'sim -ə-trē\ N. arrangement of parts so that balance is obtained; congruity. The addition of a second tower will give this edifice the *symmetry* which it now lacks.

syn-chro-nous \'siŋ -krə-nəs\ ADJ. similarly timed; simultaneous with. We have many examples of scientists in different parts of the world who have made *synchronous* discoveries.

syn-the-sis \'sin(t) -thə-səs\ N. combining parts into a whole. Now that we have succeeded in isolating this drug, our next problem is to plan its *synthesis* in the laboratory.

syn-thet-ic \sin-'thet -ik\ ADJ. artificial; resulting from synthesis. During the twentieth century, many *synthetic* products have replaced the natural products. also N.

\ə\ abut   \ᵊ\ kitten, F table   \ər\ further   \a\ ash   \ā\ ace   \ä\ cot, cart
\aů\ out   \ch\ chin   \e\ bet   \ē\ easy   \g\ go   \i\ hit   \ī\ ice   \j\ job

–t–

tac-it\\'tas -ət\\ ADJ. understood; not put into words. We have a *tacit* agreement.

tac-i-turn\\'tas -ə˛tərn \\ADJ. habitually silent; talking little. New Englanders are reputedly *taciturn* people.

tac-tile\\'tak -t²l\\ADJ. pertaining to the organs or sense of touch. His calloused hands had lost their *tactile* sensitivity.

taint\\'tānt \\v. contaminate; corrupt. Health authorities are always trying to prevent the sale and use of food *tainted* by bacteria.

tal-is-man\\'tal -ə-smən\\N. charm. She wore the *talisman* to ward off evil.

tal-on\\'tal -ən\\N. claw of bird. The falconer wore a leather gauntlet to avoid being clawed by the hawk's *talons*.

tan-ta-lize \\'tant -²l˛īz \\ v. tease; torture with disappointment. Tom loved to *tantalize* his younger brother.

tan-ta-mount \\'tant -ə˛maůnt \\ ADJ. equal in value. Your ignoring their pathetic condition is *tantamount* to murder.

tan-trum\\'tan -trəm\\N. fit of petulance; caprice. The child learned that he could have almost anything if he went into a *tantrum*.

ta-ran-tu-la\\tə˺ranch -(ə-)lə\\N. venomous spider. We need an antitoxin to counteract the bite of the *tarantula*.

tat-ter-de-ma-lion \\˛tat -ərd-i˺māl -yən\\N. ragged fellow. Do you expect an army of *tatterdemalions* and beggars to put up a real fight?

taut \\'tȯt \\ADJ. tight; ready. The captain maintained that he ran a *taut* ship.

tau-to-log-i-cal \\˛tȯt -²l˺äj -i-kəl\\ ADJ. needlessly repetitious. In the sentence "It was visible to the eye," the phrase "to the eye" is *tautological*.

tau-tol-o-gy \\tȯ˺täl -ə-jē\\N. unnecessary repetition; pleonasm. "Joyful happiness" is an illustration of *tautology*.

taw-dry \\'tȯd -rē\\ ADJ. cheap and gaudy. He won a few *tawdry* trinkets in Coney Island. also N.

te-di-um\\'tēd -ē-əm\\N. boredom; weariness. We hope this radio will help overcome the *tedium* of your stay in the hospital.

te-mer-i-ty \\tə˺mer -ət-ē\\ N. boldness; rashness. Do you have the *temerity* to argue with me?

\\ŋ\\ **sing** \\ō\\ **go** \\ȯ\\ **law** \\ȯi\\ **boy** \\th\\ **thin** \\th\\ **the** \\ü\\ **loot** \\ů\\ **foot**
\\y\\ **yet** \\zh\\ **vision** \\à, ḵ, ⁿ, œ, œ̄, ue, ū̄e, ʸ\\ *see* Pronunciation Symbols

tem-per\\'tem-pər\\ v. restrain; blend; toughen. His hard times in the army served only to *temper* his strength.

tem-po\\'tem -(ı)pō\\ N. speed of music. I find the conductor's *tempo* too slow for such a brilliant piece of music.

tem-po-ral\\'tem -p(ə-)rəl\\ ADJ. not lasting forever; limited by time; secular. At one time in our history; *temporal* rulers assumed that they had been given their thrones by divine right.

tem-po-rize\\'tem -pə-,rīz\\ v. avoid committing oneself; gain time. I cannot permit you to *temporize* any longer; I must have a definite answer today.

te-na-cious\\tə-'nā -shəs\\ ADJ. holding fast. I had to struggle to break his *tenacious* hold on my arm.

te-nac-i-ty\\tə-'nas -ət-ē\\ N. firmness; persistency; adhesiveness. It is extremely difficult to overcome the *tenacity* of a habit such as smoking.

ten-den-tious\\ten-'den -chəs\\ ADJ. having an aim; biased. The editorials in this periodical are *tendentious* rather than truth-seeking.

te-net\\'ten -ət\\ N. doctrine; dogma. I cannot accept the *tenets* of your faith.

ten-sile\\'ten(t)-səl\\ ADJ. capable of being stretched. Mountain climbers must know the *tensile* strength of their ropes.

ten-ta-tive\\'tent -ət-iv\\ ADJ. provisional; experimental. Your *tentative* plans sound plausible.

ten-u-ous\\'ten -yə-wəs\\ ADJ. thin; rare; slim. The allegiance of our allies is held by rather *tenuous* ties.

ten-ure\\'ten -yər\\ N. holding of an office; time during which such an office is held. He has permanent *tenure* in this position.

tep-id\\'tep -əd\\ ADJ. lukewarm. During the summer, I like to take a *tepid* bath.

ter-ma-gant\\'tər -mə-gənt\\ N. shrew; scolding, brawling woman. *The Taming of the Shrew* is one of many stories of the methods used in changing a *termagant* into a demure lady. also ADJ.

\\ə\\ abut   \\ᵊ\\ kitten, F table   \\ər\\ further   \\a\\ ash   \\ā\\ ace   \\ä\\ cot, cart
\\aú\\ out   \\ch\\ chin   \\e\\ bet   \\ē\\ easy   \\g\\ go   \\i\\ hit   \\ī\\ ice   \\j\\ job

ter-mi-nol-o-gy \tər -mə-'näl -ə-jē\ N. terms used in a science or art. The special *terminology* developed by some authorities in the field has done more to confuse the layman than to enlighten him.

ter-mi-nus \'tər -mə-nəs\ N. last stop of railroad. After we reached the railroad *terminus,* we continued our journey into the wilderness on saddle horses.

ter-ra-pin \'ter -ə-pən\ N. American marsh tortoise. The flesh of the diamondback *terrapin* is considered by many epicures to be a delicacy.

ter-res-tri-al \tə-'res -t(r)ē-əl\ ADJ. of the earth. We have been able to explore the *terrestrial* regions much more thoroughly than the aquatic or celestial regions.

terse \'tərs \ ADJ. concise; abrupt; pithy. I admire his *terse* style of writing.

ter-ti-ar-y \'tər -shē-er -ē\ ADJ. third. He is so thorough that he analyzes *tertiary* causes where other writers are content with primary and secondary reasons.

tes-sel-lat-ed \'tes -ə-lāt -əd\ ADJ. inlaid; mosaic. I recall seeing a table with a *tessellated* top of bits of stone and glass in a very interesting pattern.

tes-ta-tor \'tes ˌtāt -ər\ N. maker of a will. The attorney called in his secretary and his partner to witness the signature of the *testator.*

tes-ty \'tes -tē\ ADJ. irritable; short-tempered. My advice is to avoid discussing this problem with him today as he is rather *testy.*

teth-er \'teth -ər\ V. tie with a rope. Before we went to sleep, we *tethered* the horses to prevent their wandering off during the night. also V.

thau-ma-tur-gist \'thȯ -mə-ˌtər -jəst\ N. miracle worker; magician. I would have to be a *thaumaturgist* and not a mere doctor to find a remedy for this disease.

the-oc-ra-cy \thē-'äk -rə-sē\ N. government of a community by religious leaders. Some Pilgrims favored the establishment of a *theocracy* in New England.

\ŋ\ sing	\ō\ go	\ȯ\ law	\ȯi\ boy	\th\ thin	\t̲h̲\ the	\ü\ loot	\u̇\ foot
\y\ yet	\zh\ vision	\à, k̲, ⁿ, œ, œ̄, ᴜe, ᵫ, ʸ\ *see* Pronunciation Symbols

the-os-o-phy \thē-ạ̈s -ə-fē\ N. wisdom in divine things. *Theosophy* seeks to embrace the essential truth in all religions.

ther-a-peu-tic \ther -ə-'pyüt -ik\ ADJ. curative. These springs are famous for their *therapeutic* qualities.

ther-mal \thər -məl\ ADJ. pertaining to heat. The natives discovered that the hot springs gave excellent *thermal* baths and began to develop their community as a health resort. also N.

thrall \thról \N. slave; bondage. The captured soldier was held in *thrall* by the conquering army.

thren-o-dy \thren -əd-ē\ N. song of lamentation; dirge. When he died, many poets wrote *threnodies* about his passing.

thrifty \'thrif-tē \ADJ. careful about money; economical. A *thrifty* shopper compares prices before making major purchases.

throe \thrō \N. violent anguish. The *throes* of despair can be as devastating as the spasms accompanying physical pain.

throng \'thróŋ \N. crowd. *Throngs* of shoppers jammed the aisles. also V.

throt-tle \thröt -əl\V. strangle. The criminal tried to *throttle* the old man. also N.

thwart \thwò(ə)rt \V. baffle; frustrate. He felt that everyone was trying to *thwart* his plans.

thyme \tīm \ N. aromatic plant used for seasoning. The addition of a little *thyme* will enhance the flavor of the clam chowder.

tim-bre \tam -bər\ N. quality of a musical tone produced by a musical instrument. We identify the instrument producing a musical sound by its *timbre*.

ti-mid-i-ty \tə-'mid -ət-ē\N. lack of self-confidence or courage. If you are to succeed as a salesman, you must first lose your *timidity*.

tim-o-rous \tim -(ə-)rəs\ ADJ. fearful; demonstrating fear. His *timorous* manner betrayed the fear he felt at the moment.

\ə\ abut   \ᵊ\ kitten, F table   \ər\ further   \a\ ash   \ā\ ace   \ä\ cot, cart
\au̇\ out   \ch\ chin   \e\ bet   \ē\ easy   \g\ go   \i\ hit   \ī\ ice   \j\ job

tip-ple\'tip -əl\ v. drink (alcoholic beverages) frequently. He found that his most enjoyable evenings occurred when he *tippled* with his friends at the local pub. also N.

ti-rade\ tī-rād \N. extended scolding; denunciation. Long before he had finished his *tirade*, we were sufficiently aware of the seriousness of our misconduct.

ti-tan-ic\tī-tan -ik\ADJ. gigantic. *Titanic* waves beat against the shore during the hurricane.

tithe\tīth \N. tax of one-tenth. Because he was an agnostic, he refused to pay his *tithe* to the clergy. also V.

tit-il-late \tit -ᵊl-āt \ v. tickle. I am here not to *titillate* my audience but to enlighten it.

tit-u-lar\tich -(ə-)lər\ADJ. nominal holding of title without obligations. Although he was the *titular* head of the company, the real decisions were made by his general manager.

toad-y\tōd -ē\v. flatter for favors. I hope you see through those who are *toadying* you for special favors. also N.

to-ga\tō -gə\N. Roman outer robe. Marc Antony pointed to the slashes in Caesar's *toga*.

tome\tōm \N. large volume. He spent much time in the libraries poring over ancient *tomes*.

to-pog-ra-phy\tə-päg-rə-fē\ N. physical features of a region. Before the generals gave the order to attack, they ordered a complete study of the *topography* of the region.

tor-pid\tȯr -pəd\ADJ. dormant; dull; lethargic. The *torpid* bear had just come out of his cave after his long hibernation.

tor-por\'tȯr-pər\N. lethargy; sluggishness; dormancy. Nothing seemed to arouse him from his *torpor*: he had wholly surrendered himself to lethargy. **torpid**\'tȯr-pəd\ADJ.

tor-so\tȯr -(ꞏ)sō\N. trunk of statue with head and limbs missing; human trunk. This *torso*, found in the ruins of Pompeii, is now on exhibition in the museum in Naples.

tor-ti-lla\tȯr-tē -(y)ə\N. flat cake made of cornmeal, etc. As we traveled through Mexico, we became more and more accustomed to the use of *tortillas* instead of bread.

tor-tu-ous\tòrch -(ə-)wəs\ADJ. winding; full of curves. Because this road is so *tortuous,* it is unwise to go faster than twenty miles an hour on it.

touch-stone\ˈtəch -ˌstōn \N. stone used to test the fineness of gold alloys; criterion. What *touchstone* can be used to measure the character of a person?

touch-y \ˈtəch -ē\ADJ. sensitive; irascible. Do not discuss this phase of the problem as he is very *touchy* about it.

tox-ic\ˈtäk -sik\ADJ. poisonous. We must seek an antidote for whatever *toxic* substance he has eaten.

tract\ˈtrakt \N. pamphlet; a region of indefinite size. The King granted William Penn a *tract* of land in the New World.

trac-ta-ble\ˈtrak -tə-bəl\ADJ. docile. You will find the children in this school very *tractable* and willing to learn.

tra-duce\trə-ˈd(y)üs \V. expose to slander. His opponents tried to *traduce* the candidate's reputation by spreading rumors about his past.

tra-jec-to-ry\trə-ˈjek -t(ə-)rē\N. path taken by a projectile. The police tried to locate the spot from which the assassin had fired the fatal shot by tracing the *trajectory* of the bullet.

tran-quil-li-ty\tran-ˈkwil -ət-ē\N. calmness; peace. After the commotion and excitement of the city, I appreciate the *tranquillity* of these fields and forests.

tran-scend\tran(t)s-ˈend \V. exceed; surpass. This accomplishment *transcends* all our previous efforts. **tran-scen-den-tal**\ˌtran(t)s -ˌen -ˈdent -ᵊl\ADJ.

tran-scribe\tran(t)s-ˈkrīb \V. make a copy of. When you *transcribe* your notes, please send a copy to Mr. Smith and keep the original for our files. **tran-scrip-tion**\tran(t)s- ˈkrip -shən\N.

trans-gres-sion\tran(t)s-ˈgresh -ən\N. violation of a law; sin. Forgive us our *transgressions.*

tran-sient\ˈtranch -ənt\ADJ. fleeting; quickly passing away; staying for a short time. This hotel caters to a *transient* trade. also N.

tran-si-tion \tran(t)s-ˈish -ən \N. going from one state of action to another. During the period of *transition* from oil heat to gas heat, the furnace will have to be shut off.

trans-lu-cent \tran(t)s-'lüs -ᵊnt\ ADJ. partly transparent. We could not recognize the people in the next room because of the *translucent* curtains which separated us.

trans-mute \tran(t)s-'myüt \ V. change; convert to something different. He was unable to *transmute* his dreams into actualities.

trans-par-ent \tran(t)s-'par -ənt\ ADJ. permitting light to pass through freely; easily detected. Your scheme is so *transparent* that it will fool no one.

tran-spire\ tran(t)s-'pī(ə)r \V. exhale; become known; happen. In spite of all our efforts to keep the meeting a secret, news of our conclusions *transpired*.

trau-mat-ic\trə-'mat -ik\ADJ. pertaining to an injury caused by violence. In his nightmares, he kept recalling the *traumatic* experience of being wounded in battle.

tra-vail\trə-'vā(ə)l \N. painful labor. How long do you think a man can endure such *travail* and degradation without rebelling? also V.

tra-verse \ trə-'vərs \ V. go through or across. When you *traverse* this field, be careful of the bull. **tra-verse**\'tra - vərs\ N.

trav-es-ty \trav -ə-stē\N. comical parody; treatment aimed at making something appear ridiculous. The decision the jury has arrived at is a *travesty* of justice. also V.

trea-cle\trē -kəl\N. syrup obtained in refining sugar. *Treacle* is more highly refined than molasses.

trea-tise\trēt -əs\N. article treating a subject systematically and thoroughly. He is preparing a *treatise* on the Elizabethan playwrights for his graduate degree.

trek\trek \ V. travel with difficulty. The tribe *trekked* further north that summer in search of available game. also N.

trem-or\trem -ər\N. trembling; slight quiver. She had a nervous *tremor* in her right hand.

trem-u-lous \trem -yə-ləs\ ADJ. trembling; wavering. She was *tremulous* more from excitement than from fear.

tren-chant\tren -chənt\ADJ. cutting; keen. I am afraid of his *trenchant* wit for it is so often sarcastic.

tren-cher-man \tren -chər-mən\N. good eater. He is not finicky about his food; he is a *trencherman*.

trep·i·da·tion \trep -ə-dā -shən\ N. fear; trembling agitation. We must face the enemy without *trepidation* if we are to win this battle.

trib·u·la·tion \trib -yə-lā -shən\ N. distress; suffering. After all the trials and *tribulations* we have gone through, we need this rest.

tri·bu·nal \trī-byün -ᵊl\ N. court of justice. The decision of the *tribunal* was final.

trib·ute \trib -(ı)yüt\ N. tax levied by a ruler; mark of respect. The colonists refused to pay *tribute* to a foreign despot.

tri·dent \trīd-ᵊnt\ N. three-pronged spear. Neptune is usually depicted as rising from the sea, carrying his *trident* on his shoulder. also ADJ.

tril·o·gy \tril -ə-jē\ N. group of three works. Romain Rolland's novel *Jean Christophe* was first published as a *trilogy*.

trite \trīt \ ADJ. hackneyed; commonplace. The *trite* and predictable situations in many television programs alienate many viewers.

troth \träth \N. pledge of good faith especially in betrothal. He gave her his *troth* and vowed he would cherish her always.

truck·le \trək -əl\V. curry favor; act in an obsequious way. If you *truckle* to the lord, you will be regarded as a sycophant; if you do not, you will be considered arrogant.

tru·cu·lent \trək -yə-lənt\ ADJ. aggressive; savage. They are a *truculent* race, ready to fight at any moment.

tru·ism \trü -ˌiz -əm\ N. self-evident truth. Many a *truism* is well expressed in a proverb.

trum·pery \trəm -p(ə-)rē\ N. objects that are showy, valueless, deceptive. All this finery is mere *trumpery*.

trun·cate \trəŋ -ˌkāt \V. cut the top off. The top of a cone which has been *truncated* in a plane parallel to its base is a circle.

tryst \trist \ N. appointed meeting. The lovers kept their *tryst* even though they realized their danger.

tu·mult \ˈt(y)ü-ˌməlt \N. commotion; riot; noise. She could not make herself heard over the *tumult* of the mob.

\ə\ abut   \ᵊ\ kitten, F table   \ər\ further   \a\ ash   \ā\ ace   \ä\ cot, cart
\aù\ out   \ch\ chin   \e\ bet   \ē\ easy   \g\ go   \i\ hit   \ī\ ice   \j\ job

tun-dra \\'tən -drə\ N. rolling, treeless plain in Siberia and arctic North America. Despite the cold, many geologists are trying to discover valuable mineral deposits in the *tundra*.

tur-bid \\'tər -bəd\ ADJ. muddy; having the sediment disturbed. The water was *turbid* after the children had waded through it.

tur-bu-lence \\'tər -byə-lən(t)s\ N. state of violent agitation. We were frightened by the *turbulence* of the ocean during the storm.

tu-reen \tə-'rēn \ N. deep table dish for holding soup. The waiters brought the soup to the tables in silver *tureens*.

tur-gid \\'tər -jəd\ ADJ. swollen; distended. The *turgid* limb was sore and painful.

turn-key \\'tərn -ˌkē \ N. jailer. By bribing the *turnkey*, the prisoner arranged to have better food brought to him in his cell.

tur-pi-tude \\'tər -pə-ˌt(y)üd \ N. depravity. A visitor may be denied admittance to this country if he has been guilty of moral *turpitude*.

tu-te-lage \\'t(y)üt -ᵊl-ij\ N. guardianship; training. Under the *tutelage* of such masters of the instrument, he made rapid progress as a virtuoso.

tu-te-lar-y \\'t(y)üt -ᵊl-ˌer -ē\ ADJ. protective; pertaining to a guardianship. I am acting in my *tutelary* capacity when I refuse to grant you permission to leave the campus. also N.

ty-ro \\'tī -(ˌ)rō\ N. beginner; novice. For a mere *tyro*, you have produced some marvelous results.

–u–

u-biq-ui-tous \yü-'bik -wət-əs\ ADJ. being everywhere; omnipresent. You are *ubiquitous;* I meet you wherever I go.

ul-te-ri-or \əl -'tir -ē-ər\ ADJ. situated beyond; unstated. You must have an *ulterior* motive for your behavior.

ul-ti-mate \'əl -tə-mət\ ADJ. final; not susceptible to further analysis. Scientists are searching for the *ultimate* truths. also N.

ul-ti-ma-tum \əl -tə-'māt -əm\ N. last demand; warning. Since they have ignored our *ultimatum,* our only recourse is to declare war.

um-brage \'əm -brij\ N. resentment; anger; sense of injury or insult. She took *umbrage* at his remarks.

u-na-nim-i-ty \yü -nə-'nim -ət-ē\ N. complete agreement. We were surprised by the *unanimity* with which our proposals were accepted by the different groups. **u-nan-i-mous** \yü-'nan -ə-məs\ ADJ.

un-as-suag-able \ən -ə-'swā -jə-bəl\ ADJ. unable to be soothed. He was *unassuagable;* the apology did no good.

un-as-sum-ing \ən -ə-'sü -miŋ\ ADJ. modest. He is so *unassuming* that some people fail to realize how great a man he really is.

un-bri-dled \ən -'brīd -əld\ ADJ. unrestrained. He had a sudden fit of *unbridled* rage.

un-can-ny \ən -'kan -ē\ ADJ. strange; mysterious. You have the *uncanny* knack of reading my innermost thoughts.

un-con-scio-na-ble \ən -'känch -(ə-)nə-bəl\ ADJ. unscrupulous; excessive. He found the loan shark's demands *unconscionable* and impossible to meet.

un-couth \ən -'küth \ADJ. outlandish; clumsy; boorish. Most biographers portray Lincoln as an *uncouth* and ungainly young man.

unc-tion \'əŋ(k) -shən\ N. the act of anointing with oil. The anointing with oil of a person near death is called extreme *unction.*

unc-tu-ous \'əŋ(k) -chə(-wə)s\ ADJ. oily; bland; insincerely suave. Uriah Heep disguised his nefarious actions by *unctuous* protestations of his "'umility."

---

un-du-late \ ən -jə-ˌlāt \ v. move with a wavelike motion. The waters *undulated* in the breeze. **un-du-late** \ ən -jə-lət \ ADJ.

un-earth \ ən -ˈərth \ v. dig up. When they *unearthed* the city, the archaeologists found many relics of an ancient civilization.

un-earth-ly \ ən -ˈərth -lē \ ADJ. not earthly; weird. There is an *unearthly* atmosphere about his work which amazes the casual observer.

un-e-quiv-o-cal \ ən -i-ˈkwiv -ə-kəl \ ADJ. plain; obvious. My answer to your proposal is an *unequivocal* and absolute "No."

un-err-ing-ly \ ˌən-ˈe(ə)r-iŋ-lē \ ADV. infallibly. My teacher *unerringly* pounced on the one typographical error in my essay.

un-fal-ter-ing \ ən -ˈfȯl -t(ə-)riŋ \ ADJ. steadfast. She approached the guillotine with *unfaltering* steps.

un-feigned \ ən -ˈfānd \ ADJ. genuine; real. I am sure her surprise was *unfeigned*.

un-fledged \ ˌən-ˈflejd \ ADJ. immature. It is hard for an *unfledged* writer to find a sympathetic publisher.

un-gain-ly \ ən -ˈgān -lē \ ADJ. awkward. He is an *ungainly* young man.

un-guent \ ən -gwənt \ N. ointment. Apply this *unguent* to the sore muscles before retiring.

uni-for-mi-ty \ ˌyü-nə-ˈfȯr-mət-ē \ N. sameness; consistency; monotony. After a while, the *uniformity* of TV situation comedies becomes boring. **uni-form** \ ˈyü-nə-ˌfȯrm \ ADJ.

u-ni-lat-er-al \ yü -ni-ˈlat -ə-rəl \ ADJ. one-sided. This legislation is *unilateral* since it binds only one party in the controversy.

un-im-peach-a-ble \ ən -im-ˈpē -chə-bəl \ ADJ. blameless and exemplary. His conduct in office was *unimpeachable*.

un-in-hib-it-ed \ ˌən-in-ˈhib-ət-əd \ ADJ. unrepressed. The congregation was shocked by her *uninhibited* laughter during the sermon.

---

u·nique \yu̇-ˈnēk\ ADJ. without an equal; single in kind. You have the *unique* distinction of being the first student whom I have had to fail in this course.

u·ni·son \ˈyü-nə-sən\ N. unity of pitch; complete accord. The choir sang in *unison*.

un·kempt \ən-ˈkem(p)t\ ADJ. disheveled; with uncared-for appearance. The beggar was dirty and *unkempt*.

un·mit·i·gat·ed \ən-ˈmit-ə-ˌgāt-əd\ ADJ. harsh; severe; not lightened. I sympathize with you in your *unmitigated* sorrow.

un·ob·tru·sive \ˌən-əb-ˈtrü-siv\ ADJ. inconspicuous; not blatant. The secret service agents in charge of protecting the President tried to be as *unobtrusive* as possible.

un·prec·e·dent·ed \ˌən-ˈpres-ə-ˌdent-əd\ ADJ. novel; unparalleled. Margaret Mitchell's book *Gone with the Wind* was an *unprecedented* success.

un·ru·ly \ən-ˈrü-lē\ ADJ. disobedient; lawless. The only way to curb this *unruly* mob is to use tear gas.

un·sa·vory \ˌən-ˈsāv-(ə-)rē\ ADJ. distasteful; morally offensive. People with *unsavory* reputations should not be allowed to work with young children.

un·seem·ly \ən-ˈsēm-lē\ ADJ. unbecoming; inappropriate. Your levity is *unseemly* at this time.

un·sul·lied \ən-ˈsəl-ēd\ ADJ. untarnished. I am happy that my reputation is *unsullied*.

un·ten·a·ble \ən-ˈten-ə-bəl\ ADJ. unsupportable. I find your theory *untenable* and must reject it.

un·to·ward \ən-ˈtō-(ə)rd\ ADJ. unfortunate; annoying. *Untoward* circumstances prevent me from being with you on this festive occasion.

un·wit·ting \ən-ˈwit-iŋ\ ADJ. unintentional; not knowing. He was the *unwitting* tool of the swindlers.

un·wont·ed \ən-ˈwȯnt-əd\ ADJ. unaccustomed by experience. He hesitated to assume the *unwonted* role of master of ceremonies at the dinner.

up·braid \əp-ˈbrād\ V. scold; reproach. I must *upbraid* him for his misbehavior.

up·shot \ˈəp-ˌshät\ N. outcome. The *upshot* of the rematch was that the former champion proved that he still possessed all the skills of his youth.

ur-bane\ər -ˈbān \ADJ. suave; refined; elegant. The courtier was *urbane* and sophisticated. **ur-ban-i-ty**\ər -ˈban -ət-ē\N.

ur-chin\ ˈər-chən \N. mischievous child (usually a boy). Get out! This store is no place for grubby *urchins!*

ur-sine\ər -sīn \ADJ. bearlike; pertaining to a bear. Because of its *ursine* appearance, the great panda has been identified with the bears; actually, it is closely related to the raccoon.

u-sur-pa-tion\yü -sər-ˈpā -shən\N. act of seizing power and rank of another. The revolution ended with the *usurpation* of the throne by the victorious rebel leader.

u-su-ry\yüzh -(ə-)rē\N. lending money at illegal rates of interest. The loan shark was found guilty of *usury.*

u-to-pi-a\yu̇-ˈtō -pē-ə\N. imaginary land with perfect social and political system. Shangri-la was the name of James Hilton's Tibetan *utopia.*

\ŋ\ **sing**   \ō\ **go**   \ȯ\ **law**   \ȯi\ **boy**   \th\ **thin**   \t͟h\ **the**   \ü\ **loot**   \u̇\ **foot**
\y\ **yet**   \zh\ **vision**   \à, k̲, ⁿ, œ, œ̄, ᵫ, ū͞ē, ʸ\ *see* Pronunciation Symbols

—V—

vac·il·la·tion \vas -ə-lā -shən\ N. fluctuation; wavering. His *vacillation* when confronted with a problem annoyed all of us who had to wait until he made his decision.

vac·u·ous \vak -yə-wəs\ ADJ. empty; inane. The *vacuous* remarks of the politician annoyed the audience, who had hoped to hear more than empty platitudes.

vag·a·bond \'vag-ə-ˌbänd\ N. wanderer; tramp. In summer, college students wander the roads of Europe like carefree *vagabonds*. also ADJ.

va·ga·ry \vā -gə-rē\ N. caprice; whim. She followed every *vagary* of fashion.

va·grant \'vā-grənt\ ADJ. stray; random. He tried to study, but could not collect his *vagrant* thoughts. **va·gran·cy** \'vā-grən(t)-sē\ N.

vain·glo·ri·ous \(ˡ)vān-ˈglōr -ē-əs\ ADJ. boastful; excessively conceited. He was a *vainglorious* and arrogant individual.

val·e·dic·to·ry \val -ə-dik -t(ə-)rē\ ADJ. pertaining to farewell. I found the *valedictory* address too long; leave-taking should be brief. also N.

val·i·date \val -ə-dāt \V. confirm; ratify. I will not publish my findings until I *validate* my results.

val·or \'val-ər \N. bravery. He received the Medal of Honor for his *valor* in battle. **val·iant** \'val-yənt \ADJ.

vam·pire \vam ˌpī(ə)r \N. ghostly being that sucks the blood of the living. Children were afraid to go to sleep at night because of the many legends of *vampires*.

van·guard \van ˌgärd \N. forerunners; advance forces. We are the *vanguard* of a tremendous army that is following us.

van·tage \vant -ij\ N. position giving an advantage. They fired upon the enemy from behind trees, walls and any other point of *vantage* they could find.

va·pid \vap -əd\ ADJ. insipid; inane. He delivered an uninspired and *vapid* address.

var·i·e·gat·ed \ver -ē-ə-ˌgāt -əd\ ADJ. many-colored. He will not like this blue necktie as he is addicted to *variegated* clothing.

---

vas-sal \vas -əl\ N. in feudalism, one who held land of a superior lord. The lord demanded that his *vassals* contribute more to his military campaign.

vaunt \vȯnt \v. boast; brag; highly publicize. To *vaunt* this project now that its failure is known is pointless. also N.

veer \vi(ə)r \v. change in direction. After what seemed an eternity, the wind *veered* to the east and the storm abated. also N.

veg-e-tate \vej -ə-tāt \v. live in a monotonous way. I do not understand how you can *vegetate* in this quiet village after the adventurous life you have led.

ve-he-ment \vē -ə-mənt\ADJ. impetuous; with marked vigor. He spoke with *vehement* eloquence in defense of his client.

vel-lum \vel -əm\N. parchment. Bound in *vellum* and embossed in gold, this book is a beautiful example of the binder's craft. also ADJ.

ve-loc-i-ty \və-'läs-ət-ē\N. speed. The train went by at a considerable *velocity*.

ve-nal \vēn -ᵊl\ ADJ. capable of being bribed. The *venal* policeman accepted the bribe offered him by the speeding motorist whom he had stopped.

ven-det-ta \ven-det -ə\N. feud; private warfare. The *vendetta* continued for several generations despite all attempts by authorities to end the killings.

ven-dor \'ven-dər\N. seller. The fruit *vendor* sold her wares from a stall on the sidewalk.

ve-neer \və-'ni(ə)r \ N. thin layer; cover. Casual acquaintances were deceived by his *veneer* of sophistication and failed to recognize his fundamental shallowness. also v.

ven-er-a-ble \ven -ər(-ə)-bəl\ADJ. deserving high respect. We do not mean to be disrespectful when we refuse to follow the advice of our *venerable* leader.

ven-er-ate \ven -ə-rāt \v. revere. In China, the people *venerate* their ancestors.

ve-ni-al \vē -nē-əl\ADJ. forgivable; trivial. We may regard a hungry man's stealing as a *venial* crime.

ven-i-son \'ven-ə-sən\N. the meat of a deer. The hunters dined on *venison*.

\ŋ\ **sing**   \ō\ **go**   \ȯ\ **law**   \ȯi\ **boy**   \th\ **thin**   \t̲h̲\ **the**   \ü\ **loot**   \u̇\ **foot**
\y\ **yet**   \zh\ **vision**   \á, k̲, ⁿ, œ, œ̄, ue, ūe̲, ʸ\ *see* Pronunciation Symbols

vent \vent\ N. a small opening outlet. The wine did not flow because the air *vent* in the barrel was clogged. also v.

ven·tral \ven -trəl\ V. abdominal. We shall now examine the *ventral* plates of this serpent.

ven·tril·o·quist \ven-'tril-ə-kwəst\ N. someone who can make his or her voice seem to come from another person or thing. This *ventriloquist* does an act in which she has a conversation with a wooden dummy.

ven·ture·some \'ven-chər-səm\ ADJ. bold. A group of *venturesome* women were the first to scale Mt. Annapurna.

ven·tur·ous \vench -(ə-)rəs\ ADJ. daring. The five *venturous* young men decided to look for a new approach to the mountain top.

ven·ue \'ven-ˌyü\ N. location. The attorney asked for a change of *venue;* he thought his client would do better if the trial were held in a less conservative county.

ve·ra·cious \və-rā -shəs\ ADJ. truthful. I can recommend him for this position because I have always found him *veracious* and reliable. **ve·rac·i·ty** \və-ras -ət-ē\ N.

ver·bal·ize \'vər-bə-ˌlīz\ v. to put into words. I know you don't like to talk about these things, but please try to *verbalize* your feelings.

ver·ba·tim \ˌ(i)vər-'bāt -əm\ ADV. word for word. He repeated the message *verbatim*. also ADJ.

ver·bi·age \vər -bē-ij\ N. pompous array of words. After we had waded through all the *verbiage,* we discovered that the writer had said very little.

ver·bose \ˌ(i)vər-bōs \ADJ. wordy. This article is too *verbose;* we must edit it.

ver·dant \vərd -ᵊnt\ ADJ. green; fresh. The *verdant* meadows in the spring are always an inspiring sight.

verge \'vərj\ N. border; edge. Madame Curie knew she was on the *verge* of discovering the secrets of radioactive elements. also v.

ver·i·si·mil·i·tude \ˌver-ə-sə-'mil-ə-ˌt(y)üd\ N. appearance of truth; likelihood. Critics praised her for the *verisimilitude* of her performance as Lady Macbeth. She was completely believable.

\ə\ abut   \ᵊ\ kitten, F table   \ər\ **further**   \a\ ash   \ā\ ace   \ä\ cot, cart
\aů\ out   \ch\ chin   \e\ bet   \ē\ **easy**   \g\ go   \i\ hit   \ī\ ice   \j\ job

ver·i·ty\'ver -ət-ē\ N. truth; reality. The four *verities* were revealed to Buddha during his long meditation.

ver·nac·u·lar\və(r)-'nak-yə-lər\ N. living language; natural style. Cut out those old-fashioned thee's and thou's and write in the *vernacular*. also ADJ.

ver·nal\'vərn -ᵊl\ ADJ. pertaining to spring. We may expect *vernal* showers all during the month of April.

ver·sa·tile\'vər -sət-ᵊl\ ADJ. having many talents; capable of working in many fields. He was a *versatile* athlete; at college he had earned varsity letters in baseball, football, and track.

ver·tex\'vər -teks \ N. summit. Let us drop a perpendicular line from the *vertex* of the triangle to the base.

ver·tig·i·nous\(ᵣ)vər-'tij -ə-nəs\ ADJ. giddy; causing dizziness. I do not like the rides in the amusement park because they have a *vertiginous* effect on me.

ver·ti·go\'vərt -i-gō \ N. dizziness. We test potential plane pilots for susceptibility to spells of *vertigo*.

verve\('vərv \ N. enthusiasm; liveliness. She approached her studies with such *verve* that it was impossible for her to do poorly.

ves·tige\'ves -tij\ N. trace; remains. We discovered *vestiges* of early Indian life in the cave.

vex\'veks \ V. annoy; distress. Please try not to *vex* your mother; she is doing the best she can.

vi·a·ble\'vī -ə-bəl\ ADJ. capable of maintaining life. The infant, though prematurely born, is *viable* and has a good chance to survive.

vi·ands\'vī -əndz\ N. food; provisions. There was a cache of *viands* at the campsite.

vi·car·i·ous\vī-'ker -ē-əs\ ADJ. acting as a substitute; done by a deputy. Many people get a *vicarious* thrill at the movies by imagining they are the characters on the screen.

vi·cis·si·tude\və-'sis -ə-t(y)üd \ N. change of fortune. I am accustomed to life's *vicissitudes,* having experienced poverty and wealth, sickness and health, and failure and success.

vict·uals\'vit -ᵊlz\ N. food. I am very happy to be able to provide you with these *victuals*.

vie\\vī \ v. contend; compete. When we *vie* with each other for his approval, we are merely weakening ourselves and strengthening him.

vig-i-lance\\vij -ə-lən(t)s\ N. watchfulness. Eternal *vigilance* is the price of liberty.

vi-gnette\vin-'yet\ N. picture; short literary sketch. *The New Yorker* published her latest *vignette*.

vig-or\'vig-ər\ N. active strength. Although he was over seventy years old, Jack had the *vigor* of a man in his prime. **vig-or-ous**\'vig-(ə-)rəs\ ADJ.

vil-i-fy\\vil -ə-ˌfī \ v. slander. Why is he always trying to *vilify* my reputation?

vin-di-cate\\vin -də-ˌkāt \ v. clear of charges. I hope to *vindicate* my client and return him to society as a free man.

vin-dic-tive \vin-'dik -tiv\ ADJ. revengeful. He was very *vindictive* and never forgave an injury.

vi-per\\vī -pər\ N. poisonous snake. The habitat of the horned *viper*, a particularly venomous snake, is in sandy regious like the Sahara or the Sinai peninsula.

vi-ra-go\və-'räg -ˌ(ˌ)ō\ N. shrew. Rip Van Winkle's wife was a veritable *virago*.

vir-ile\\vir -əl\ ADJ. mainly. I do not accept the premise that a man is *virile* only when he is belligerent.

vir-tu-o-so\ˌvər -chə-'wō -ˌ(ˌ)sō\ N. highly skilled artist. Heifetz is a violin *virtuoso*.

vir-u-lent \\vir -(y)ə-lənt\ ADJ. extremely poisonous. The virus is highly *virulent* and has made many of us ill for days.

vi-rus\\vī -rəs\ N. disease communicator. The doctors are looking for a specific medicine to control this *virus*.

vis-age\\viz -ij\ N. face; appearance. The stern *visage* of the judge indicated that he had decided to impose a severe penalty.

vis-cer-al\'vis-ə-rəl\ ADJ. felt in one's inner organs. She disliked the *visceral* sensations she had whenever she rode the roller coaster.

vis-cous\\vis -kəs\ ADJ. sticky; gluey. Melted tar is a *viscous* substance. **vis-cos-i-ty**\vis-'käs -ət-ē\ N.

vi-sion-ar-y \\'vizh -ə-ner -ē\\ ADJ. produced by imagination; fanciful; mystical. He was given to *visionary* schemes which never materialized. also N.

vi-ti-ate \\'vish -ē-āt \\v. spoil the effect of; make inoperative Fraud will *vitiate* the contract.

vit-re-ous \\'vi -trē-əs\\ADJ. pertaining to or resembling glass. Although this plastic has many *vitreous* qualities such as transparency, it is unbreakable.

vit-ri-ol-ic \\'vi -trē-'äl -ik\\ ADJ. corrosive; sarcastic. Such *vitriolic* criticism is uncalled for.

vi-tu-per-a-tive \\vī-'t(y)ü -p(ə-)rət-iv\\ ADJ. abusive; scolding. He became more *vituperative* as he realized that we were not going to grant him his wish.

vi-va-cious \\və-'vā -shəs\\ADJ. animated; gay. She had always been *vivacious* and sparkling.

vi-vi-sec-tion \\viv -ə-'sek -shən\\ N. act of dissecting living animals. The Society for the Prevention of Cruelty to Animals opposed *vivisection* and deplored the practice of using animals in scientific experiments.

vix-en \\'vik-sən\\N. female fox; ill-tempered woman. Aware that she was right once again, he lost his temper and called her a shrew and a *vixen*.

vi-zier \\və-'zi(ə)r\\N. powerful Muslim government official. The *vizier* decreed that all persons in the city were to be summoned to the ceremony.

vo-cif-er-ous \\vō-'sif -(ə-)rəs\\ADJ. clamorous; noisy. The crowd grew *vociferous* in its anger and threatened to take the law into its own hands.

vogue \\'vōg \\N. popular fashion. Slacks became the *vogue* on many college campuses.

vol-a-tile \\'väl -ət-ºl\\ ADJ. evaporating rapidly; lighthearted; mercurial. Ethyl chloride is a very *volatile* liquid.

vo-li-tion \\vō-'lish -ən\\ N. act of making a conscious choice. She selected this dress of her own *volition*.

vol-u-ble \\'väl -yə-bəl\\ ADJ. fluent; glib. He was a *voluble* speaker, always ready to talk.

vo-lu-mi-nous \\və-'lü-mə-nəs\\ADJ. bulky; large. Despite her family burdens, she kept up a *voluminous* correspondence with her friends.

vo-lup-tuous\və-ˈləp -chə-(-wə)s\ADJ. gratifying the senses. The nobility during the Renaissance led *voluptuous* lives.

vo-ra-cious\vȯ-ˈrā -shəs\ADJ. ravenous. The wolf is a *voracious* animal.

vo-ta-ry\ˈvōt -ə-rē\N. follower of a cult. He was a *votary* of every new movement in literature and art.

vouch-safe\vau̇ch-ˈsāf \V. grant condescendingly; guarantee. I can safely *vouchsafe* you a fair return on your investment.

vul-ner-a-ble\ˈvəln -(ə-)rə-bəl\ADJ. susceptible to wounds. Achilles was *vulnerable* only in his heel.

vy-ing\ˈvī -iŋ\V. contending. Why are we *vying* with each other for his favors? **vie** V.

—W—

waft\ 'wäft \ v. move gently, as if impelled by wind or waves. Daydreaming, he gazed at the leaves which *wafted* past his window. also N.

wag-gish \ wag -ish\ ADJ. mischievous; humorous; tricky. He was a prankster who, unfortunately, often overlooked the damage he could cause with his *waggish* tricks.

waif\ 'wāf\ N. homeless child or animal. Although he already had eight cats, he could not resist adopting yet another feline *waif*.

waive\ wāv \ v. give up temporarily; yield. I will *waive* my rights in this matter in order to expedite our reaching a proper decision.

wal-low\ 'wäl-(,)ō\ v. roll in; indulge in; become helpless. The hippopotamus loves to *wallow* in the mud.

wan\ wän \ ADJ. having a pale or sickly color; pallid. Suckling asked, "Why so pale and *wan*, fond lover?" also v.

wane \ wān \ v. grow gradually smaller. From now until December 21, the winter equinox, the hours of daylight will *wane*. also N.

wan-gle\ 'waŋ-gəl\ v. bring about by manipulation or trickery. She tried to *wangle* an invitation to the party.

wan-ton \ wȯnt -ᵊn\ ADJ. unruly; unchaste; excessive. His *wanton* pride cost him many friends. also N.

war-ble\ 'wȯr-bəl\ v. sing melodiously; trill. Every morning the birds *warbled* outside her window. also N.

war-rant\ 'wȯr-ənt\ v. justify; authorize. Before the judge issues the injunction, you must convince her this action is *warranted*.

war-ran-ty \ wȯr -ənt-ē\ N. guarantee; assurance by seller. The purchaser of this automobile is protected by the manufacturer's *warranty* that he will replace any defective part for five years or 50,000 miles.

war-y \ wa(ə)r -ē\ ADJ. very cautious. The spies grew *wary* as they approached the sentry.

wast-rel \ wā -strəl\ N. profligate. He was denounced as a *wastrel* who had dissipated his inheritance.

wax\ 'waks\ v. increase; grow. With proper handling, his fortunes *waxed* and he became rich.

\ŋ\ **sing**   \ō\ **go**   \ȯ\ **law**   \ȯi\ **boy**   \th\ **thin**   \th̲\ **the**   \ü\ **loot**   \u̇\ **foot**
\y\ **yet**   \zh\ **vision**   \à, k̲, ⁿ, œ, œ̄, ue, ū̄, ʸ\ *see* Pronunciation Symbols

way-lay\\'wā-ˌlā\\v. ambush; lie in wait. They agreed to *waylay* their victim as he passed through the dark alley going home.

wean\\'wēn\\v. accustom a baby not to nurse; give up a cherished activity. He decided he would *wean* himself away from eating junk food and stick to fruits and vegetables.

weath-er\\'weth-ər\\v. endure the effects of weather or other forces. He *weathered* the changes in his personal life with difficulty, as he had no one in whom to confide.

welt\\'welt\\N. mark from a beating or whipping. The evidence of child abuse was very clear; Jennifer's small body was covered with *welts* and bruises.

wel-ter\\'wel -tər\\v. wallow. At the height of the battle, the casualties were so numerous that the victims *weltered* in their blood while waiting for medical attention. also N.

whee-dle\\'hwēd -ᵊl\\v. cajole; coax; deceive by flattery. She knows she can *wheedle* almost anything she wants from her father.

whelp\\'hwelp\\N. young wolf, dog, tiger, etc. This collie *whelp* won't do for breeding, but he'd make a fine pet.

whet\\'hwet \\v. sharpen; stimulate. The odors from the kitchen are *whetting* my appetite; I will be ravenous by the time the meal is served.

whim-si-cal\\'hwim -zi-kəl\\ADJ. capricious; fanciful; quaint. *Peter Pan* is a *whimsical* play.

whin-ny\\'hwin-ē\\v. neigh like a horse. When he laughed through his nose, it sounded as if he *whinnied*. also N.

whit\\'hwit \\N. smallest speck. There is not a *whit* of intelligence or understanding in your observations.

whorl\\'hwȯr(ə)l \\N. ring of leaves around stem; ring. Identification by fingerprints is based on the difference in shape and number of the *whorls* on the fingers.

wi-ly\\'wī -lē\\ADJ. cunning; artful. He is as *wily* as a fox in avoiding trouble.

wince\\'win(t)s \\v. shrink back; flinch. The screech of the chalk on the blackboard made her *wince*.

\ə\ abut	\ᵊ\ kitten, F table	\ər\ further	\a\ ash	\ā\ ace	\ä\ cot, cart
\au̇\ out	\ch\ chin	\e\ bet	\ē\ easy	\g\ go	\i\ hit	\ī\ ice	\j\ job

wind-fall\'win(d)-ˌföl\ N. unexpected lucky event. This huge tax refund is quite a *windfall*.

win-now\'win-(ˌ)ō\ V. sift; separate good parts from bad. This test will *winnow* out the students who study from those who don't bother.

win-some\'win(t) -səm\ ADJ. agreeable; gracious; engaging. By her *winsome* manner, she made herself liked by everyone who met her.

with-er\'with-ər\ V. shrivel; decay. Cut flowers are beautiful for a day, but all too soon they *wither*.

wit-less\'wit -ləs\ ADJ. foolish; idiotic. Such *witless* and fatuous statements will create the impression that you are an ignorant individual.

wit-ti-cism\'wit -ə-ˌsiz -əm\ N. witty saying; facetious remark. What you regard as *witticisms* are often offensive to sensitive people.

wiz-ard-ry\'wiz -ə(r)-drē\ N. sorcery; magic. Merlin amazed the knights with his *wizardry*.

wiz-en\'wiz -ᵊn\ V. wither; shrivel. The hot sun *wizened* all the trees and plants.

wont\'wönt \ N. custom; habitual procedure. As was his *wont*, he jogged two miles every morning before going to work.

world-ly\'wər(-ə)l -dlē\ ADJ. engrossed in matters of this earth; not spiritual. You must leave your *worldly* goods behind you when you go to meet your Maker.

wraith\'rāth \ N. ghost; phantom of a living person. It must be a horrible experience to see a ghost; it is even more horrible to see the *wraith* of a person we know to be alive.

wran-gle\'raŋ-gəl\ V. quarrel; obtain through arguing; herd cattle. They *wrangled* over their inheritance.

wrath\'rath\ N. anger; fury. She turned to him, full of *wrath*, and said, "What makes you think I'll accept lower pay for this job than you get?"

wreak\'rēk \ V. inflict. I am afraid he will *wreak* his wrath on the innocent as well as the guilty.

wrench\'rench\ V. pull; strain; twist. She *wrenched* free of her attacker and landed a powerful kick to his kneecap.

---

wrest\\rest \ v. pull away; take by violence. With only ten seconds left to play, our team *wrested* victory from their grasp.

writhe\'rīth\v. squirm, twist. He was *writhing* in pain, desperate for the drug his body required.

wry\'rī\ADJ. twisted; with a humorous twist. We enjoy Dorothy Parker's verse for its *wry* wit.

—xyz—

xe-no-phile\zen -ə₁fīl \N. one attracted to foreign people, manners, and styles. She was a *xenophile* who spent all her time exploring foreign cultures.

xe-no-pho-bi-a\zen -ə-'fō -bē-ə\N. fear and hatred of anything foreign. His *xenophobia* prevented him from learning anything about the customs of people in other countries.

yen\'yen\N. longing; urge. She had a *yen* to get away and live on her own for a while.

yeo-man\yō -mən\ N. man owning small estate; middle-class farmer. It was not the aristocrat but the *yeoman* who determined the nation's policies.

yoke\'yōk\v. join together, unite. I don't wish to be *yoked* to him in marriage, as if we were cattle pulling a plow. also N.

yo-kel\yō -kəl\N. country bumpkin. At school, his classmates regarded him as a *yokel* and laughed at his rustic mannerisms.

za-ny\'zā-nē\ADJ. crazy; comic. I can watch the Marx brothers' *zany* antics for hours.

zeal-ot\zel -ət\N. fanatic; person who shows excessive zeal. It is good to have a few *zealots* in our group for their enthusiasm is contagious.

ze-nith\'zē -nəth\ N. point directly overhead in the sky; summit. When the sun was at its *zenith,* the glare was not as strong as at sunrise and sunset.

zeph-yr\zef -ər\N. gentle breeze; west wind. When these *zephyrs* blow, it is good to be in an open boat under a full sail.

\ə\ abut \ᵊ\ kitten, F table \ər\ further \a\ ash \ā\ ace \ä\ cot, cart
\aů\ out \ch\ chin \e\ bet \ē\ easy \g\ go \i\ hit \ī\ ice \j\ job